GEORGETOWN UNIVERSITY ROUND TABLE ON LANGUAGES AND LINGUISTICS 2001

Linguistics, Language, and the Real World: Discourse and Beyond

Deborah Tannen
and
James E. Alatis
Editors

Georgetown University Press
Washington, D.C.

Georgetown University Press, Washington, D.C.
© 2003 by Georgetown University Press. All rights reserved.
Printed in the United States of America

10 9 8 7 6 5 4 3 2 1   2003

This volume is printed on acid-free offset book paper.

ISBN 0-87840-904-1
ISSN 0186-7207

In honor of
JAMES E. ALATIS, DEAN OF THE SCHOOL OF LANGUAGES AND LINGUISTICS
1973–1994,
WHO NURTURED AND SUSTAINED THE GEORGETOWN UNIVERSITY ROUND TABLE ON
LANGUAGES AND LINGUISTICS FOR OVER THREE DECADES

Contents

Introduction

Deborah Tannen
Co-chair, GURT 2001

Even before I joined its faculty in 1979, I admired Georgetown University because of the Georgetown University Round Table on Languages and Linguistics. I had regarded this alluring meeting with a combination of awe and envy throughout my graduate student days, as I saw my professor, John Gumperz, fly off to take part and return to write up his papers for inclusion in the volume. I could hardly have imagined then that eventually I would be fortunate enough not only to take part in but to organize three Round Tables: the 1981 meeting, "Analyzing Discourse: Text and Talk"; the 1985 meeting, "Languages and Linguistics: The Interdependence of Theory, Data, and Application," held in conjunction with the LSA/TESOL Institute that I directed at Georgetown in the summer of 1985; and finally the current one, "Linguistics, Language, and the Real World: Discourse and Beyond"—exactly two decades after the first. I suggested to my co-chair, James E. Alatis, that he write a brief history of the Round Table to be included in this volume, partly because I myself wished to learn the history of these meetings. I am personally grateful for his insight and wisdom. No one is better placed to bring this history into present awareness.

What Jim Alatis does not emphasize in his brief account is the enormous role he himself has played in establishing the Georgetown University Round Table (affectionately if somewhat unaesthetically called GURT) as a major force in the development of the field of linguistics. The role of GURT in the rise of sociolinguistics and discourse analysis as subfields of linguistics is an exemplary case of the importance of GURT meetings and volumes, and also Jim Alatis's vision. In his historical survey, Dr. Alatis notes the establishment of the sociolinguistics program in the Georgetown University Linguistics Department in 1970, thanks to a grant from the National Science Foundation, but he neglects to mention that he himself was the driving force behind the winning of that grant.

Throughout his tenure as dean of Georgetown University's School of Languages and Linguistics (SLL), Dr. Alatis also has been the force behind GURT by ensuring funding, frequently organizing meetings himself, and—in years he did not do so—selecting an organizer from the SLL faculty and lending his decanal support in every way possible. I remain personally grateful to him for the matchless opportunity to play a role by organizing three GURTs. I also would like to take this opportunity to honor Dr. Alatis's unrelenting efforts and contribution to the Round Table tradition leading up to GURT 2001, which I have had the honor of co-chairing with him.

Given his unique role in supporting the Round Table from the time he assumed the position of dean of the School of Languages and Linguistics in 1973, the name James E. Alatis will always be associated with the Georgetown University Round Table. Yet this is the last GURT in which Dr. Alatis played an official role. Administration of future Round Tables will reside with Georgetown University's linguistics department. In light of this transition, I was able to convince Jim Alatis to allow me to dedicate this volume to him, so it may stand as concrete recognition of his incomparable contribution to maintaining the Round Table for nearly three decades.

GURT 2001, "Linguistics, Language, and the Real World: Discourse and Beyond," was designed to contribute to the field of linguistics in two ways: to advance research in the field of discourse analysis and to bring linguistic insight to bear on issues of importance to American society at large. This Round Table thus continues a tradition not only in the field of sociolinguistics but also of the Round Tables, as Dr. Alatis outlines in his brief history, which follows this Introduction.

GURT 1981 addressed the topic "Analyzing Discourse: Text and Talk." In my introduction to that volume, I define *discourse* as "language in context across all forms and modes." GURT 2001 promises to extend work in discourse "beyond" the analysis of language to include examination of how language affects issues of importance to the world at large. Robin Lakoff remarks in a note to her chapter, "As in previous years, GURT 2001 served as a reminder to all of us of the importance and centrality of sociolinguistics." Indeed, she continues, "as Labov remarked many years ago, the field might be better off if what we call 'sociolinguistics' were recognized as, in fact, the central concern of the field, under the name of 'linguistics,' and if what is commonly referred to as 'core linguistics,' on the other hand, had been given a hyphenated or complex name like 'autonomo-linguistics.'" In this spirit, let us think of this and the other papers in this volume as contributions to "linguistics" proper.

Into the 1980s, GURT meetings were composed of all-plenary, all-invited papers. The economics began to change, however, and beginning in 1988 GURT meetings became a combination of concurrent sessions composed of papers refereed on the basis of submitted abstracts and a smaller number of invited plenary speakers. The present volume is composed entirely of plenary addresses. Following is a brief overview of what lies in store.

Overview
The volume opens with two essays that address fundamental and underresearched aspects of discourse. First, Frederick Erickson gives us "Some notes on the musicality of speech." Throughout his long scholarly career, Erickson has

been a leading researcher into the rhythmic nature of spoken discourse and its importance in understanding the outcomes of interaction—including, prominently, the paper he delivered at GURT 1981 in which he transcribed the conversation he analyzed in musical notation (Erickson 1982). In the essay in this volume, Erickson begins his demonstration of both the musical nature of speech and the usefulness of a quasi-musical transcription of discourse by examining cadential sequences in well-known Western musical compositions that, he argues, deliberately imitate speech. He then examines the rhythmic patterns in speech recorded at a dinner-table conversation and in first-grade and fifth-grade classrooms. The cadential organization of spoken discourse makes listener response possible by signaling "transition relevance" (cuing a speaker's willingness to transfer a speaking turn) and "listening response relevance" (an invitation to provide a sign of listenership such as "mhm" or "uh huh"). Given listeners' inevitable ebb and flow of attention, Erickson notes, the ability to not only interpret but also anticipate customary patterns of prosodic emphasis makes possible both comprehension and participation in interaction.

In "Laughing while talking," Wallace Chafe gives us the first (as far as I know) detailed linguistic account of a phenomenon that has been little studied by linguists but is pervasive in conversation: laughter. Based on audiotaped examples of laughter in naturally occurring conversation, he begins with the phonetics of laughter, examining its components (such as number of expulsion-of-air pulses and quality of vocalic articulation). Next he considers laughter as the expression of emotion, the "feeling of nonseriousness," and examines its properties (such as its lack of voluntary control and its universality and contagiousness). He then considers the function of nonseriousness in conversational interaction, both in response to intentionally nonserious performance such as joke-telling and other forms of verbal play and also in more frequent instances of laughter in the course of conversational interaction to replace unpleasant emotions, to evince ridicule, to serve as a conversational lubricant, and so on. Thus, Chafe suggests—and demonstrates by his own analysis—that research into the forms and functions of laughter in conversation can add to our understanding of human cognition and interaction.

The third chapter is my own: "Power maneuvers or connection maneuvers? Ventriloquizing in family interaction." Like all the papers that follow, this chapter has relevance to a specific domain of the "real world" of our theme (in this case, family interaction), while also adding to our general understanding of discourse in interaction. It grows out of two of my ongoing and interrelated theoretical interests: framing in discourse—a process I regard as central to the discursive creation of meaning, identity, and human relationships—and the interplay of hierarchy and connection, which I see as a corrective to the tendency to focus on power in discourse to the exclusion of the inextricably intertwined dimension of solidarity, or connection. Here I approach these interwoven threads through analysis of a linguistic strategy I call "ventriloquizing" in tape recordings taken from a larger project in which dual-career couples with children tape-recorded all of their interaction over a week. I examine instances in which one family member communicates to a second by speaking through, to, or as a third. For example, a mother might ventriloquize her infant child by saying, in her husband's presence and in a baby-talk register, "My diaper is dirty!" My analysis focuses on how these interactions are simultaneously "control maneuvers" and "connection maneuvers." My goal is to better understand family discourse, as well as to investigate how creative framing of utterances allows speakers to integrate the dynamics of power and solidarity, or control and connection, in their discourse.

The next four chapters address a range of "real-world" domains by examining narrative discourse. William Labov, who ushered in three decades of linguistic analysis of narrative with a seminal paper that has been the foundation of all subsequent structural analyses of narrative in our field (Labov and Waletzky 1967), here revisits the topic in "Uncovering the event structure of narrative." He begins with an examination of the event structure of a narrative told by a seventy-three-year-old man living in a small midwestern town about a frightening experience he recalls from his teen years. Labov then examines a narrative told in the context of testimony before the South African Truth and Reconciliation Commission. In that testimony, the speaker recounts events leading up to the murder of an innocent black couple—a murder in which the speaker participated but for which he would like to downplay his responsibility. Labov shows that analysis of the underlying event structure of the narrative "helps to accomplish the initial goals of the Truth and Reconciliation Commission: to discover what was done and who was responsible." At the same time, Labov contributes to the linguistic analysis of discourse by advancing our understanding of "the process by which narratives are created, transmitted, and understood."

Deborah Schiffrin, author of the classic essay "Tense Variation in Narrative" (Schiffrin 1981), also returns here to the topic of narrative. Her essay, "Linguistics and history: Oral history as discourse," addresses the intersection of linguistics and history by comparing two different accounts of a single experience by a Holocaust survivor. While briefly interned at a Budapest prison before being sent to Auschwitz, Susan Beer encountered a fellow prisoner named Hannah Szenes (sometimes spelled Senesh), a now legendary but then unknown young Hungarian Jewish emigrant to Palestine who had been captured (and later was tortured and executed) after parachuting into Hungary on a failed rescue mission. Schiffrin compares Beer's accounts of her meeting with Szenes as taken from two separate interviews and presented in two different modes. One excerpt comes from an interview conducted in 1984; the other appears on a website titled "Women and the Holocaust," in which Beer's account of her meeting with Szenes is excerpted from an interview conducted in 1982. As Schiffrin shows, even though the two texts were told by the same speaker about the same event, they "speak in different voices," reflect different stances, and include different aspects of the truth. By viewing oral history through the perspective of discourse analysis, Schiffrin demonstrates "the impact of transcription and other modes of presenting texts, the intertextual relevance of personal and historical themes, and the display of identity through referring terms and event-types." Thus, Schiffrin's analysis sheds light on issues of linguistic as well as historical concern.

We again encounter a single speaker saying "the same thing" in different contexts in Alessandro Duranti's "The voice of the audience in contemporary American political discourse." Having accompanied and videotaped congressional candidate Walter Capps as he campaigned in California, Duranti compares multiple instances on a single day when Capps told "the same" joke and made "the same" political points to different audiences. By analyzing the varied rhetorical strategies Capps uses in different contexts, Duranti shows not only how the candidate sculpts his speech to accommodate a variety of audiences but also how the different audiences impose their own interpretations on the same words—interpretations that at times diverge from Capps's own intentions. This phenomenon poses a dilemma for the speaker, who must choose between his own "voice" and the "voice of the audience": Will he reassert control of his own meaning or "go along" with the audience—an especially tempting choice when their reaction displays enthusiastic approval of the meaning they heard. Duranti's chapter demonstrates that an ethnographically informed discourse analysis can contribute to an understanding of political discourse, as well as to an understanding of the moral dilemma between "pleasing others and asserting oneself" that is central to "the construction of human agency through talk."

The chapter by Robin Lakoff dovetails with Schiffrin's and Labov's in compelling ways. Lakoff also addresses the intersection of historical events and narrative, and she also is concerned with varying versions of the same "text." Her focus, however, is on narrative in the larger sense of a socially agreed-upon storyline that connects divergent events, rather than a particular story told by a single speaker about a personal experience. The narratives Lakoff addresses are news stories about current events—"public stories"—in which different groups of citizens agree on details, interpretations, and evaluations that differ markedly from those to which other groups of citizens ascribe. Lakoff contrasts two pairs of public stories. One is the O. J. Simpson saga, in which celebrity athlete Simpson was tried and acquitted for the murder of his former wife, Nicole, and her friend Ron Goldman. The other is the political fate of President Bill Clinton and his wife, now-Senator Hillary Clinton. With respect to Simpson, Lakoff shows that the black and white communities in the United States accepted as truth irreconcilably contrasting narratives. Similarly irreconcilable are the stories—that is, the network of facts, interpretations, and evaluations—about the Clintons that are embraced as truth by divergent groups of Americans. For Lakoff, these sets of stories are "about" race and gender, respectively, and she sees the competition for narrative rights that they represent as both reflecting and aggravating social discord. Lakoff suggests that understanding public discourse as a struggle for narrative rights can shed light on the frequently remarked and frequently bemoaned rise of incivility in public discourse.

The last three chapters all address, in different yet related ways, the intersection of language and public institutions. Heidi E. Hamilton—whose ground-breaking analysis of the language of an Alzheimer's patient (Hamilton 1994) established her as a leading scholar in the domain of discourse and medicine— examines the accounts given by patients to explain why they fail to comply with their doctors' advice regarding management of their diabetes. Echoing Lakoff's observation that dominant voices suppress the narrative rights of subordinate voices in news stories, Hamilton demonstrates in "Patients' voices in the medical world: An exploration of accounts of noncompliance" how patients' voices are similarly though inadvertently suppressed in medical encounters. Starting from the premise that physicians sincerely wish to help their patients, Hamilton surmises that doctors treating patients for diabetes would be better able to help patients comply with medical advice if they better understood their patients' reasons for noncompliance. Yet these reasons, which patients volunteered in postexamination interviews, did not emerge in interaction with their doctors. Hamilton's analysis of the contents and structure of patients' accounts shows that they know what they need to do to manage their diabetes but are hampered by an identifiable range of real-life obstacles, which they explain by reference to an identifiable set of excuses and justifications. With this understanding as background, Hamilton then presents examples of physician-patient interactions to show how patients' admissions of noncompliance could (but don't) provide an opportunity for physicians to address the reasons for noncompliance. Her analysis of patients' accounts is useful not only for the domain of doctor-patient communication but also for a wide range of human interactions in which accounts of various types are given. Moreover, Hamilton's chapter joins with those of Schiffrin and Duranti to elucidate how discourse varies in response to different contexts.

In "Discourse of denial," Shirley Brice Heath also presents a structural analysis of account-type discourse: the discursive strategies employed by well-intentioned policymakers and educators in denying the import of research findings. Heath draws on her own encounters with such policymakers in bringing to their attention her own research in two divergent contexts: first, a decade of investigations into the impact of community-based, arts-centered learning environments on high-risk youth; second, her work with linguists and literacy specialists attempting to help Papua New Guinea villagers address their concerns about potentially disastrous threats to their environment. With regard to high-risk youth, Heath notes that educators and policymakers deny the well-documented promise of community-based youth programs in part because they see such programs in opposition to, and consequently a threat to, school-based programs. Interestingly (and sadly), Heath notes the power of narrative as a denial strategy, as when a policymaker simply tells an engaging narrative that disputes the research findings. Heath then examines the linguistic strategies (in her terms, "stylistic maneuvers") by which these narratives effectively sidestep the research. Shifting to Papua New Guinea, Heath shows that villagers presented clear evidence that "a wide range of texts in several languages could be made accessible to villagers, so long as oral patterns of information transmission were honored." Yet educators, linguists, and literacy "experts" questioned the evidence because of their unwavering commitment to the necessity of literate skills such as decoding written texts and individuals' abilities to read aloud and use written texts in public. Again, Heath's chapter demonstrates that discourse analysis can help elucidate and address the most pressing problems in the real world, while enhancing our understanding of interpersonal interaction.

The volume ends with a success story. In "Implementing a district-wide foreign language program: A case study of acquisition planning and curricular innovation," G. Richard Tucker and Richard Donato report on their successful six-year consulting experience with a public school district in Pittsburgh, Pennsylvania, that resulted in the planning and implementation of a system-wide Spanish language program. By discussing the steps involved in selecting the target language and incorporating active participation by all senior administrators in every aspect of program planning and implementation, Tucker and Donato provide an in-depth glimpse of successful researcher-policymaker collaboration. They describe the program, which was completing its fifth full year in 2001, as well as their documentation of the students' success in learning Spanish. Among the themes that emerge in the account, the notion of "empowerment" stands out, as the authors note the unanimous reports of satisfaction at feeling "ownership" of the program among teachers, department heads, principals, and others.

Taken together, then, the chapters in this volume contribute to the field of discourse analysis by enhancing our understanding of language in interaction, at the same time that they illustrate that linguistics can address real-world problems, in both private and public domains. In his brief history of the Round Table, James E. Alatis notes that GURT was founded following World War II as a way to address what is surely the most pressing problem humans face: to ensure world peace. This noble purpose is even more urgent as I write this introduction; the rise of international terrorism and the proliferation of nuclear as well as chemical and biological weapons capability constitute threats to world peace as grave as any since the Cuban missile crisis brought the world to the brink of nuclear war. Perhaps we have become more jaded in our faith in the ability of languages and linguistics to create peace in the world. If the goal of world peace seems ever more elusive, the goal of using our linguistic expertise to address human problems in society at large seems ever more urgent. As Robin Lakoff observes in the note to her paper, this goal is neither more nor less than the business of linguistics. That is the optimistic hope of this volume.

REFERENCES

Erickson, Frederick. 1982. Money tree, lasagna bush, salt and pepper: Social construction of topical cohesion in a conversation among Italian-Americans. In *Analyzing discourse: Text and talk: Georgetown University Round Table on Languages and Linguistics 1981*, edited by Deborah Tannen. Washington, D.C.: Georgetown University Press, 43–70.

Hamilton, Heidi Ehernberger. 1994. *Conversations with an Alzheimer's patient.* Cambridge: Cambridge University Press.

Labov, William, and Joshua Waletzky. 1967. Narrative analysis: Oral versions of personal experience. In *Essays on the verbal and visual arts*, edited by June Helm. Seattle: University of Washington Press, 12–44. Reprinted in *Journal of Narrative and Life History* 7 (1997): 395–415.

Schiffrin, Deborah. 1981. Tense variation in narrative. *Language* 57 (1): 45–62.

A brief history of the Georgetown University Round Table on Languages and Linguistics

James E. Alatis
Co-chair, GURT 2001

In 1919—just after World War I—the brilliant Jesuit internationalist Rev. Edmund A. Walsh, S.J., went to Europe and became convinced of the need for a school to train students for America's foreign service, hoping that if people could sit around a table and resolve their differences diplomatically, wars could be avoided. To that end, he founded the School of Foreign Service at Georgetown University. Thirty years later, in 1949, Father Walsh went back to Europe after World War II and came to the conclusion that if people were going to discuss their problems diplomatically, they should know each other's languages. He therefore founded the Institute of Languages and Linguistics as part of the School of Foreign Service. This Institute later became the School of Languages and Linguistics.

The man to whom Father Walsh turned to implement his plan for a language-competent American society was Professor Leon Dostert. Professor Dostert was born in France in 1904 and was brought to the United States after World War I by American soldiers for whom he had served as an interpreter. During World War II he was commissioned in the U.S. Army as a major and assigned as liaison officer for General Giraud, an interpreter in French for General Eisenhower. Professor Dostert was promoted to the rank of colonel in 1945; after the war, he became chief of the language division of the Nuremberg War Crimes Tribunal. There he introduced the idea of simultaneous interpretation and translation. He then served as director of simultaneous interpretation at the United Nations and played a significant part in the organization and training of interpreters. After that he returned to Georgetown at Father Walsh's request. In addition to establishing the Institute of Languages and Linguistics—including a state-of-the-art "multilingual room" and language laboratory—in 1949, Dr. Dostert began the annual Georgetown University Round Table on Languages and Linguistics (GURT), and the series of monographs that reported the proceedings of the Round Table each year.

Legend has it that the first Round Table meeting was so small that all the participants could sit comfortably at the same round table. At those early meetings the themes focused on linguistics as applied to language teaching, testing, humanistic study, and allied subjects. During the years when the institute became the School of Languages and Linguistics (SLL), with Dr. Robert Lado as its first dean from 1960 to 1973, the themes were chosen to examine the major linguistics topics of the time—such as contrastive linguistics, generative grammar, transformation theory, tagmemic description, semantics, and syntax.

In 1973 I succeeded Dr. Lado as dean of the School of Languages and Linguistics. Having previously worked in the U.S. Department of State and the U.S. Office of Education in language research and materials development for the less commonly taught languages, I tried to foster a close relationship between GURT and the federal linguists. A pre-GURT session was added to the program, featuring the government-based Interagency Language Roundtable (ILR) and examining language use in the public sphere as well as the classroom. The Round Table meetings were timed to include a weekend, to open the program to language teachers in the area. This cross-fertilization between classroom and academia led to fruitful explorations of topics such as bilingual education, standard English, and the teaching of English to speakers of other languages (TESOL).

One of the major developments in linguistics in the 1960s was the emergence of sociolinguistics. The Georgetown University Round Table became a forum for this subfield of linguistics when it was still in its infancy. In 1969 the School of Languages and Linguistics won a $460,000 Departmental Science Development Grant from the National Science Foundation, with which it set up a sociolinguistics program within the linguistics department. Among the new faculty members were Roger Shuy, the director of the program, and Ralph Fasold, both of whom had collaborated earlier in researching African-American English in Detroit and Washington, D.C. The increasing theoretical importance and social relevance of sociolinguistics was reflected in several key GURTs. First was the historic 1972 GURT organized by Roger Shuy around the theme "Sociolinguistics: Current Trends and Prospects." Next was the 1981 GURT organized by Deborah Tannen with the theme "Analyzing Discourse: Text and Talk," followed by the 1984 GURT organized by Deborah Schiffrin titled "Meaning, Form, and Use in Context: Linguistic Applications."

GURT 2000, which I co-chaired with Heidi Hamilton, was titled "Linguistics, Language, and the Professions: Education, Journalism, Law, Medicine, and Technology." It combined the sociolinguistic and applied themes that have characterized the focus of GURT and the focus of the Georgetown University linguistics department, under whose auspices succeeding GURTs will reside. The meeting that gave rise to the current volume, GURT 2001, was co-chaired with Deborah Tannen.

Since its beginnings as a response to wartime experiences of language needs, the Georgetown University Round Table has been a forum for presenting cutting-edge scholarly work and for examining changing national needs in languages and linguistics. It began with the idealistic hope that research in linguistics would lead to practical, peaceful solutions to human conflict. May this fine tradition continue forever.

Some notes on the musicality of speech[1]

Frederick Erickson
University of California, Los Angeles

Since the beginnings of systematic descriptive linguistics early in the twentieth century, linguists have mentioned the importance of pitch, volume, and timing in the conduct of talk. These music-like features of speaking have been called prosody, intonation, and paralanguage.

The temporal organization of speech's musicality has received less attention than some other aspects of the music of talk. One research group that has been investigating the timing of speech comparatively across examples from adult speakers of English, German, and Italian has been a set of faculty and students at the University of Konstanz (see Auer 1992). Pitch and timing in mother-infant interaction have been investigated recently by a research group at the University of Edinburgh (see Trevarthen 1999) and over a long period of time by Stern, Jaffe, Feldstein, and others (see Jaffe and Feldstein 1970; Beebe et al. 1985).

Chafe has shown special interest in the ways intonation contours function to communicate referential meaning in speaking, with each continuous intonation contour typically demarcating a single chunk of key information within a sequence of oral discourse (Chafe 1994). In his discussion of intonation units, Chafe likens them to phrase units in Western music of the classical era, giving an example from a piano sonata of Mozart. Just as the music listener's expectations are guided by the harmonic sequence, timing, and melodic contour of music to hear a connected set of notes as a whole, in speech the intonation unit marks for a hearer a whole entity in discourse.

Van Leeuen has emphasized the emotional connotations of pitch contours. He compared the characteristic speech patterns of disc jockeys on radio stations with different audiences—a "top forty" popular music station and a "beautiful music" station (Van Leeuen 1999: 104). The "top forty" disc jockey communicates a sense of excitement by a pattern of successive rising intonations in his speech, whereas the "beautiful music" disc jockey communicates a sense of relaxed friendliness by a pattern of successive falling intonations in his speech. Van Leeuen compares these contrasting examples of pitch patterns in speaking with contrasting melodic phrases from two Christian hymns—one in a martial spirit (which has successive rising intonations) and one in a more contemplative spirit (which has successive falling intonations).

Georgetown Anniversary

In the paper I delivered in a plenary session at the Georgetown University Round Table 1981, I illustrated the relationship between timing and discourse topics in speech during a dinner conversation by using quasi-musical notation (i.e., notation that displayed speech rhythms but not pitch) to show the relative temporal location of stressed syllables within intonation units (Erickson 1982b). By coincidence Scollon, at the same conference, presented a paper that used a similar kind of quasi-musical notation to illustrate the timing of speech in discourse at the breakfast table (Scollon 1982). Scollon and I—both with considerable education and performance experience as musicians—were able to use our Western musical intuitions in preparing transcripts of speech accompanied by quasi-musical notation. In my case, I had been prepared for this work by an undergraduate major in composition and music history and a master's degree in music history.

In one earlier paper and in a few later papers (Erickson 1982a, 1992, 1996) I used quasi-musical notation to illustrate the timing of talk in school classroom interaction as well as in family dinner conversation. I argue in those papers that the musicality of speech focuses the listener on key information points in the speech stream and cues moments of what conversational analysts have called "transition relevance" at which turn exchange between speakers is appropriate (see Ford and Thompson 1996). In other work (Erickson 1979, 1986; Erickson and Shultz 1982) as well as in an extended discussion in Erickson (1992) I have shown how such moments of transition relevance also are moments at which it is especially appropriate for listeners to provide some form of nonverbal and/or verbal listening response.

Issues in Quasi-Musical Notation of Speech

The transcribing that Scollon and I have done is based on our experience as musicians. As an undergraduate music major I was taught to transcribe the pitches and rhythms of melodies that were played as a kind of listening test. I also took courses in ethnomusicology—the study of musical practices other than those in the tradition of Western art music. Often those other musics are performed without the use of a notation system, and one of the basic skills of ethnomusicologists becomes transcribing audiotapes of musical performances into Western musical notation, with some accommodation in that notation to the distinctive characteristics of the particular music being transcribed. Because non-Western musics don't "fit" neatly into the Western notation system, there are arguments among ethnomusicologists about transcription approaches that are analogous to arguments about transcription among phoneticians in linguistics. In the use of Western musical notation to show the rhythms of speech, the "fit" between the speech phenomena being represented by the notation system is even looser, in some respects, than that between non-Western and Western music. Accordingly, the rendering of speech rhythm patterns into a quasi-musical transcription produces an approximation to the phenomena being described.

Just as an ethnomusicologist can be criticized for cramming non-Western rhythm patterns into the conventions of Western notation (and, even more fundamentally, for "hearing" the non-Western music in ways influenced by the Western notation system, thus making phenomenological/perceptual acoustic mistakes), so one can question the accuracy and appropriateness of a quasi-musical transcription of speech. Questions have been raised about the accuracy of my transcriptions: Are the patterns they show actually occurring in nature or are they an artifact of the transcriber/analyst's illusions in hearing and in using a particular representation system (Western musical notation) for a purpose other than that for which it was developed by musicians?

In particular, I have argued that there is a cadential pattern in the timing of speech (and of co-occurring kinesic activity—gesture, gaze shifts, and posture shifts). Stressed syllables (as well as peaks of gestures, gaze shifts, and major posture shifts) more often than not occur at a regular timing interval, akin to the cadence of marching soldiers and the regular beating of the heart. Not every stressed syllable or arm extension falls on this "beat," but enough do so to produce an auditory and visual temporal gestalt—and underlying regular "beat," as in Western music. Byers (1972) also has noted a cadential timing structure in the conduct of social interaction among adults. I first demonstrated cadential timing patterns in a study of academic advisor-student conversations in junior colleges (Erickson and Shultz 1982). In that work my coauthor and I were able, through the analysis of frame-numbered cinema film, to note the precise timings of the onset of body motion (in the right and left arms, head, and torso) and the onset of volume-stressed syllables in speech. Cinema film is exposed at 1/24th of a second, so our transcriptions of the cadence patterns in kinesic prosody and speech prosody were accurate to 1/24th of a second. We also found a cadence rate of approximately four "beats" over ten seconds, with some variation across twenty-six cases (four beats plus or minus two beats per ten seconds), but some regular "beat interval" invariably was apparent in the speech of the advisors and students, in every instance we analyzed. On the basis of that initial work I began to use musical notation as a way of illustrating the cadential timing patterns in speech.

Ontogeny of Timing in Human Social Interaction

Some recent work on the developmental origins of prosody in speaking—through the study of interaction between infants and their caretakers—suggests that Scollon and I were not just "making things up" in our approach to rendering speech rhythms in quasi-musical notation. The research group at the University of Edinburgh has been using sound spectrograph prints to identify cadence-like patterns in mother-infant speech that can be represented by two-beat "measures" in musical notation. Figure 1.1 presents an example from Malloch (1999/2000: 33).

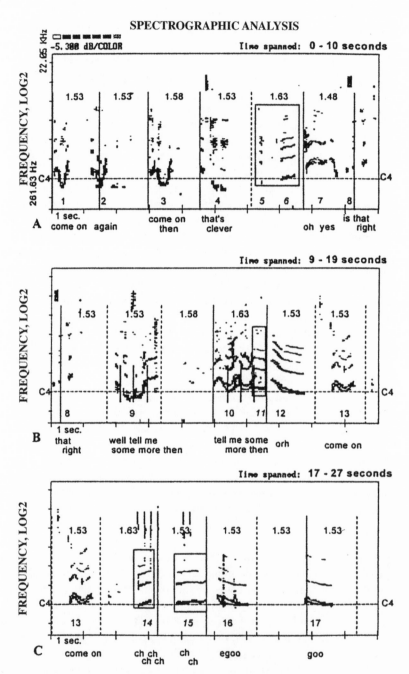

Figure 1.1. Laura (6 weeks) and her mother vocalising together.

The mother speaks to the infant in brief bursts, each of which is approximately 1.53 seconds in duration, plus or minus a maximum of 0.1 seconds. In the transcription below each burst of speech has its own line:

Mo: Come on . a-

gain . .

Come on then

That's clever

. . . .

Oh yes . is

that right .

well tell me some more then

. . . .

tell me some more then

Ch: o:::rh . .

Mo: . come on .

. come on .

Ch: ch ch ch ch

. ch .

. egoo .

In this example one can see the origins of turn-taking in conversation, with each turn-unit lasting approximately 1.5 seconds.

Using a different kind of spectrograph print, Gratier (1999/2000: 108) shows that an instance of vocalizing between another mother and infant also reveals a regular, cadential "beat," with the "line of best fit" for each beat indicated by vertical arrows in the spectrograph chart in Figure 1.2. As in the example from Malloch, the rate of the successive "beats" is roughly four in every ten seconds (recall that this is the same rate I discovered in my films of adult academic advisors and their college age advisees).

Similar cadential timing phenomena have been noted in a series of studies by Beebe et al. (1985). An implication of this finding is that as a child grows, nursery rhymes and songs provide interactional "scaffolding" practice for the acquisition of speech because the stress patterns in those rhythmically stylized genres map over the slightly less stylized but nonetheless regular patterns of timing in the conduct of ordinary talk.

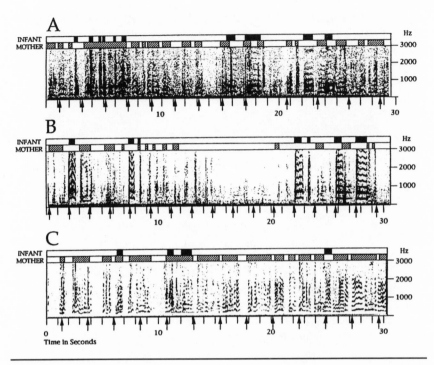

Figure 1.2. Sample spectographs of mothers' and infants' vocalisations.

I recall an example from one of my own children. Len, at approximately twenty-two months—at that point speaking only a few recognizable words—would sing the nursery rhyme song "Baa baa black sheep" with perfectly tuned pitch and regular cadential rhythm. The transcript below can be read aloud with an accent on each syllable that appears on the left margin:

> baa baa
>
> baa baa
>
> baa baa
>
> fuvvy .
>
> fuvvy
>
> fuvvy
>
> fuvvy
>
> fuvvy

What Len was doing was to change words at a major structure point in the harmonic sequence of the music (the return to the tonic chord after the sequence tonic, tonic-6, subdominant/)—a point that also was a turning point in the grammatical structure of the text (baa baa black sheep, have you any/). Where "wool" would be in the text is precisely where he shifted from "baa" to "fuvvy," and he made the shift on the next cadential "beat" after the last "baa" in his sequence. That is a point in time at which a noun is uttered that contains key information: have you any [bananas/money/fame/wool].

The example shows not only that Len was in the midst of acquiring mastery of sentence-level syntax and poem/discourse level syntax (using a very limited vocabulary as a scaffold toward further acquisition) and that this simplified syntax was leading up to a key point of new information ("wool") in the sentence/poem he was reciting (by a bricoleur-like approximation). The example also shows that he was getting to that key point of information at a point in real time that was part of an overall pattern in timing—a moment in time that was made especially clear and predictable by the cadence-like structure of the poetry he was approximating in his singing/speaking. Just as we see a cadence regularity in the mother-infant babbling sequences in the sound spectrograph examples from Malloch and Gratier, so we see it in this solo performance by a slightly older infant—and we shall see cadence patterns repeatedly in the examples that follow in the remainder of this paper, examples taken from the speech of adults and of older children and examples of song performed by adults. At this point I begin to consider a series of examples of song that are especially speech-like.

Timing in Ritual Speech: An Example from the Latin Mass

The custom of using speech-like song in religious ritual is widespread. It occurs in many non-Western musical traditions. In the Judeo-Christian tradition, passages from Scripture are declaimed by repeating a few melodic formulas over and over. So-called Gregorian chant or "plainsong"—a Christian descendent of the Jewish synagogue practice of reciting expository texts from the Torah and the prophets and singing the poetic texts of the Psalms—is a musical genre that directly influenced composers of Western art music. The melodic formulas of chant also were used to organize the exchange of turns in dialogue between a ritual leader (the priest or bishop celebrating Mass) and the congregation. The dialogue that occurs between celebrant and congregation at a liturgical high point in the Latin Mass, at the beginning of the long prayer of consecration, is reproduced below. In this example of ritual speech (whether spoken or sung), the words of each utterance and the turns at talk are predetermined. Each turn is a single intonation unit.

Celebrant:	**Do**minus vo**bis**cum
People:	Et cum **Spi**ritu tuo
Celebrant:	**Sur**sum **cor**da

Here is the same dialogue in contemporary English:

Celebrant:	The **Lo::rd** be **with** you
People:	And **also** with you . .
Celebrant:	**Lift** up your **hearts** .
People:	We **lift** them up to the **Lord**
Celebrant:	Let us give **thanks** to the Lord our **God** . .
People:	It is **right** to give Him **thanks** and praise .
Celebrant	It is a **good** and joyful thing to give thanks . . .

In this sequence, whether spoken or sung, the words presented in boldface receive pitch and volume stress. When you read this sequence aloud, stressing the boldface words, you see that this sequence produces an approximate cadence that enables celebrant and congregation to know when to begin each next line in the dialogue. Those "next moments" are redundantly cued by the melodic formulas when sung and by the prosody when spoken, as well as by the grammar of each utterance.

Musical Composition that Imitates Speech: Recitative in Opera, Oratorio, and Cantata

An additional line of evidence for the musicality of speech and for the appropriateness of quasi-musical notation as a rough illustration of speech rhythms comes from a musical genre within the tradition of Western art music. The kind of transcribing that Scollon and I had done in our GURT 1981 papers was prefigured among Western composers at the beginning of the Baroque era. This genre developed as composers sought to craft musical lines for singers that imitated closely the timing, pitch organization, and volume stress patterns of naturally occurring speech. This kind of speech/song was called "recitative." The recitative genre was employed in early opera and in oratorio (an unstaged performance of musical pieces that are very similar to those presented with staging and costume in opera).

In writing in the style of recitative, the composers used their native-speaker intuitions about speech to portray it musically—the opposite of what Scollon and I had done in our papers at GURT 1981. In preparing the current paper it occurred to me that a discussion of the ways in which composers have "realized" naturally occurring speech in musical notation since the early Baroque era might shed some light on the musicality of speech itself.

The recitative genre was invented in Florence near the end of the last decade of the sixteenth century, when a group of humanist scholars who called themselves the *Camerata* were trying to re-create the musical declamation they knew had been used by the ancient Greeks in the performance of their plays. Vincenzo Galilei (father of the physicist Galileo Galilei) was a member of this group, as was the composer Guilio Caccini. In 1600 Caccini published the text and musical score of the first opera, *Euridice*. The libretto was based on the story of the tragically fated love between Orpheus and Euridice.

Figure 1.3 presents the first example of recitative in the opera. Euridice appears onstage in the midst of a group of singing nymphs and shepherds. She declares the joys of love:

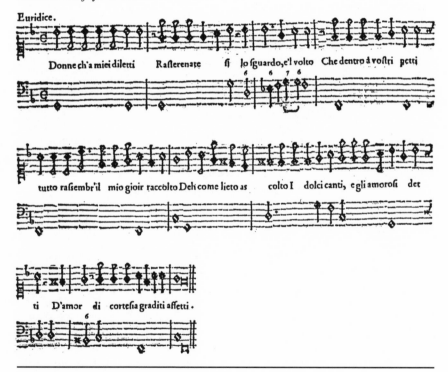

Figure 1.3. Excerpt from G. Caccini opera, *Orfeo*

Readers who can read music, even though the notation appears archaic, can see how the melodic shape of the first phrase is extremely simple: recitation on a single note (B-flat) for the first half of the phrase, followed by a melodic skip downward of a minor third, is followed by a rise of a whole step and then a half-step.

One hundred thirty years later, at the close of the Baroque era that had been begun with Caccini's first opera, the form of recitative had become a bit more complex melodically and harmonically. Yet the stylized singing in imitation of speech still kept close to the timing and pitch contours in actual speaking. Figure 1.4 depicts an example from one of the secular cantatas of J. S. Bach, published in approximately 1732. This cantata (an oratorio in miniature) would have been performed in the mansion of a nobleman, in a large gallery or reception room in which the relatively small audience of gentry would be seated, talking together before the performance. Ordinarily such a cantata would begin with an instrumental introduction, followed by a flowery, deferential address to the audience, sung as a prologue. In this case there is no instrumental introduction, and a mock prologue begins abruptly—"Schweigt stille (be quiet!) . . plaudert nicht (stop chattering . . .):

Schweigt stille . . . . Plaudert nicht . . . und höret

Be quiet!   *Stop chattering*   *and let's listen*

was jetzt und geschicht

to what I'm telling you about what's happening

Da kommt Herr Schlendrian . . .

There comes Herr Schlendrian . . .

Cantate.

„Schweigt stille, plaudert nicht.‟

Figure 1.4. Excerpt from J. S. Bach cantata, *Schweigt Stille, Plaudert Nicht*

The prologue's voice rises with a skip of a fourth upward and then falls back ("Schweigt stille—be quiet!"). As the audience laughs, presumably, at being addressed so impertinently, the voice then rises a minor third and falls a half-step ("Plaudert nicht—stop chattering"), completing the first intonation unit and repeating the injunction to the audience to stop talking. Then the voice rises an augmented fourth (which provides special harmonic emphasis as well as pitch emphasis) and, from a high note followed by a fall, returns to the exact pitch on which the first intonation unit began. The second phrase's grammatical units are each marked by a separate melodic contour:

und höret . . . . was jetzt und geschicht

(verb-subjunctive) (object of verb)

Again, one can see a cadence-like timing organization in the sequence of pitch and volume-stressed syllables: The key words *stille-plaudert-höret* all occur on the musical "beat."

Figure 1.5 presents another example by Bach, from the oratorio *St. Matthew Passion*. The evangelist/narrator describes Jesus in Bethany, at dinner in the home of Simon the leper.

Da nun Jesus war zu Bethanien

Now Jesus was at Bethany

Im hause Simonis des Aussätzigen

In the house of Simon the leper

In each of the two intonation units, key information is marked diacritically by the peaks of melodic emphasis and by the timing at which each of these peaks occurs. For example, the /tha/ of "Bethanien" is placed at the top of the melodic line that precedes it, and /tha/ also is sung at the beginning of the last measure of the first musical phrase/intonation unit. Thus, the pitch/rhythm-emphasized sylla-bles help the hearer locate crucial information nouns in the two intonation units, which enables the hearer to disambiguate during the real-time performance of the uttering, as if to answer questions such as the following:

Figure 1.5. Excerpt from J. S. Bach oratorio, *Mattäuspassion*

Da nun Jesus war / zu Be**tha**nien

(Where was Jesus? / In Bethany.)

im **Hau**se / **Simon**is / des **Aus**sätzigen

(In whose house? / That of Simon. / Who was he? / The leper.)

As in the preceding example, the core syllables in the words containing crucial new information all fall on the cadential "beat": Bethany-house-Simon-leper.

Figure 1.6 presents an example from Bach's contemporary, Handel, in a recitative from the oratorio *Messiah.*

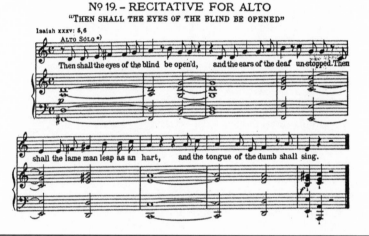

Figure 1.6. Excerpt from G. F. Handel oratorio, *Messiah*

Notice that key nouns and verbs in the text receive pitch and volume emphasis and that these stressed syllables occur on a cadential "beat"—on either the first or third quarter note in each measure:

Then shall the

eyes of the

blind be

opened

. . . and the

ears of the

deaf un

stopp-ed

. . .   then shall the lame

man   leap as an

hart   and the

tongue of the

dumb

. . .   shall

sing

This sequence of stressed words sets up the succeeding chain of expectations for the hearer, and each new expectation is fulfilled on the next cadential "beat," as indicated in the italicized column below:

(Then shall the what?

The eyes.

Of whom?

The blind.

Be what?

Opened.

And the what?

The ears.

Of whom?

Of the deaf.

Be what?

Unstopped.)

Again, the key information nouns appear on a cadential "beat": "eyes-blind-opened." The cadence tells the listener exactly where in the continuous stream of chronological time to listen for the new information—that is, where in time the immediately subsequent "next" will occur.

Recitative continued in opera during the Classic period that succeeded the Baroque, through Mozart and even past Beethoven into the early Romantic period. In the middle of the nineteenth century, however, recitative was melded into the *aria* genre, and the clear distinction between *aria* and *recitative* became blurred. At the time of World War I, a genre similar to recitative reappeared in the chamber music of Arnold Schoenberg. Figure 1.7 presents an example from Schoenberg's suite *Pierrot Lunaire*. The vocal line is uttered without definite pitch but with rising and falling intonation and regular rhythm, in a style that Schoenberg invented and called *sprechstimme* (spoken voice).

Although this atonal music sounds different, on the surface, from the recitative of the late Baroque, Schoenberg's underlying approach to a musical portrayal of speech is similar to that of earlier composers. Notice how key information nouns receive pitch stress and rhythm stress, marking the deliberately enigmatic and paradoxical sense of the symbolist poetic text:

1. Mondestrunken.

Figure 1.7. Excerpt from A. Schoenberg suite/song cycle, *Pierrot Lunaire*

	den			that	
Wein	den man mit		**wine**	which one with	
Augen trinkt	. .	giesst	**eyes** drinks	. .	pours at
Nachts		der	**night**		the
Mond		in	**moon**		in
Wo:::gen		nieder	**waves**		down

To conclude this discussion of a set of examples that were literally musical, notice that in these instances of musical attempts to imitate naturally occurring speech, stressed syllables—those bits of speech that were given special prominence within the overall speech stream—appeared more often than not at a regularly spaced temporal interval: a cadence-like "beat." As I note in my introductory remarks on the use of quasi-musical notation to portray speech rhythms, the cadence-like pattern of timing is apparent to the hearer even though not every stressed syllable falls on what would be notated as a "beat" in Western music. Enough of the stressed syllables do fall on the "beat" that as a series those syllables (together with gestures and other aspects of body motion and gaze direction) sketch a rhythmic *gestalt*—a cadence. Such a *gestalt* is apparent within each of the examples of recitative that I have presented.

The *gestalt* by which a sense of cadence in speaking is experienced leads the hearer to expect crucial new information at an anticipated "next" point in real time, and this temporal placement of new information is especially clear in the musical notation of recitative—the musical genre whose purpose is to simulate the patterns of naturally occurring speech. The significance of this point can hardly be overstated. This relation of "next" is not simply a matter of sequence, of adjacency in an abstract sense of formal succession, outside the contextual circumstances of real time. Instead, it is a sequential pattern that is realized concretely within real-time performance so that interactional partners can anticipate the chronological location of each successive "next" moment in time, as that "next" moment is about to happen.

Examples from the Dinner Table and the Classroom

Returning from the foregoing excursus to an examination of the ways in which Western music has deliberately imitated speech, I now consider further examples in which naturally occurring speech shows aspects of the organization of sound in music. The first example comes from a study of discourse in a dinner-table conversation (Erickson 1992).

During the course of the dinner, the topic of how much things cost came up. At the table were gathered the five children of the Pastore family, together with their parents and a guest who was a graduate student research assistant. The old-est son, B-1, began to list items that were paid for on a monthly basis. His younger brothers (B-2, B-3, B-4), his younger sister (S-1), and his mother (M) all contributed items to the overall list that was being sketched in talk. Invariably, the list-item nouns were uttered on a cadential "beat." This pattern was evident whether the speaker uttering the noun was the oldest son or some other member of the family.

B-1: I don't have to pay	taxes on a house
B-1: I don't have to pay	mortgage
B-1: I don't have to pay	all kinds/
S:	a water bill
B-1: I don't have to pay	all kinds of stuff like that
B-2: You don't have to pay for a car	
	'n the insurance
B-4:	electric bill
B-1: I don't have to keep two	cars on the road
M:	electric bill
	gas
	insurance

The quasi-musical transcript that appears in Figure 1.8 shows the timing of utterance of the list-item nouns. It also shows the ways in which other utterances (those of commentary and laughter) appear in the overall performance in a time frame that is consistent with the list-item nouns, which were the main focus of attention during the collective production of the list by the family members.

The accuracy of the musical notation in the transcript was tested with a MacSpeech Lab I voice analyzer, which produces a digitized display of waveforms in speech along a timeline calibrated in microseconds. This display allows the researcher to locate the temporal "center" of each major volume burst (i.e., stressed syllable) in the speech stream. Analysis of the audio channel from the videotaped conversation shows a basic cadential interval of 1.7 seconds between most stressed syllables, with variation from that unit of no more than 0.3 seconds, or 20 percent of that time interval. The machine analysis also shows that the musi-cal transcript was accurate to within less than 0.3 seconds per "beat"—usually absolutely accurate, and never as much as 0.3 seconds different from the cadential timing locations indicated by the digital readout of the MacSpeech Lab I software.

Table 1.1. Rhythm of List-item Nouns in the Discourse

I don't have to pay (for)

(15a)	B-1:	táxes	
(15b)	B-1:	mórtgage	
(15c)	B-1:	áll kinds	
(18)	S:	wáter bill	
(15d)	B-1:		all
		kinds of stuff	
(19)	B-2:	cár	in-
		surance	
(15e)	B-1:	cárs	
(20)	M:		e-
		léctric bill	
		gás	in-
		surance	
(21)	B-3:	fíve kids	
(24)	B-1:	fíve kids	
(27)	M:	shóes	
		clóthes	

Source: Erickson 1994

Table 1.1 presents the list-item nouns from the foregoing strip of conversation.

Compare this sequence of list-item nouns with the sequence of stressed syllables in the recitative from Handel's oratorio *Messiah*. In the Handel example, two nouns that receive pitch and timing stress are followed by a verb that receives pitch and timing stress (eyes-blind-opened, ears-deaf-unstopped). In the Pastore family's list of items that cost money, one noun follows another. Yet in both examples—one from dinner-table speech and the other from speech-like singing of recitative—the words that received pitch and timing prominence within the speech (song) stream were those that contained important new information. These words appeared one information-unit at a time across a series of "next" moments that occurred with a temporal regularity that was almost metronomic.

The next example comes from a bilingual first-grade classroom in which much of the instruction was in Spanish (Erickson 1982a). A child stands before the chalkboard at the front of the room and points to cards on which are written the Arabic numerals from 1 through 10. The teacher says a number word, and the child is to point to that number as the teacher utters the Spanish word that designates it. In this interaction, the cadential rhythm signals turn exchange relevance, in that the rhythm of speech marks the appropriate next moments for pointing to a number card or for saying a number word. Each number word—*cinco, seis, quatro*—is said by the teacher on the cadential beat, and on the immediately subsequent beat the child who is answering points to the card showing the number that has just been named by the teacher. This rhythm not only

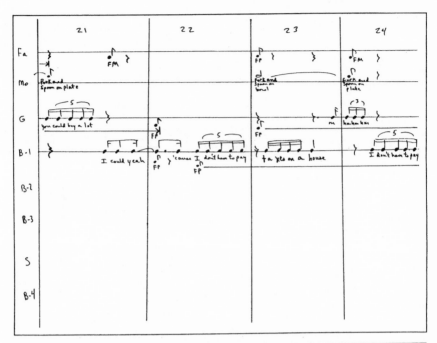

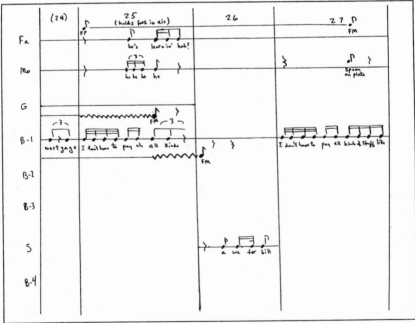

Figure 1.8 continues on facing page.

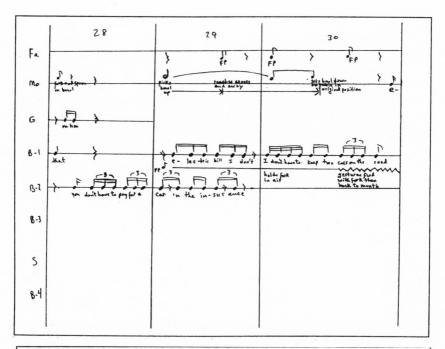

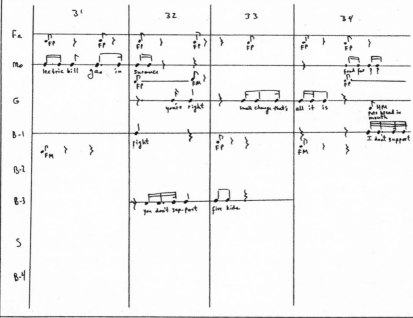

Figure 1.8.

Excerpt from family diner table conversation. Reprinted with permission by John Benjamins N.A. Inc. Originally published in *The contextualization of language*, edited by Peter Auer and Aldo di Luzio, 1992, pp. 265–397.

marks the next moments at which a card should be pointed to, it also shows the rest of the children in the room where and when to direct their visual attention in a next moment.

The importance of timing for signaling moments of transition relevance that also are moments at which key information is to be communicated (in this instance, by pointing) is underscored by what another child, Ernesto, is doing (see Figure 1.9). Ernesto has just previously had a turn at the chalkboard, pointing to the numbers on the cards in the next moment after the teacher had said the name of a number. He wants to continue doing this exercise but is told by the teacher to go to his seat and let another child have a turn as answerer. Ernesto sits down in frustration. As the answer moments come for his successor (the next student designated by the teacher as answerer/pointer), Ernesto fills the answer slots by using two pencils to tap out a rhythm pattern on the wooden surface of his desk. The time for the answer slots is cued by the teacher's prosodic emphasis on the first syllable of the numeral words (*cinco, seis, quatro*). Ernesto's tapped "answers" at his seat (as shown in measures 2, 3, and 4 of Figure 1.9) are done simultaneously with the pointings to each number card by the designated "answerer" at the front of the room.

In the next example from a kindergarten/first-grade classroom (Erickson 1996), the teacher's prosodic emphasis cues the moments of appropriateness for answering questions just asked. The conversation depicted in Figure 1.10 occurred at the beginning of the morning on the third day of the new school year.

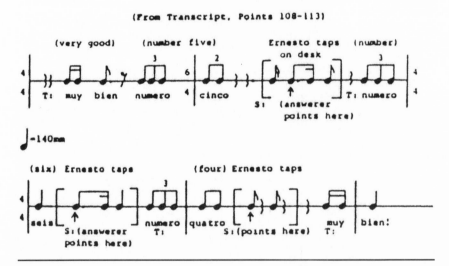

Figure 1.9.

Question-and-answer sequence, first-grade classroom. Reprinted with permission of Academic Press, *Communicating in the classroom*, ed. Louise Cherry Wilkinson, 1982, pp. 153–81.

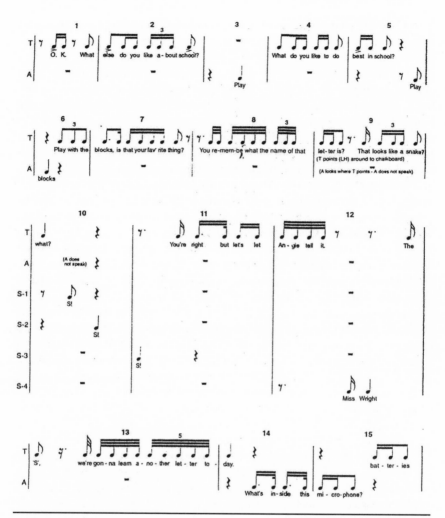

Figure 1.10. Rhythmic organization of questions and answers about school and letter name

In measures 2 and 5 the teacher asks questions of a kindergartner in which the informationally crucial words receive pitch and volume stress on the cadential beat:

What **else** do you   **like** about school?

What do you like to do **best** in school?

The child's answers came on the next beat after a one-beat pause at the ends of the teacher's questions:

> . . . .
>
> **play**
>
> . . . play
>
> **blocks**

This information (about the child's preferences) was known to the child but not to the teacher. In measure 8 the teacher asks the child, Angie, a "teacher-like" *known information* question—one to which the teacher already knows the answer: "You remember what the name of that letter is?" Angie hesitates (see measure 9) and the teacher prompts, sketching the shape of the letter in the air with her forefinger: " . . the one that looks like a snake?" If Angie had followed the timing pattern of her previous two answers ("play," "play blocks"), she would have uttered the answer "S" on the first beat of measure 10. Instead she pauses, and in rapid succession Student 1, Student 2, and Student 3 answer in her stead. Student 1 anticipates the next "beat" slightly, and Student 2 and Student 3 utter their answers exactly on the following two beats (measures 10 and 11). Thus, the example shows how the underlying cadential "beat" enables interlocutors to anticipate the next moments at which turn exchange is appropriate within successive question-answer sequences. If Student 1, Student 2, and Student 3 had not known how to "read" the timing cues in the teacher's utterance of the question about the letter S, they would not have been able to steal Angie's turn and answer. It is precisely their capacity to anticipate a tactically crucial *next moment*, as signaled by speech prosody, that this example shows us.

In a final classroom example, shown in Figure 1.11, four fifth graders are reporting to a new student teacher what they have been learning about whales in a research project. Notice again how key information nouns appear in prosodically emphasized syllables that also are rhythmically located "on the beat."

The four children sit side by side in a row at a table in the school lunchroom, facing the practice teacher who sits across the table from them. Brandon is seated at one end of the row, and Jessica is seated at the opposite end of the row. In line 4, as Brandon says "some people believe," he smiles and glances along the row of students all the way across toward Jessica. In an argument that had occurred six weeks previously (before school was interrupted by a teacher strike), Jessica had been the chief proponent of the position that killer whales should be considered taxonomically as dolphins rather than as whales. By his glance and by the prosodic timing of his words, Brandon sets up (in lines 4 and 7) an opposition between *some people* (i.e., Jessica) and *scientists* (i.e., people who concur with Brandon). Schematically, we can see Brandon's structuring of the contrasting

(1) B: ..   and they have like this

(2) thing   on their back   . .   called a

(3) dorsal fin   . . . .   and um . .

(4) some people believe that the

(5) killer whales are actually . the biggest

(6) dolphin   . . . .   but

(7) scientists have proved   . .

(8) proved in studies that is not

(9) TRUE

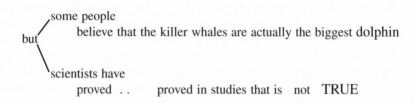

Figure 1.11. Four fifth-grade students reporting to a student teacher

propositions concerning taxonomy—Jessica's and his. The force of Brandon's argument is supported by the prosodic emphasis on "**some**" and "**dol**phin," with "**scien**tists" and "**proved**" and "not **true**."

In Chafe's terms (1994), multiple centers of interest and shifting foci of attention are apparent within and between the successive intonation units in this example. The timing of uttering here not only affords emphasis as a means of highlighting the literal, referential meanings of particular words, as it had in the preceding examples from the classroom and the dinner table (as well as in the examples of musical recitative). Here the timing of uttering goes beyond functioning as a denotative marker of clarification to function as a marker of contrast in a discourse move of persuasion. Thus, Brandon's attempt at rhetorical persuasion was given added force by the timed points of emphasis in his speech.

Conclusion

I have argued that there is a cadential organization in the real-time performance of speech. These cadences occur as roughly equal intervals in clock time (for which the term in ancient and modern Greek is *kronos*). Their function is to mark moments of special tactical relevance in speaking and listening—moments of "opportunity" (for which the term in ancient and modern Greek is *kairos*). Various tactically important things can occur in these *kairos* moments. They can be moments of "transition relevance," in which turn exchange among interlocutors is appropriate. They can be moments of "listening response relevance," at which verbal and/or nonverbal listening response by an interlocutor is appropriate (on this point, see especially Erickson 1986).

As I have demonstrated through examples in the foregoing discussion, certain *kairos* moments that are pointed to by the cadential timing of speech are moments within intonation units at which crucial new information is communicated, as key information nouns and verbs are uttered and as a new rhetorical point is made. All of these functions of *kairos* moments (marking transition relevance, listening-response relevance, key information, and rhetorical emphasis) are apparent in machine recording of talk, as illustrated by the examples of sound spectrograph printouts of mother-infant dialogue. They also are apparent in the western European musical genre of recitative, in which composers from the sixteenth through the early nineteenth centuries used their native-speaker intuitions about speech prosody to construct in musical notation an imitation of ordinary talk. The various functions of timing in speech also are made apparent in quasi-musical notation that indicates the real-time occurrence of talk, marking the temporal location of points of volume and pitch emphasis within the speech stream.

The main implication of this argument is that it is necessary for listeners to hear prehensively, to "listen for" crucial *kairos* moments in the speech stream, because that stream, taken as a whole, contains more information than can be handled cognitively through uniform monitoring of it across time. I am assuming that an ebb and flow of attention—which can anticipate customary patterns of prosodic emphasis used in a given community of speaking practices—is an important aspect of linguistic and interactional competence. I contend that the cadential patterns in speaking that I have illustrated here "tell" the hearer where in time to focus attention, and in so doing those speech rhythms (and the hearer's capacities to "read" them as attentional cues) provide a foundation for the articulation of conjoint social action that is necessary for the real-time conduct of talk—the performed social organization of talk in face-to-face interaction.

Note

1. Audio and video examples from this essay can be accessed at Frederick Erickson's website: www.gseis.ucla.edu/faculty/pages/ferickson.html.

REFERENCES

Auer, Peter. 1992. Introduction: John Gumperz' approach to contextualization. In *The contextualization of language,* edited by Peter Auer and Aldo di Luzio. Amsterdam and Philadelphia: John Benjamin Publishing Co., 1–38.

Beebe, Beatrice, Joseph Jaffe, Stanley Feldstein, Kathleen Mays, and Deborah Alson. 1985. Inter-personal timing: The application of an adult dialogue model to mother-infant vocal and kinesic interactions. In *Social perception in infants,* edited by Tiffany M. Field and Nathan Fox. Norwood, N.J.: Ablex, 249–68.

Byers, Paul. 1972. From biological rhythm to cultural pattern: A study of minimal units. Ph.D. diss., Columbia University.

Chafe, Wallace. 1994. *Discourse, consciousness, and time.* Chicago: University of Chicago Press.

Erickson, Frederick. 1979. Talking down: Some cultural sources of miscommunication in interracial interviews. In *Research in nonverbal communication,* edited by Aaron Wolfgang. New York: Academic Press, 99–125.

———. 1982a. Classroom discourse as improvisation: Relationships between academic task structure and social participation structure in lessons. In *Communicating in the classroom,* edited by Louise C. Wilkinson. New York: Academic Press, 155–81.

———. 1982b. Money tree, lasagna bush, salt and pepper: Social construction of topical cohesion in a conversation among Italian-Americans. In *Analyzing discourse: Text and talk,* edited by Deborah Tannen. Washington, D.C.: Georgetown University Press, 43–70.

———. 1986. Listening and speaking. In *Language and linguistics: The interdependence of theory, data, and application. Georgetown University Round Table on Languages and Linguistics 1985,* edited by Deborah Tannen and James E. Alatis. Washington, D.C.: Georgetown University Press, 294–319.

———. 1992. They know all the lines: Rhythmic organization and contextualization in a conversational listing routine. In *The contextualization of language,* edited by Peter Auer and Aldo di Luzio. Amsterdam/Philadelphia: John Benjamin Publishing Co., 365–97.

———. 1996. Going for the zone: The social and cognitive ecology of teacher-student interaction in classroom conversations. In *Discourse, learning, and schooling,* edited by Deborah Hicks. Cambridge and New York: Cambridge University Press, 29–62.

Erickson, Frederick, and Jeffrey Shultz. 1982. *The counselor as gatekeeper: Social interaction in interviews.* New York: Academic Press.

Ford, Cecilia, and Sandra A. Thompson. 1996. Interactional units in conversation: Syntactic, intonational, and pragmatic resources for the management of turns. In *Interaction and grammar,* edited by Elinor Ochs, Emanuel A. Schegloff, and Sandra A. Thompson. Cambridge: Cambridge University Press.

Gratier, Maya. 1999/2000. Expressions of belonging: The effect of acculturation on the rhythm and harmony of mother-infant vocal interaction. *Musicae Scientiae: Journal of the European Society for the Cognitive Sciences of Music* (special issue 1999/2000): 93–122.

Jaffe, Joseph, and Stanley Feldstein. 1970. *Rhythms of dialogue.* New York: Academic Press.

Malloch, Stephen. 1999/2000. Mothers and infants and communicative musicality. *Musicae Scientiae: Journal of the European Society for the Cognitive Sciences of Music* (special issue 1999/2000): 29–58.

Scollon, Ron. 1982. The rhythmic integration of ordinary talk. In *Analyzing discourse: Text and talk. Georgetown University Roundtable on Language and Linguistics 1981,* edited by Deborah Tannen. Washington, D.C.: Georgetown University Press, 335–49.

Trevarthen, Colwyn. 1999. Musicality and the intrinsic motive pulse: Evidence from human psychobiology and infant communication. *Musicae scientiae: Journal of the European Society for the Cognitive Sciences of music* (special issue 1999/2000): 155–215.

Van Leeuen, Theo. 1999. *Speech, music, sound.* New York: St. Martin's Press.

Laughing while talking

Wallace Chafe
University of California, Santa Barbara

Like many linguists who are interested in discourse, I have spent a great deal of time transcribing speech, and like many others I have frequently come across instances of laughing. The easy way out is just to ignore them, or to write nothing more than the word "laugh" in parentheses, but transcribers often go farther than that, perhaps writing something like "heh heh heh heh" or "mh hih hih huh" (*cf.* Jefferson 1985). In Santa Barbara there has been a tradition of writing each pulse of laughter with "@," as in:

(1)   @@@@@@=,

In this case there were six laugh pulses. The equals sign shows that the last pulse was lengthened, and the comma shows a final rising pitch contour. There is a need, however, for additional transcription conventions that will capture more of the variety to be found in this special kind of sound. I make a few suggestions in this essay, but more are needed to cover the full range of variation.

Sooner or later one may wonder when and why people make sounds like these. The literature on laughter is extensive (see Ruch and Ekman 2001 for a review), but as far as I know the topics I discuss here still have not been adequately covered. My own interest goes back to the 1970s; at that time I wrote a paper on the subject that was published some years later (Chafe 1987). I have a particular reason for returning to it now: a developing interest in ways in which language expresses emotions. In this essay I try to make a case that laughter does indeed express an emotion. First, however, I say a few things about the sound itself, the phonetics of laughter. My examples are excerpts from the Corpus of Spoken American English that is being compiled at the University of California, Santa Barbara—specifically, the selections from that corpus that have been made available by the Linguistic Data Consortium at the University of Pennsylvania.

The Phonetics of Laughter

Laughter is produced by a spasmodic expulsion of air from the lungs. Its predominant physical effect is to remove air from the lungs more forcefully than is done during relaxed breathing or ordinary speech. As these explosive pulses of air

travel upward through the larynx, they usually set the vocal folds to vibrating—
which is to say that laughter usually is voiced, although voiceless laughter does
occur. This forceful depletion of air is necessarily followed by a pulse of inhal-
ing, the recovery phase, which often is audible as well.

In example (2a) there was first a single voiceless pulse with audible glottal
friction, which I have indicated with the lowercase "h" at the beginning. This
voiceless pulse was followed by five voiced pulses with a rising pitch at the end,
indicated with the comma. In (2b) there was a single pulse from the other speaker, whose lips were closed, as shown with the superscript "m". The pitch this time
fell, as shown by the period. Finally, in (2c), there was an audible inhalation to
recover the lost air, as shown with the capital "H."

(2) a   Pamela: h @@@@@,

b   Darryl: @^{m}.

c   Pamela: H

Sometimes during the final inhalation the vocal folds vibrate to produce ingressive voicing, as in (3c), where it is indicated with an exclamation point following
the capital "H." Ingressive voicing is perceptually distinguishable from egressive
voicing and voiceless inhalation. In (3c) it was preceded by a 0.4-second pause.
The square brackets in (3a) and (3b) indicate overlapping pulses.

(3) a   Jamie: @[@@],

b   Pete: [@@@]@.

c   Jamie: (.4) H!

In (4) there is a more complex sequence, in which a single pulse in (4a) was followed in (4b) by six pulses, the third and fifth of which were weaker than the others (as shown with smaller type). There was an inhalation in (4c), followed in (4d)
by six pulses with a change in vowel quality in the middle, and then a voiced
inhalation in (4e). In (4f) there was a sniff and one more pulse, and in (4g) eleven
pulses, followed by a voiced inhalation in (4h).

(4) a   @.

b   (.2) @@@@@@,

c   (.3) H

d   (.3) @^{e}@^{e}@^{e}@^{a}@^{a}@^{a},

e   (.5) H!

f   (.3) H^{n} @,

g   (.3) @ .. @@@@@@@@@@,

h   H!

At the opposite extreme from the extensive laughing in (4), there may be nothing more than a single pulse, as in (5).

(5)   @,

These laugh sounds are surrounded by speech, of course, and occasionally they are simultaneous with it, as in (6)—where the last part of (6a), all of (6b), and a portion in the middle of (6c) were pronounced with forceful expulsions of air superimposed on the speech sounds. I have shown this laughing that is simultaneous with speech in boldface and underlined.

(6)   a   [That's what] **she does,**

b   **she gets real embarrassed,**

c   and she just gigg**les like** a goofball.

Once these spasmodic pulses of air reach the upper part of the vocal tract, they are modified in the mouth. The variety of oral articulations is more restricted than in speech, but several options exist. For example, there are vocalic laughs and consonantal laughs. With vocalic laughs the airstream passes through the mouth relatively freely, whereas with consonantal laughs it is shut off, usually by closing the lips, so that it passes only through the nose. There is an illustration of this bilabial laughter in (7), shown with a superscript "m" (*cf.* 2b).

(7)   ... (.3) @^{m}@^{m}@^{m},

With regard to vocalic articulation, there is a popular idea that laughs are pronounced as "ha ha ha," or "ho ho ho," or "he he he." What I have been finding in real life is that most laughs appear to have the tongue in the position of approximately a low schwa. Laughs are not as cleanly periodic as ordinary vowels, and it is difficult to identify formants that would aid in identifying their vowel quality. Sometimes, however, variations in vowel quality are clearly perceptible, as in (4d)—repeated as (8)—where the superscripts show roughly the vowel change.

(8)   (.3) @^{e}@^{e}@^{e}@^{a}@^{a}@^{a},

Although much more could be said about the phonetics of laughter, I mention just two additional considerations. Laughing typically is accompanied by the adjustment of facial muscles that we call smiling. It is unnatural to laugh without smiling at the same time. Smiling affects the nature of the resulting sound, and generally it is possible to hear that people are smiling as they talk. In (9a) Pamela was smiling; in (9b), which began with an inhalation, she was not. The smiling faces at the beginning and end of (9a) are an obvious transcription device.

(9) a   Pamela: ☺Of whatever it was I was doing before I was,☺

    b   H before my number came up.

One might be tempted to suppose that smiling alone, without pulses of laughter, is the mildest form of laughter itself: one end of a laugh continuum. It is more likely, however, that the function of smiling is broader than that of laughing, a more general expression of happiness and good feeling—more akin to the emotion expressed by dogs when they wag their tails.

The phonetics of laughter involves the production, propagation, and perception of this special kind of sound, but those are not the only aspects that should ultimately be describable in physical terms. Surely there are accompanying brain states and processes. It is impossible to predict how long it will be before we can relate laughing to specific neural events. In the meantime, as in other cases, we will have to rely on our ability to observe and describe introspectively what we experience when we laugh and when we hear others laugh. As in other cases, an eventual understanding of physical events in the brain, helpful though it will be, still will not elucidate the quality of the experience itself.

Laughter as the Expression of an Emotion

I have suggested that laughing expresses an emotion. This emotion is not usually included in a class with anger, fear, sadness, or joy, but I suggest that it does belong in such a list. We even fail to have a word for it that would be parallel to words such as "anger" or "fear." We do have the word "humor," but it applies to some of the stimuli that produce this emotion, not the emotion itself. In this essay, for reasons that will become clear, I refer to this emotion as "the feeling of nonseriousness."

This nonserious feeling shares with the more generally recognized emotions at least five properties:

- It is not under voluntary control.
- It fades slowly.
- It is contagious.
- It comes in degrees.
- It is universal.

First, the feeling of nonseriousness is not under voluntary control in the sense that we usually do not put ourselves into it by an act of will, just as we do not voluntarily make ourselves sad or joyful. It usually is triggered by external events or, sometimes, by events inside ourselves. It is true that actors may have the ability to call up emotions in themselves voluntarily or to let their emotions be triggered by events in a play, and thus to sound as if they are authentically experiencing them. But the feeling of nonseriousness is no different from other emotions in this regard.

Second, this feeling fades slowly. It affects our experience over relatively long intervals, as compared to the rapid turnover of ideas in focal consciousness, where there is a replacement every second or two. Each Monday my local newspaper carries next to its editorial page a column by Dave Barry. When I open the paper on Monday I read that column first, and it is quite effective in producing the feeling of nonseriousness in me. If I then turn to another columnist or letters to the editor or editorials, I find myself unable at first to take them seriously. This feeling is slow to dissipate, and at least for a few minutes any serious consideration of politics or any other serious topic is impossible. Again, the feeling of nonseriousness shares this property of slow fading with other emotions.

The third property is contagiousness, as is well known and easily observable. In (10) there is an example of shared hilarity, with three people laughing together.

(10) a   Pete: (.3) @^{m} [1@^{m}1],

    b   Jamie: [2[1@1]@@2] @@ h @$_@$@@@,

    c   Harold: [2@@@@2] @@@,

    d   Pete: @^{m}@^{m}@^{m}@^{m},

    e   Jamie: (.45) h @@@,

    f   (.73) @,

    g   (1.25) H

Television sitcom producers believe that adding a laugh track to their product, or producing it in front of a live audience that already has been stimulated into the feeling of nonseriousness artificially, will help to create that state among millions of people in their broader audience.

The fourth property is the observation that emotions come in degrees. We experience them more or less. We can be more or less angry, more or less afraid, more or less happy—and similarly, we can experience the feeling of nonseriousness to a greater or lesser degree. Some of these degrees even have names. The word "chuckle" captures a mild degree of amusement that usually is limited to one person, "hilarity" a stronger emotion that is shared, as in (10).

The fifth property is universality. Emotions, including the feeling of nonseriousness, are experienced by humans everywhere. People in different cultures may differ in many ways, but everyone experiences emotions. Two obvious disclaimers are necessary. First, different cultures certainly can differ with regard to what triggers emotions. Events that produce anger, or the feeling of nonseriousness, in one culture may not produce the same emotion in another. Some cultures may even encourage anger, or the nonserious feeling, more than others. It would be surprising, however, to find a culture in which people were never angry, or never experienced the feeling of nonseriousness. A second disclaimer is needed for individual differences. Just as some people are more prone to anger than others, so there are some who experience the feeling of nonseriousness more easily and more often. If there are some who never experience it at all, that condition borders on the pathological. Here too, however, this feeling is just like other emotions.

If laughing does express an emotion, then, how can that emotion be characterized? It is impossible to describe an emotion as one might describe a physical object. An emotion is an experience, and there is no way to put such an experience into words—even less into some formal representation. Even if we eventually are able to associate particular emotions with particular neural processes, that will not tell us what the experience itself is like.

Nevertheless, there is one very important and obvious thing we can say about the feeling of nonseriousness: It is pleasant. If anger, fear, and sadness are unpleasant, this feeling is the opposite. In that respect it belongs in a class with aesthetic experiences, certain drug-induced experiences, and sex. It is interesting that these are experiences that people go out of their way to have, and even pay money for. People pay to visit art museums and concerts, to buy drugs, and to have sex. They also pay for books and movies and other products that make them laugh. Creating the feeling of nonseriousness in large numbers of people is an extremely profitable business. It is one of the best sources of pleasure available to people, among other reasons because it lacks the undesirable side effects that may accompany drugs and sex.

The Function of Nonseriousness

Now, however, we come to the big questions: What is it, exactly, that produces this feeling in people? And why should whatever it is create an emotion that brings together a peculiar conjunction of properties: a spasmodic expulsion of air from the lungs along with enjoyment? Depletion of air and euphoria: Why should those two be linked?

The suggestion I set forth in Chafe (1987) was that this feeling is an emotion that keeps us from taking seriously—and from taking action with respect to—experiences that it would be inappropriate to take seriously, or to act on. It does so by physically disabling us through the expulsion of air and by psychologically disabling us through a feeling of pleasure that distracts us from serious thought. It is useful to think of this phenomenon in terms of various worlds that people can know about and interact with. All humans have an idea of a normal world: a world they believe to be real, a world that conforms to their expectations of how things really are. Different people have different conceptions of this normal world, but everyone has some conception of it. Suppose we use the word "serious" to characterize experiences that conform to this world of normal expectations. People take newly encountered experiences seriously if these experiences contribute to their knowledge of this normal world.

Evidently there are two kinds of experience that are not taken seriously in this sense. One kind comes under the heading of play. Athletic contests and other kinds of games—although there may be a sense in which people take them seriously indeed—are nonconsequential in the sense that they fail to affect people's lives in a serious way. There is a difference between a baseball game and a wartime battle. In both, two sides are contesting with each other, but it is only in the battle that people lose their lives and property is devastated. If there were a game in which the members of the losing team were lined up and shot, we would certainly want to say that things turned serious at that point: that people were no longer playing. That is the perspective that allows us to say that play is nonconsequential.

Athletic contests, however, are still full of action. People do things. What is further removed from the normal, serious, consequential world is the world associated with laughter, where the things people experience or imagine are inappropriate for action. If both play and whatever it is that triggers the feeling of nonseriousness are nonconsequential, the latter goes a step further in being what might be called nonactionable as well. What triggers the feeling of nonseriousness is either imagining or actually encountering a world that is judged to be inappropriate to act on. At the same time, however, it is a world that has some kind of pseudo-plausibility. We recognize a pseudo-logic by which the existence of such a world could somehow be entertained. The feeling of nonseriousness is a safety valve that keeps us from acting on that pseudo-plausible but nonactionable world by depleting air from our lungs and at the same time distracting us with a feeling of euphoria.

We can look first at an example in which a pseudo-plausible world was imagined, not real. The context of (11) was as follows: People had been talking about dancing. Within that general topic they introduced and developed more specific topics that involved dancing in some way. In (11) Miles introduced one such topic by asking a question of Harold, and Harold's wife Jamie and a friend named Pete then commented on Harold's response.

(11) a Miles: (5.0) What are you planning on doing with dancing Harold.

   b   (.9) You were taking some classes last fall?

   c Harold: I'll take a few more,

   d Jamie: (.3) [You will?]

   e Harold: [As a] it turns out as a spouse I get in free.

   f Pete: Oh really.

g   Harold: So,

h   Pete: [That's not] bad.

i   Jamie: [To group classes,]

j   Pete: (.5) Hm.

k   Harold: So,

l   I should [do that].

m   Miles: [Oh really?]

n   Jamie: Mhm,

The topic of Harold's free dance lessons was now open for further development. Everything that had been said up to this point was serious, but Miles changed that by saying what's in (12).

(12)   Miles: (1.2) That's why you married her.

Miles thereby shifted the conversation into an imaginary world in which Harold had married Jamie so he could have free dance lessons.

It is of some interest that we use the word "funny" in two ways: for something that produces the feeling of nonseriousness but also for something that fails to conform to our normal world, something that would be inappropriate to take seriously or act on. Thus, we can say that (12) introduced a "funny" world in the latter sense: a world in which Harold married Jamie to get free dance lessons—conforming to the pseudo-logic that people marry people for some benefit, and free dance lessons are a benefit. It was easy to recognize that this was not a world to take seriously, and Miles made that clear to everyone by laughing the laughs in (13): first a three-pulse chuckle, then a basic laugh with six pulses, then another three-pulse chuckle.

(13) a   Miles: (1.2) That's why you married her.

b   .. @@@.

c   (.3) @@@@@@,

d   .. @@@.

The feeling of nonseriousness then spread contagiously to others in the conversation. The first to join in was Jamie. In (14a) she smiled as she joined Miles in his funny world, suggesting that free dance lessons were not really such a great benefit. In (14b) she added a single pulse of laughter, which overlapped four more pulses by Miles in (14c). Miles recovered his breath with a voiced inhalation in (14d), and there was another single and high-pitched pulse by Jamie in (14e).

(14) a   Jamie: ☺Some benefit huh?☺

    b   [@],

    c   Miles: [@] @@@.

    d   .. H!

    e   Jamie: (0.2) @,

Harold then kept the funny world alive by suggesting in (15) that, although free dance lessons may not have been a wonderful benefit, they were at least something.

(15)   Harold: It's better than nothing,

His comment elicited more laughter from Miles and Pete in (16).

(16) a   Miles: (.6) @^{m},

    b   @. @[@@@=],

    c   Pete: [@^{m}@^{m}@^{m}@^{m}@^{m}@^{m}]@^{m},

The feeling of nonseriousness continued, kept alive by further fictional evaluations of Jamie's and Harold's marriage, until this episode ran its course. The same conversation exhibited other nonserious episodes, also initiated by Miles. To that extent, and especially because of Miles's presence, it could be characterized as a light-hearted conversation. In other conversations, depending on the participants, episodes such as this may be more or less frequent, or they may be lacking altogether.

The most interesting finding, however, may be that most of the laughing in conversations is not like this example, not the result of someone trying deliberately to produce the feeling of nonseriousness. Usually the laughing just happens in the ordinary course of what is being talked about. Most of the laughing people do in their daily lives is not in response to deliberate humor or jokes at all. This observation stems especially from works by Robert Provine (e.g., Provine 2000), and what I have found confirms what he wrote. I have found also that the stimulus for nonseriousness need not be an imagined world at all—that it is probably more often a real world that for some reason the speaker wants to avoid taking seriously or does not want others to take seriously.

Laughing at Unpleasantness

During one conversation a woman named Lynne had been talking about how she took lessons in shoeing horses. She said that the students did not start with live horses, which they might injure through inexperience. At first they used legs that had been cut from dead horses. Then she said what is transcribed in (17).

(17) a   Lynne: I mean you have this h . . . (2.1) piece of **horse**,

     b   @@H **I mean this** leg that's-

     c   oh it's just gross.

     d   H

This was not an imagined world; Lynne really did work with these pieces of horse. But as she told about it she laughed, and by laughing she was able to mitigate its seriousness. Without the laughter there would have been nothing but a disgusting experience. With laughter, a bit of the edge was removed from that disgustingness.

Prior to the excerpt in (18), Roy and Marilyn had been talking about a book they had read in which the author described how humans had become the dominant force on earth, replacing the world of nature. They found that idea depressing. In (18d) Marilyn said explicitly, "Then it gets really depressing." After that both Marilyn and her friend Pete engaged in a great deal of laughter. Why should all this laughter accompany talk about a depressing idea? Again, placing this topic in a nonserious world was a way of mitigating its unpleasantness.

(18) a   Roy: And then he goes on,

     b   for the rest of book,

     c   to [absolutely],

     d   Marilyn: [Then it gets really] depressing @.

     e   Roy: [2heartless2][3ly3],

     f   Pete: [2@Oh2] [3@good3].

     g   Marilyn: [3@3] [4@@@@4] [5@=

     h   Pete: [4@ @oh @gee @4]

Associating laughter with unpleasant experiences may seem paradoxical, but it makes sense if one understands the feeling of nonseriousness as an emotion whose function is specifically to prevent experiences from being taken seriously. In a variety of examples I have found it associated with experiences that might variously be characterized as awkward, confusing, disastrous, disgusting, embarrassing, illegal, insulting, stupid, threatening, or unethical, and doubtless other adjectives could be added to this list. To mention an extreme case, during the Vietnam War I was told that when some Vietnamese women saw pictures of atrocities inflicted on Vietnamese children, they broke into laughter. To take those pictures seriously was more than they could bear, and their laughter must have given them a way of dealing with their extreme distress.

These examples raise the question of whether the feeling of nonseriousness can be experienced simultaneously with other emotions such as disgust, depression, or horror, or whether it serves to replace such unpleasant emotions with a feeling that is enjoyable. Is it, in short, a mask to hide unpleasantness (*cf.* Ekman 1973), or is it a genuine, though perhaps only temporary, replacement of an unpleasant emotion? I am inclined to fàvor the latter interpretation, but the question is open for further study.

Laughing and Ridicule

In the Western tradition of laughter and humor studies there is an old idea associated with what has been called the "superiority theory." Keith-Spiegel (1972: 6) summarized this view in the following way: "The roots of laughter in triumph over other people (or circumstances) supplies the basis for superiority theories. Elation is engendered when we compare ourselves favorably to others as being less stupid, less ugly, less unfortunate, or less weak. According to the principle of superiority, mockery, ridicule, and laughter at the foolish actions of others are central to the humor experience." The truth is that ridicule is only one of many triggers for laughter, but it is interesting that people in the ancient Mediterranean world regarded it as so important. Perhaps that shows more about them than about laughter itself.

The fact is, however, that we do sometimes find laughing an accompaniment to ridicule. We even have expressions such as "laughing at" or "making fun" of someone. Prior to (19), Pamela had been talking about how, when she was a girl, she had trouble understanding a definition of the word "paradox." In (19e) she said, "I sort of bit my teeth into that one." Whatever she may have meant, her friend Darryl found it a "funny" thing for her to say, and he laughed. Pamela could have proceeded to explain what she meant, but instead she joined in the laughter herself—perhaps because it was contagious, perhaps because she wished to follow the lead of her partner.

(19) a   Pamela: (.6) Well,

b   that was age twelve.

c   (.3) So that

d   (.2) that was very close to Devon's age when,

e   (.9) H I sort of (.2) bit my teeth into that one.

f   Darryl: (.5) Bit your teeth hunh?

g   Pamela: H And then,

h   [1yeah.]

i   As I went1]

j   Darryl: [1@@@@@1]@,

k Pamela: (.3) @@@[2@@@@2],

l   Darryl: [2@@@2]@@,

m Pamela: H (.2) I=

n Darryl: H @h@,

o Pamela: [took] a bite?

p Darryl: [@@]

q   **Is** is that **like** (.2) **cutting** it [in the] nip?

r Pamela: [@@],

s Darryl: @@@@@@@[@@],

t Pamela: [H]

u   (1.6) H I= (.2) I get a [little **ahead of myself**.]

v Darryl: [@@@@@ H],

w   **Yeah I guess you do**,

x   @@@@@,

y   H

Laughing as a Lubricant

The last use of laughter to be illustrated here involves what I think of as lubricating the interaction between separate minds. The act of influencing another person not through overt persuasion but simply by providing information the other person did not previously have—by inserting one's own knowledge into another's mind—can be a mild imposition. In a small way, one is trying to make the other person's mind conform to one's own. People sometimes laugh for no other purpose than to remove the seriousness of this imposition.

The example in (20) illustrates, in part, an attempt to steer the flow of a conversation. At the same time it shows how the mildly impositional nature of doing so was mitigated with laughter. Jamie had been telling how she became annoyed at a neighbor who had a large number of ill-behaved children. She said that the way she reacted to those children made her feel like an old lady—a role that made her uncomfortable. In (20a) she then tried to steer the conversation away from that uncomfortable topic by saying explicitly, "New subject." But then she laughed, and by laughing she reduced the slight presumptuousness that might otherwise have been associated with steering a conversation.

(20) a Jamie: New subject,

    b   @@,

    c Pete: Hm.

    d Jamie: @@,

    e   H!

Conclusion

My purpose has been to suggest why a linguist interested in natural discourse might find it rewarding to look carefully and systematically at laughing. My main points have been these. Humans often experience an emotion that might be called, in lieu of a better term, a feeling of nonseriousness. Laughing is an overt expression of this emotion, and its most conspicuous manifestations include forcefully expelling air from the lungs and simultaneously feeling pleasure. This seemingly odd combination makes sense if we hypothesize that the feeling of nonseriousness functions to prevent us from taking seriously experiences that have some kind of pseudo-plausibility but that it would be inappropriate to take seriously. In Chafe (1987) I called laughter a "disabling mechanism." Expelling air keeps us from acting in a physical way, while euphoria distracts us intellectually. Laughing in conversations sometimes is a response to a deliberate attempt to put people in this state, but more often it is a response to something that just happens to arise in the course of the conversation and that is, for one reason or another, judged inappropriate for seriousness. Often this judgment is associated with a desire to mitigate an experience that would be undesirable or unpleasant if it were taken seriously. Studying in detail the many and varied occurrences of laughing while talking can add significantly to our understanding of human thought and interaction.

References

Chafe, Wallace. 1987. Humor as a disabling mechanism. *American Behavioral Scientist* 30: 16–25.
Ekman, Paul. 1973. Cross-cultural studies of facial expression. In *Darwin and facial expression: A century of research in review*, edited by Paul Ekman. New York: Academic Press, 169–222.
Jefferson, Gail. 1985. An exercise in the transcription and analysis of laughter. In *Handbook of discourse analysis. Volume 3: Discourse and dialogue*, edited by Teun van Dijk. New York: Academic Press, 25–34.

Keith-Spiegel, Patricia. 1972. Early conceptions of humor: Varieties and issues. In *The psychology of humor: Theoretical perspectives and empirical issues*, edited by Jeffrey H. Goldstein and Paul E. McGhee. New York: Academic Press, 3–39.

Provine, Robert R. 2000. *Laughter: A scientific investigation*. New York: Viking.

Ruch, Willibald, and Paul Ekman. 2001. The expressive pattern of laughter. In *Emotion, qualia, and consciousness*, edited by Alfred Kaszniak. Tokyo: World Scientific Publishing, 410–25.

Power maneuvers or connection maneuvers? Ventriloquizing in family interaction[1]

Deborah Tannen
Georgetown University

Family interaction has long been the object of study by scholars in a wide range of fields, but their ranks have been joined by linguists and linguistic anthropologists relatively recently. Especially prominent have been researchers concerned with understanding children's acquisition of language, such as Shoshana Blum-Kulka (1997) and Elinor Ochs and her colleagues and students (Ochs, Pontecorvo, and Fasulo 1996; Ochs and Taylor 1992a, 1992b, 1995; Ochs et al. 1992). These studies have examined conversational interaction recorded around the dinner table—a logical choice because family members typically gather and talk over dinner and because the bounded nature of the activity, as well as the physical orientation around a table, facilitate recording.

My own recent research interest in family interaction (Tannen 2001, 2003) has developed out of my ongoing interest in the language of conversational interaction in general and of interpersonal relationships in particular (Tannen 1984, 1986, 1990). It draws on and contributes to two theoretical frameworks I have been developing: first, the ambiguity and polysemy of power and solidarity (Tannen 1994), and second, the linguistic framing of verbal interaction. I have been developing these frameworks both as a continuation of my overriding goal of understanding what drives interactional discourse and as a corrective to the widespread tendency to focus on power in discourse. I have argued that in studying interaction, we need to understand power (or hierarchy, or control) not as distinguished from solidarity (or connection, or intimacy) but as inseparable from and intertwined with it. Because relationships among family members are intensely hierarchical and intensely connected, family interaction is an ideal site for exploring the ambiguity and polysemy of power and solidarity. In keeping with my ongoing interest in framing in discourse, I have been examining the interplay of hierarchy and connection through a type of interactional framing—a phenomenon I call ventriloquizing.

To gain access to talk that goes on in the private world of families, my colleague Shari Kendall and I designed a project in which we enlisted four families who agreed to tape-record their own interactions, at home and at work, for a week. Drawing on a subset of the tape recordings of home interaction, I have been examining conversational interchanges in which one family member (usually the mother) communicates to a second (either the father or a child) by speaking through, for, or to a third (typically a small child or a pet). The canonical form of what I call ventriloquizing is an interchange in which, for example, a mother holding an infant might say to her husband in a high-pitched, baby-talk register, "Daddy, my diaper is dirty!" She is speaking *as* the child to encourage the father to change the baby's diaper. I also examine related strategies by which, for example, a mother may communicate to her husband by speaking *through* the child— still using a high-pitched baby-talk register but framing the utterance as addressed *to* rather than as the child. Thus, the hypothetical mother could have reminded her husband to change the baby's diaper by saying to the infant, "You have a dirty diaper, don't you? Yes, you do!"

I begin this chapter by briefly recapping my theoretical framework of power and solidarity. Readers who have encountered this discussion elsewhere are encouraged to skip to the succeeding section, in which I explore the intertwined nature of power and solidarity in the context of the crucial family role of mother. I then turn to the conversational strategy, ventriloquizing. After identifying this strategy as a type of constructed dialogue that creatively manipulates the framing of utterances, I examine four examples that emerged in the tape recordings of interaction made by two of the four families in our project. In each case, I demonstrate that the conversational strategies are simultaneously power maneuvers and connection maneuvers. The first example I discuss is an instance of canonical ventriloquizing, the second and third are ventriloquizing-like interactions, and the fourth is a complex blending of both. My analysis and discussion add, I hope, to our understanding of the discourse analysis of interaction in general as well as the specific understanding of family interaction.

The Ambiguity and Polysemy of Power and Solidarity

Researchers routinely interpret interaction, in the family and elsewhere, as a struggle for power. For example, in a book titled *Power in Family Discourse,* Watts (1991: 145) defines power as "the ability of an individual to achieve her/his desired goals." Similarly, in a book about family conversation Varenne (1992: 76) explains, "The power we are interested in here is the power of the catalyst who, with a minimal amount of its own energy, gets other entities to spend large amounts of their own."[2] Millar, Rogers, and Bavelas (1984) write of "control maneuvers" and note that in family therapy, "Conflict takes place within the power dimension of relationships." My claim is that family interaction (including conflict) also takes place within the intimacy dimension, and we also can speak of—indeed, need to speak of—"connection maneuvers."

Elsewhere (Tannen 1994) I explore and argue for what I call the ambiguity and polysemy of power and solidarity—or, in different terms, of status or hierarchy and of connection or intimacy. Here I briefly recap this analysis.

In conventional wisdom, as well as in research tracing back to Brown and Gilman's (1960) classic study of power and solidarity, Americans have had a tendency to conceptualize the relationship between hierarchy (or power) and connection (or solidarity) as unidimensional and mutually exclusive (see Figure 3.1).

Family relationships are at the heart of this conception. For example, Americans frequently use the terms "sisters" and "brothers" to indicate "close and equal." If a woman says of her friend, "We are like sisters," the implication is, "We are as close as siblings, and there are no status games, no one-upping between us." In contrast, hierarchical relationships are assumed to preclude closeness. Thus, in military and workplace contexts, most Americans regard as self-evident that friendships across levels of rank are problematic and discouraged if not explicitly prohibited.

I suggest that in reality the relationship between power (or hierarchy) and solidarity (or connection) is not a single dimension but a multidimensional grid (see Figure 3.2).

This grid represents the dimensions of hierarchy and connection as two intersecting axes. One axis (which I represent as the vertical one) stretches between hierarchy and equality; the other (which I represent as the horizontal axis) stretches between closeness and distance. The same linguistic strategy can operate on either axis to create power, connection, or both. For example, in conversation, if one person begins speaking while another is speaking, this overlap can be an interruption (an attempt to display or create power or status over the other speaker) or a cooperative expression of enthusiastic listenership (an attempt to display or create solidarity or connection). It also can be both, as when speakers share a conversational style by which an aggressive struggle for the floor is part of friendly competition in a political argument among friends.

In the context of family interaction, imagine an interchange in which one person announces, "I'm going to take a walk," and a second replies, "Wait, I'll go with you. I just have to make a phone call first." This response could be intended (or experienced) as a power maneuver: The second person is limiting the freedom of the first to take a walk at will. But it could also be intended (or experienced) as a connection maneuver—a bid to do something together, to express and reinforce the closeness of the relationship. In fact, it is an inextricable combination of both. Living with someone in a close relationship requires accommodations that limit freedom. Thus, solidarity entails power.

power	solidarity
asymmetry	symmetry
hierarchy	equality
distance	closeness

Figure 3.1. Unidimensional model

Mother: A Paradigm Case of the Ambiguity and
Polysemy of Power and Connection

If the family is a key locus for understanding the complex and inextricable relationship between power (negotiations along the hierarchy-equality axis) and connection (negotiations along the closeness-distance axis), nowhere does this relationship become clearer than in the role of a key family member, mother. It surfaces both in the language spoken to mothers and in the language spoken by mothers. For example, Hildred Geertz (1989 [1961]: 20), writing about *The Javanese Family,* notes that in Javanese there are "two major levels of language, respect and familiarity." (I would point out that, in light of the grid presented in Figure 3.2, these are two different dimensions: Respect is situated on the hierarchy-equality axis, whereas familiarity is a function of the closeness-distance axis.) Geertz observes that children use the familiar register when they speak with their parents and siblings until about age ten or twelve; they gradually shift to the respect register in adulthood. Geertz adds, however, "Most people continue to speak to the mother in the same way as they did as children; a few shift to respect in adulthood" (Geertz 1989 [1961]: 22). This observation leaves open the question of whether mothers are addressed in the familiar rather than the respect register because they receive less respect than fathers or because their children feel closer to them. I suspect it is both at once, and trying to pick them apart would be futile.

Although the lexical distinction between respect and familiar registers is not found in the English language, there are phenomena in English that parallel those

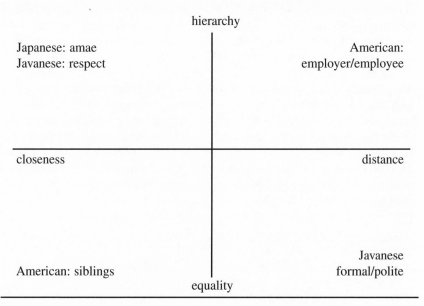

Figure 3.2. Multidimensional model

described by Geertz. Ervin-Tripp, O'Connor, and Rosenberg (1984) looked at the forms of "control acts" in family discourse to gauge power in that context. They found that "effective power and esteem were related to age" (134). Again, however, "the mothers in our sample were an important exception to the pattern. . . ." (135). The authors note that mothers in their caregiving role "received nondeferent orders, suggesting that they expected compliance and believed their desires to be justification enough." As with the Javanese example, one could ask whether children use more bald imperatives when they speak to their mothers because they have less respect for them or because they feel closer to them, or both. In other words, children's use of nondeferent orders to their mothers, like Javanese children's use of the familiar register with their mothers, is both ambiguous and polysemous with regard to power and solidarity.

Power Lines—or Connection Lines—in Telling Your Day

Blum-Kulka (1997) and Ochs and Taylor (1992a, 1992b, 1995) identify a ritual that typifies dinner conversation in many American families—a ritual that Blum-Kulka dubs "Telling Your Day." When the family includes a mother and father (as the families recorded in these studies did), mothers typically encourage children to tell their fathers about events experienced during the day.

Ochs and Taylor (1992b: 310) give the examples of a mother who urges, "Tell Dad what you thought about gymnastics and what you did," and another who prompts, "Chuck, did you tell Daddy what happened at karate when you came in your new uniform? What did Daisy do for you?" The authors note that in a majority of the instances recorded in their study, fathers responded to the resultant stories by passing judgment, assessing the rightness of their children's actions and feelings, and thereby setting up a constellation the researchers call "father knows best." The family power structure, Ochs and Taylor observe, is established in these storytelling dynamics. Just as Mother typically prompted a child to tell Daddy what happened, older siblings were much more likely to urge younger ones to tell about something that happened than the other way around. Children were most often "problematizees"—the ones whose behavior was judged by others. Rarely were they "problematizers"—the ones who questioned others' behavior as problematic. This pattern puts children firmly at the bottom of the hierarchy. Fathers were the most frequent problematizers and rarely were problematizees. In keeping with the findings of Ervin-Tripp, O'Connor, and Rosenberg (1984), mothers found themselves in the position of problematizees (the ones whose behavior was held up for judgment) as often as they were problematizers (the ones who were judging others).

In this revealing study, Ochs and Taylor identify a crucial dynamic in middle-class American families by which the family exhibits a power structure with the father at the top. They further show that mothers play a crucial role in setting up this dynamic: "Father as problematizer," they argue, is "facilitated. . . by the active role of mothers who sometimes (perhaps inadvertently) set fathers up as potential problematizers—by introducing the stories and reports of children and mothers in the first place and orienting them towards fathers as primary recipients" (329). For me the word "inadvertently" is crucial. I believe that the father-knows-best dynamic results from gender differences in assumptions about the place of talk in a relationship and that it reflects the inextricable relationship between power and connection. In my view the mother who asks her children what they did that day is trying to create closeness and involvement by exchanging details of daily life—a verbal ritual frequently observed to characterize women's friendships, as I explain elsewhere (Tannen 1990). It is a connection maneuver. And when the mother encourages her children to tell their day to their father, she is trying to involve the father with the children in much the way she herself created involvement. However, the father who does not ask, "How was your day?" is not evincing lack of interest in being close to his children. Rather, he does not assume that closeness is created by the verbal ritual of telling the details of one's day.[4] So fathers, looking elsewhere for reasons their wives are urging their children to report their activities, may well conclude that they are being asked to evaluate and judge the children's behavior. Thus, it is not the mothers' initiation of the "Telling Your Day" routine in itself that sets fathers up as family judge. Instead, the "father knows best" dynamic is created by the interaction of divergent gender-related patterns.

Ventriloquizing: Reframing through Constructed Dialogue

The ambiguity and polysemy of power and solidarity provides the theoretical background against which I have been examining ventriloquizing in the tape recordings of family interaction. A few words are in order about the phenomenon I am calling ventriloquizing. Schiffrin (1993) identifies a discourse strategy she calls "speaking for another." For example, in a conversation among a married couple and their neighbor who is visiting in their home, the wife supports the neighbor's refusal to accept the husband's offer of candy by saying, "She's on a diet." The wife thus speaks for the neighbor, addressing her husband on the neighbor's behalf. My notion of ventriloquizing is a related phenomenon by which a person speaks not only *for* another but *as* another. This would have been the case if the wife had said "I'm on a diet," where "I" represented not herself but the neighbor. One could imagine the wife doing so in a teasing or genuinely mocking way, perhaps imitating her neighbor's habitual way of declining offers of sweets.

I am interested in ventriloquizing as an instance of two phenomena I have been examining for many years: constructed dialogue and framing. Constructed dialogue is my term for animating speech in another's voice (Tannen 1989). Ventriloquizing is a special case of constructed dialogue in that a ventriloquizing speaker animates another's voice *in the presence of that other.* It also is a kind of frameshifting in that a speaker "frames" an utterance as coming from another.

To illustrate what I mean by ventriloquizing and to demonstrate the significance of this strategy in family interaction, I move now to examples taken from the tapes and transcripts of two of the four families who recorded their talk for a week. In discussing these examples, I explore ventriloquizing as a framing device that simultaneously serves the needs for power and solidarity—that is, for connection and for control.

Ventriloquizing and Related Strategies in Family Interaction

Example (1)—Ventriloquizing the dogs. The first example, identified by research team member Cynthia Gordon, comes from a family composed of a mother, Clara; a father, Neil; a child of nearly four, Jared; and two small dogs, pugs named Rover and Rickie. (All names, in this and other examples, are pseudonyms.) At the time of this exchange, Clara has been home with Jared and is frustrated because he has refused to pick up his toys—a point of frequent contention in this family. She indirectly chastises Jared for his failure by animating the dogs, using the first-person plural in a high-pitched, baby-talk register. (Instances of ventriloquizing on which my analysis focuses are highlighted in boldface.)

(1) Clara: [to dog] What (do) you have.
[high pitched] Come again?
Rover and Rickie! You guys, say,
[extra high pitch] **"We're naughty,**
but we're not as naughty as Jared,
he's naughtiest.
We—we just know it!"
Okay, careful there Jared.

By using the high-pitched, baby-talk register and speaking in the first-person plural ("we"), Clara frames her utterance as the dogs' discourse. In other words, she speaks as the dogs. In animating the dogs, she does not specify an addressee, but Jared clearly is the intended recipient of the communication. When she addresses Jared directly ("Okay, careful there Jared"), she speaks at a far less marked pitch level—more as one would address an adult rather than a child.

In one sense, Clara's conversational move is a control maneuver: She is chastising her son and trying to get him to pick up his toys. Yet by ventriloquizing the dogs, she turns her chastisement into a connection maneuver as well. Ventriloquizing introduces a note of humor because the dogs obviously can neither speak nor understand the words she is putting in their mouths. Furthermore, ventriloquizing is a form of teasing, an affectionate speech move. Moreover, the indirectness, teasing, and humor deflect the confrontation and modulate the criticism—and that in itself is a connection maneuver.

Examples (2) and (3)—Ventriloquizing-like constructed dialogue. Examples (2) and (3), identified by research team member Alexandra Johnston, are not canonical cases of ventriloquizing, but illustrate a related strategy insofar as they involve a mother speaking to her husband through her daughter. These examples come from a family in which we call the mother Kathy, the father Sam, and their two-year-old daughter Sophie.

The context for the interchange in example (2) is a disagreement between the parents that was not clear from the audiotapes. What is clear is that Sam has been displeased with Kathy and that he has just entered the room drinking a Coke. In this family, as Johnston observed, there is an ongoing conflict between Kathy and Sam concerning Coca-Cola: Sam likes to drink it, but Kathy disapproves because she regards it as unhealthful and because she believes that the father's Coke-drinking habit strains the family's budget. (If he buys several Cokes a day from the machine at his workplace, the monthly cost becomes significant.) When Sam appears, Coke in hand, Kathy addresses her response not to Sam but to their daughter:

(2) Did Daddy get a Coke 'cause Mommy's being mean?

Like the highlighted lines in example (1), this line is spoken in a high-pitched, baby-talk register. Thus, the paralinguistic and prosodic features of the utterance frame it as ventriloquizing-like. Furthermore, the conversational move is much like ventriloquizing in that Kathy is communicating to a second party, Sam, through a third party, Sophie, even though she is speaking *to* Sophie, not *as* her.

The utterance in example (2) is a power maneuver insofar as Kathy is positioning herself as the family member in charge of nutrition—a position Johnston (2001) observed her to take habitually—and passing judgment on Sam's choice of drink. But it is also a connection maneuver, as Kathy admits in a subordinate clause that she has been "mean" to Sam. The lexical choice "mean" belongs to the baby-talk register as much as the high pitch and sing-song prosody. By speaking as a child, Kathy criticizes Sam but also indirectly apologizes for a prior offense, introducing a note of irony as well by characterizing herself, an adult, as "mean"—a characteristic more often associated with children. By addressing herself to Sophie, indirectly characterizing herself as a child, and indirectly apologizing, Kathy frames her criticism in a less confrontational way and introduces a note of nonseriousness that mitigates the criticism and the confrontation. Thus, Kathy's criticism is both a power maneuver and a connection maneuver.

Indeed, an apology is by nature simultaneously a power maneuver and a connection maneuver, in that it operates on both the hierarchy/equality dimension and the closeness/distance dimension. By seeking forgiveness for and admitting fault in a prior move, an apology pursues reconciliation and rapprochement. In this sense, it operates on the connection dimension. But admitting fault and seeking forgiveness also position the apologizer as one-down. In this sense, it operates on the hierarchy dimension, negotiating power relations.

Example (3) comes from the same family. Here again, the mother expresses criticism of her husband by addressing their preverbal child. Another ongoing point of conflict between this couple is the father's tendency to wake up late. His job allows him flexible work hours, so he can arrive when he wishes. But if he arrives at work late, he leaves their daughter at her daycare center late (about which the daycare center staff complain), and he returns home in the evening late as well. On this morning, however, the father is not heading for work; he is about to go on a ski trip with a group of friends. In his excitement (or perhaps his anxiety) about the impending trip, he wakes up inordinately early and awakens his wife and daughter earlier than they normally arise.

Kathy uses this unusual circumstance as an occasion to register not only her annoyance at being awakened earlier than necessary but also her dissatisfaction with Sam's habitual sleep schedule. She registers her complaint to Sam by addressing herself to Sophie in baby-talk register:

(3) Tell Daddy to wake up this early on other days.

This utterance is a power maneuver insofar as Kathy is positioning herself as a critic and judge of her husband's behavior—hence one-up on the hierarchy dimension. But on that same dimension, speaking in a baby-talk register positions Kathy as one-down. Yet it operates on the connection dimension as well: Because a parent obligatorily feels connected to a child, by positioning herself as a child through the way she speaks Kathy obligates Sam to feel connected to her instead of angry at her. It is a connection maneuver in another way, too: By referencing this morning as one of many, Kathy reinforces the family's alignment as a single unit. Furthermore, like all indirect criticism, it deflects the confrontation.[5] And as in the previous examples, confrontation is deflected because the baby-talk register introduces a note of nonseriousness. Just as it is amusing to pretend dogs are speaking, it is amusing to tell a preverbal two-year-old to tell her father a line of dialogue she is not yet able to produce. (This child doesn't even say "Daddy"; instead, she calls her father "Da da.") In all these ways, Kathy's ventriloloquizing negotiates hierarchy and connection in her family.

Examples (4) and (5)—Ventriloquizing and related strategies as complex framing. Examples (4) and (5) also were identified by Alexandra Johnston. Example (4) illustrates how Kathy uses a combination of ventriloquizing-like utterances and canonical ventriloquizing to join an interaction between Sam and Sophie and thereby blend power and connection in complex and intriguing ways. Prior to this interaction, Kathy had been home with Sophie when she heard the arrival of Sam's car and began to prepare Sophie to welcome her father home ("Daddy's home"). Sam, however, was tired and hungry and sat down to eat something. When Sophie tried to climb into his lap, he snapped at her. Sophie began to cry, and she continued to cry despite Sam's attempts to soften his voice and mollify her ("Wanna come up?").

Example (4) is Kathy's response to this interchange between Sam and Sophie. Kathy explains to Sam why Sophie is crying, indirectly chastising him for causing this reaction. At the same time, she explains Sophie's own feelings to her and suggests how she might, when she learns to talk, use words rather than tears to express those feelings and get her way:

> (4) Kathy: She got her feelings hurt.
>
>   . . .
>
>   I think she just wanted
> some Daddy's attention.
> You were missing Daddy today, weren't you?
> You were missing Daddy, weren't you?
> Can you say,
> **"I was just missing you Daddy,**
> **that was all?"**
>
> Sophie: [*cries*] Nnno.
> Kathy: And I don't really feel too good.
> Sophie: [*cries*] No.
> Kathy: No, she doesn't feel too good either.

Kathy's repeated explanations of why Sophie is crying move progressively closer to Sophie's point of view. In the first line ("She got her feelings hurt"), Kathy speaks about Sophie to Sam; in this utterance, mother and daughter are linguistically distinct. Kathy next addresses Sophie directly ("You were missing Daddy, weren't you?"), bringing herself into alignment with the child. She then models for Sophie what the child might say to articulate her own feelings ("Can you say, 'I was just missing you, Daddy, that was all?'"). Here Kathy animates Sophie's feelings but linguistically marks the fact that she is doing so by beginning, "Can you say?" This introducer separates her point of view from her child's.

Kathy's next line ("And I don't really feel too good") continues to merge Kathy with Sophie linguistically; Kathy is speaking but says "I"—meaning Sophie. This move may be interpreted either as still modified by "Can you say?" or as a new, canonical ventriloquized utterance, in which Kathy is not just suggesting to Sophie what she might say but is actually speaking as Sophie. In any case, Kathy is expressing Sophie's point of view by using the first-person pronoun. Finally, Kathy mitigates her alignment with Sophie and reorients to Sam by addressing him and referring to Sophie rather than animating her ("No, she doesn't feel too good either"). Thus, Kathy moves progressively closer to Sophie, discursively, by gradually shifting from referring to Sophie in the third person to ventriloquizing her—that is, merging her persona with Sophie's by animating Sophie's voice. Moreover, by communicating to both Sophie and Sam in the same utterances, Kathy is connecting the three of them as a family.

Kathy's explanation of why Sophie is crying ("She got her feelings hurt") is an indirect criticism of Sam because it entails the assumption that a father should not hurt his daughter's feelings. After a short spate of intervening talk, Kathy makes this injunction more explicit. (Note that the utterances transcribed in example (5) as "ROW ROW" are not the word "row" as in the children's song "Row, row, row your boat" but a verbalization meant to reproduce the sound of a dog growling, pronounced to rhyme with "how" and "growl.")

> (5) Kathy: Why are you so edgy?
> Sam: 'Cause I haven't eaten yet.
> Kathy: Why didn't you get a snack
> on the way home or something?
> Save your family a little stress.
> Sophie: Mm
> Kathy: **Yeah give us a break, Daddy.**
> **We just miss you.**
> **We try to get your attention**
> **and then you come home**
> **and you go ROW ROW ROW ROW**.
> Sophie: Row row!

Although the "we" in "We just miss you" could indicate that Kathy and Sophie both miss Sam, the continuation ("We try to get your attention. . . ") makes clear that Kathy is speaking for (and as) Sophie. Then, still speaking as Sophie, she mimics how Sam comes across from Sophie's point of view: "You go ROW ROW ROW ROW." In this utterance, Kathy is animating Sophie animating Sam. So the linguistic strategy by which Kathy tells Sam that he should alter his behavior (a control maneuver) also linguistically merges the three of them (a connection maneuver).

In sum, by speaking as, to, and through Sophie, Kathy creates involvement between Sophie and her father, explains Sophie's feelings both to Sam and to Sophie herself, explains to Sam why he's been unfair to Sophie, and aligns herself with her daughter as a team. (She could have aligned with Sam by telling their daughter to let Daddy eat, as another mother in our study did in the same situation.) Finally, by speaking for Sophie, who cannot yet speak, Kathy enters into the alignment between Sam and Sophie and thus frames the three of them as a single unit—a family.

Conclusion

I have shown that ventriloquizing and related ventriloquizing-like strategies allow a speaker to address a second party by speaking as, to, or through a third. In this type of constructed dialogue, speakers frame and reframe their utterances as they balance the needs for connection and for control. I have suggested that the concept of "connection maneuver" is needed to compliment the more commonly observed notion of "power maneuver" by showing how ventriloquizing simultaneously serves both power and connection. Thus, the analysis advances our understanding of the interrelationship between the dynamics of power and solidarity, or control and connection. It also expands and deepens our understanding of how verbal strategies create and manipulate framing in the discourse of conversational interaction in general and of family interaction in particular.

NOTES

1. The project I report on here was supported by a grant from the Alfred P. Sloan Foundation to me and Shari Kendall. The families who participated are middle-class, dual-career couples with children. I am grateful to the foundation and our project officer, Kathleen Christensen, for their support; to my co-principal investigator, Shari Kendall; and to the generous families who participated in the project. I also thank Alexandra Johnston and Cynthia Gordon, the research team members who worked with the families whose talk I have cited here and transcribed and identified the examples that I cite. The power-connection grid was first presented in Tannen (1994) and is reproduced here with permission from Oxford University Press. The theoretical background on power and solidarity as it applies to mothers is based on selections previously included in Tannen (2003). The analysis of family interaction that I present here is new.

2. Blum-Kulka's *Dinner Talk* (1997) compares American, Israeli, and American-Israeli families. She discusses parents' dual and sometimes conflicting needs to socialize their children in the sense of teaching them what they need to know and also to socialize with them in the sense of enjoying their company. This perspective indirectly addresses the interrelationship of power and connection in the family.

3. I have struggled, through many papers, with the best way to acknowledge Brown and Gilman's original conception of power solidarity without misrepresenting it, especially given my objections (Tannen 1998, 2002) to the academic convention of obligatorily posing one's work in opposition to work that came before. On one hand, Brown and Gilman acknowledge that relationships can be both equal and solidary or unequal and solidary. Yet they also claim that power governs asymmetrical relationships in which one is subordinate to another, whereas solidarity governs symmetrical relationships characterized by social equality and similarity.

4. Moreover, unlike many mothers, a father may not regard closeness as the most important barometer of his relationship with his children. See Henwood (1993) for evidence that women tend to judge the mother-daughter relationship by how close it is.

5. It should be noted that many people are more irritated by indirect criticism than by direct criticism, precisely because it seems intended to do the work of criticism without taking responsibility for it. A metaphor I have used elsewhere (Tannen 1986) is that such indirect criticism can be perceived metaphorically as being shot by a gun with a silencer: The injury is felt but the source is camouflaged.

REFERENCES

Blum-Kulka, Shoshana.1997. *Dinner talk: Cultural patterns of sociability and socialization in family discourse.* Mahwah, N.J.: Erlbaum.
Brown, Roger, and Albert Gilman. 1960. The pronouns of power and solidarity. In *Style in language,* edited by Thomas Sebeok. Cambridge, Mass.: MIT Press, 253–76.
Ervin-Tripp, Susan, Mary Catherine O'Connor, and Jarrett Rosenberg. 1984. Language and power in the family. In *Language and power,* edited by Cheris Kramarae, Muriel Schultz, and William M. O'Barr. New York: Sage, 116–35.
Geertz, Hildred. 1989 [1961]. *The Javanese family: A study of kinship and socialization.* Prospect Heights, Ill.: Waveland Press.
Henwood, Karen L. 1993. Women and later life: The discursive construction of identities within family relationships. *Journal of Aging Studies* 7 (3): 303–19.
Johnston, Alexandra. 2001. *Mother knows best: Negotiating parental and household manager identities in caretaking talk.* Paper presented at annual meeting of American Anthropological Association, Washington, D.C., November 28.
Millar, Frank E., L. Edna Rogers, and Janet Beavin Bavelas. 1984. Identifying patterns of verbal conflict in interpersonal dynamics. *Western Journal of Speech Communication* 48: 231–46.
Ochs, Elinor, and Carolyn Taylor. 1992a. Mothers' role in the everyday reconstruction of "Father Knows Best." In *Locating power: Proceedings of the Second Berkeley Women and Language Conference,* edited by Kira Hall, Mary Bucholtz, and Birch Moonwomon. Berkeley, Calif.: Berkeley Women and Language Group, 447–63.
———. 1992b. Family narrative as political activity. *Discourse and Society* 3 (3): 301–40.
———. 1995. The "father knows best" dynamic in family dinner narratives. In *Gender articulated,* edited by Kira Hall and Mary Bucholtz. New York and London: Routledge, 97–120.
Ochs, Elinor, Clotilde Pontecorvo, and Alessandra Fasulo. 1996. Socializing taste. *Ethnos* 61 (1–2): 7–46.
Ochs, Elinor, Carolyn Taylor, Dina Rudolph, and Ruth Smith. 1992. Storytelling as a theory-building activity. *Discourse Processes* 15: 37–72.
Schiffrin, Deborah. 1993. "Speaking for another" in sociolinguistic interviews: Alignments, identities, and frames. In *Framing in discourse,* edited by Deborah Tannen. New York and Oxford: Oxford University Press, 231–63.
Tannen, Deborah. 1984. *Conversational style: Analyzing talk among friends.* Norwood, N.J.: Ablex.
———. 1986. *That's not what I meant! How conversational style makes or breaks relationships.* New York: Ballantine.
———. 1989. *Talking voices: Repetition, dialogue, and imagery in conversational discourse.* Cambridge: Cambridge University Press.
———. 1990. *You just don't understand: Women and men in conversation.* New York: HarperCollins.
———. 1994. The relativity of linguistic strategies: Rethinking power and solidarity in gender and dominance. In *Gender and discourse.* Oxford and New York: Oxford University Press, 19–52.
———. 1998. *The argument culture: Stopping America's war of words.* New York: Ballantine.
———. 2001. *I only say this because I love you: How conversational style can make or break family relationships throughout our lives.* New York: Random House.
———. 2002. Agonism in academic discourse. *Journal of Pragmatics* 34 (10–11): 1651–69.
———. 2003. Gender and family interaction. In *Handbook on language and gender,* edited by Janet Holmes and Miriam Meyerhoff. Cambridge, Mass., and Oxford, UK: Basil Blackwell.
Varenne, Herve. 1992. *Ambiguous harmony: Family talk in America.* Norwood, N.J.: Ablex.
Watts, Richard J. 1991. *Power in family discourse.* Berlin: Mouton de Gruyter.

Uncovering the event structure of narrative

William Labov
University of Pennsylvania

Oral narratives of personal experience have provided one of the most fruitful areas for the study of discourse because the structure of these speech events is unusually clear and well defined.[1] This definition rests on a conception of *narrative* as one of many ways of reporting past events that have entered the biography of the narrator. An oral narrative of personal experience employs temporal junctures in which the surface order of the narrative clauses matches the projected order of the events described (Labov and Waletzky 1967). If the order of the clauses is reversed, the inferred order of the reported events changes.

Narratives that use this principle of temporal organization are characterized by a well-articulated structure that follows, as I hope to show, from certain structural principles that are necessarily involved in narrative construction. This essay will attempt to use that structure to make inferences about the relation of a narrative as it is told to the underlying events as the speaker experienced them. The first part will use a narrative told by an older resident of a small town in Michigan, reporting a terrifying experience of his boyhood, to develop the tools for locating the underlying structure of events. The second part will apply these tools to the analysis of testimony before the South African Truth and Reconciliation Commission in which one of the perpetrators of the crimes involved deals with the responsibility for a series of murders.

In the great majority of cases, the only information available on the nature of the reported events is in the narrative itself: There is no independent evidence on what actually happened.[2] At first glance it might seem that the original events cannot be recovered and that the narrative must be considered an entity in itself, disjoined from the real world. Nevertheless, there are good reasons why the effort should be made to reconstruct the original events from the narrative evidence. Inferences about the original events will lead us to greater insights into how the narrator transforms reality in reporting it to others. Retracing these transformations tells us more about the character of the narrators; the norms that govern the assignment of praise or blame; and, in more serious cases, the narrator's complicity in the events themselves.

This essay rests on a set of findings about speakers' behavior that are the result of examining large numbers of narratives of personal experience. The first finding is that it is useful to begin with the premise that the narrators do not lie. This is obviously incorrect because speakers often do lie—and in ways that we cannot detect. Nevertheless, we can make considerable progress by beginning with this premise because of three properties that tend to minimize the occurrence of lies: They are (1) dangerous, since they are frequently exposed by events outside of the control of the narrator; (2) inconvenient, since they require much more effort than reporting the events themselves; and (3) unnecessary, since there are more efficient means of transforming reality in the interests of the narrator. The second finding is that the transformation of events is often incomplete. The linguistic devices that narrators use to affect the listener's view of motivation, praise, blame, and culpability often change the semantic interpretation of the original events—but in so doing leave traces that allow the analyst to reconstruct an underlying, untransformed series. This is particularly true of the simplest and most common transformation: deletion of one or more events in the series. Just as phonemes are coarticulated with their neighboring phonemes, the clauses used to report events are interconnected with the clauses used to report neighboring events, in ways that prohibit complete elimination of information on the deleted event.

The overall framework for the study of narrative that I use is given in (1). The underlined elements are familiar (Labov and Waletzky 1967; Labov 1972). I will be dealing here with aspects that are not so familiar, which are shown in bold type.

(1)   The insertion of the narrative into the framework of conversational turn-taking by an *abstract*.

The orientation of the listener to the time, place, actors, and activity of the narrative.

The temporal organization of the *complicating action* through the use of temporal juncture.

The differential evaluation of actions by a juxtaposition of real and potential events through the use of irrealis predicates.

The validation of the most reportable event by enhancing credibility through the use of objective witnesses.

The assignment of praise or blame for the reportable events by the **integration** or **polarization** of participants.

The **explanation** of the narrative through a chain of causal relations from the most reportable event to the orientation.

The **transformation** of the narrative in the interests of the narrator through deletion of objective events and insertion of subjective events.

The **termination** of the narrative by returning the time frame to the present through the use of a *coda*.

Event Structure of a Small-Town Narrative

Let us consider first a narrative told by a seventy-three-year-old man from South Lyons, Michigan, recorded by Claire Galed at the 1973 Linguistic Institute.

(2)   The first man killed by a car in this town
          Interviewer: Claire Galed
          Speaker: "Ross Hawkins," age 73, South Lyons, Michigan

Abstract

Shall I tell you about the first man got kilt—killed by a car here . . . Well, I can tell you that.

Orientation

a   He—eh—'fore-'fore they really had cars in town
b   I think it was a judge—Sawyer—it was a judge in—uh-
c   I understand he was a judge in Ann Arbor
d   and he had a son that was a lawyer.

Complicating action

e   And this son—I guess he must've got drunk
    because he drove through town with a chauffeur
    with one of those old touring cars without, you know—
    open tops and everything, *big* cars, first ones—
f   and they—they come thr-through town in a—late in the night.
g   And they went pretty fast, I guess,
h   and they come out here to the end of a—
    where—uh—Pontiac Trail turns right or left in the road
i   and they couldn't make the turn
j   and they turned left
k   and they tipped over in the ditch,
l   steerin' wheel hit this fellow in the heart, this chauffeur,
m   killed him.

Evaluation

n   And—uh—the other fellow just broke his thumb—
    the lawyer who [hh] was drunk.
o   They—they say a drunk man [laughs] never gets it [laugh].

    p Maybe I shouldn't say that,
    q I might get in trouble.

We have no difficulty in understanding this narrative in terms of its main point, established in the evaluation section n–q. Big-city lawyers are the problem, and the blame is clearly assigned to the drunken lawyer, who escaped with minor injuries. The narrator makes a little joke about the fact that he, a small-town person, might get into trouble by criticizing these city folks with their chauffeurs and big, modern, fancy touring cars. It is the most familiar theme of American culture: the simplicity, honesty, and competence of small-town people against the sophistication, corruption, and incompetence of big-city people.

We can examine the construction of this narrative more closely by looking at the causal sequence of events narrated. The analysis begins with *reportability* and *the most reportable event* (Labov 1997). The notion of reportability is well known to be relative to the immediate social situation, age, and other cultural parameters. A *reportable event* is defined here not in absolute terms but in relation to the narrative situation. Given the fact that the unmarked turn in a conversation is a single completed sentence, a narrative is marked by the fact that it is normally much longer than this. The narrative speaker therefore holds the floor and occupies social space for a longer time than a conversational participant who is not telling a narrative. As Sacks (1992: II, 3–5) points out, other participants may take turns during the narrative, but the performance of the narrative effectively is a claim to return the assignment of speakership to the narrator until the narrative is completed.

(3)   Definition: A *reportable event* is one that justifies automatic reassignment of speaker role to the narrator.

            Implication: To be an acceptable social act, a narrative of personal experience must contain at least one reportable event.

Among these reportable events, one can usually identify a *most reportable event*—designated as e_0—as the event that is least expected and has the greatest effect on the needs and desires of the participants in the narrative. This event is the least compatible with a potential intervention, "So what?"

The most reportable event is usually the one that the story is about. It is a nontrivial fact that the speaker rarely constructs the narrative with the most reportable event as the first of the complicating actions.[3] Where, then, is the narrator to begin? Every event is preceded by an unlimited number of prior events. The question of where to begin must be posed and answered by every narrator, and it is not infrequently made explicit.

The answer to the question of where to begin is related to a second basic concept that governs narrative: credibility. The overall credibility of the narrative rests on the listeners' belief that the most reportable event did take place in real time. The less credible the event, the less likely it is to be awarded automatic speaker reassignment.[4]

A fundamental paradox of narrative rests on the inverse relationship of credibility and reportability. To the extent that the most reportable event is uncommon and unexpected, it is less credible than more common and expected events. Therefore there is a strong motivation to precede e_0 with another event that explains it—that is, an event that is related to e_0 as cause to effect. Credibility is thus enhanced by introducing events that answer the question, "How did this (perhaps incredible) event come about?" Having done so, the narrator then faces the question of whether this preceding event needs explaining. This is a recursive process, in which the narrator must (consciously or unconsciously) follow the chain of events from the most reportable backward in time.

Where does the process stop? The narrator stops when he or she reconstructs an event for which the question, "How did this event happen?" is inappropriate. This is in fact the *orientation*.

(4) Narrative construction

(a) The narrator first selects a most reportable event, e_0, which the narrative is going to be about.

(b) The narrator then selects a prior event, e_{-1}, that is the efficient cause of e_0, which answers the question about e_0, "How did that happen?"

(c) The narrator continues the process of Step 4(b), recursively, until an event e_{-n} is reached for which the question of Step 4(b) is not appropriate.

(d) The narrator then provides information on e_{-n}: the time and place, the identity of the actors, and their behavior as the orientation to the narrative.

A narrative is therefore created as the narrator's theory of causality. In the narrative of Ross Hawkins, the most reportable event is (m), the death of the chauffeur. In following the causal chain backward, we find that the chauffeur was killed because (l) the steering wheel hit him in the heart, because (k) the car tipped over in the ditch, because (i–j) they turned left but couldn't make the turn because (g) they were going pretty fast because (e) the judge's son got drunk.[5] Why did he get drunk? No further explanation is needed because it is assumed that's the kind of thing that big-city lawyers do. Clause (e) is headed by a statement that would ordinarily be a part of the orientation (*he must've got drunk*) and subordinates to it the first complicating action (*he drove through town with a chauffeur*). It is not simply this first action that is subordinated to *because* but the whole succeeding narrative (e–m). It is this whole series of events that leads the narrator to make this inference.

The net effect of this causal sequence is to assign responsibility for the death of the chauffeur to the (drunken) lawyer. Let us examine this question more closely by listing the activities of each actor, clause by clause, in the participant analysis table (5).

(5)   Participant analysis table for part 1 of "The first man killed by a car in this town"

	e gets drunk	f drove through	g came through	h went fast	j came out	k turned left	tipped over	l hit him	m killed him
Judge									
Judge's son	(y)	x	x	x	x				
Chauffeur		y	y	y	y	y		z	z
Car		z	x	x	x	x	y		
Steering wheel								y	y

The actors named in the narrative are the judge (who plays no further role), his son, the chauffeur, the car, and the car's steering wheel. The causal relations are assigned here not by the theory inherent in the narrative but by our understanding of causal relationships in the real world. Active causal agents are denoted by y and patients directly affected by z; other participants are denoted by x. The first action is in parentheses, since the narrator qualifies it with "I guess he must've." Here the active agent is the judge's son. He is not the active agent for the five succeeding clauses, however. It is clear that the chauffeur was driving the car because in (l) the steering wheel hit him in the heart and (m) killed him. Yet the general understanding of most listeners—and my own when I first heard the narrative—is that the (drunken) lawyer was responsible. Otherwise, the assumption that he must have been drunk, first stated in (e) and elaborated in the evaluation section (n–q), is completely unmotivated.

How does the narrative transfer the responsibility implied in (e) to the succeeding actions and the events as a whole? It took several years of study of this narrative before I realized how this was achieved. This reassignment of responsibility is the work of the zero causative verb *drove*. The semantic composition of this complex item is indicated in (6). *Push* and *drive* both indicate transverse[6] motion, but *drive* indicates that an agent causes an entity that has its own source of power to move transversely. This entity may be a self-powered machine (boat, train, car) or be powered by coupling with other animate agents (wagon, coach).

(6)   The semantics of *drive*

        push "cause something to move [transversely]"

        $drive_1$ "cause a machine to move [transversely, under its own power]"

        $drive_2$ "cause a person to drive"

        = "cause a person to cause a machine to move [transversely, under its own power]"

The most common case is $drive_1$, with a single human participant, the agent. But there is a $drive_2$, which involves a second participant. English $drive_2$ is used with subjects who have ordered, directed, or otherwise motivated other agents to $drive_1$ a machine. *$Drive_2$* is the linguistic device that creates the causal link for the listener. The further course of the narrative shows that the narrator had no knowledge of the actual situation of the judge's son and the chauffeur as they drove through the town in the middle of the night. Nonetheless, the zero causative effectively evokes the image that the (drunken) son was responsible—most likely ordering the chauffeur, against his will, to drive faster and faster. It also is consistent, however, with the possibility that the son was asleep in the back of the car. As we follow the participant diagram, step by step, it is clear that in fact the chauffeur is the active agent—in driving through the town, in going fast, in turning left, in not making the turn—until the car itself becomes the active agent, and the steering wheel kills the driver. Yet $drive_2$ is appropriate because regardless of whether the judge's son had given a direct order, the action was taken in his behalf.[7]

The narrator then achieves this reassignment of responsibility through two features of the narrative. The first narrative action is subordinated to the supposition *he must've got drunk*. The unstated but implied logic of *must* is that no other explanation would account for the series of events that followed. The homonymity of $drive_1$ and $drive_2$, combined with this unstated inference, allows the listener to sustain the implication that the judge's son was the active agent. The narrator's interpretation is sustained by an ambiguity that is a specific feature of English. In *He drove through town with a chauffeur*, drive is a zero causative in that the additional causal relationship has no overt marker, as it would in a French translation (*Il s'est fait conduire à travers la ville par un chauffeur.*)

The overt subject of the narrative is the chauffeur—the first person killed by a car in South Lyons. Normally the principal characters of a narrative are introduced as a major part of speech in a narrative clause: subject, direct object, predicative noun. The choice of the zero causative verb reduces the chauffeur to the object of a prepositional phrase—*he drove through town with a chauffeur*—and assigns agency to the lawyer. Furthermore, this entire construction is placed in a subordinate causal clause. As the story progresses, it turns out that the chauffeur is even less an active agent. Mr. Hawkins continues with a further extension of the opposition of big-city to small-town morality. Mr. Hawkins' father was the local magistrate responsible for cleaning up the situation created by these big-city people.

(7)   Part 2 of "The first man killed by a car in this town"

Complicating action 2
r   But—uh—anyway, they called up my dad.

Orientation 2
s   And I lived across from the City Hall there.
t   And he was justice for most of his life, and—uh—justice of the peace, you know.

Complicating action 2
u   And they says, "Mr. Hawkins, ya—we want you to get t-livery barn, get Mr. Drury to get you a liv—a buckboard and a livery st—and have you drive it out there and get that 'n' bring him t'town to—eh—you know, f'r whatever they had to do," funeral home or what.

Complicating action 2
v   So my dad said it—let me go with him.

Orientation 2
w Of course I was over twelve.
x   I don't know how—probably fifteen maybe.

Complicating action 2
y   And so we went out there,
z   and we picked up that man in a buckboard.

Evaluation
aa   Well, there was two men on the front seat,
       so I had to lay back there with that man,
bb   and his feet was floppin' over the edge [laughs]
       where the gate goes down if there was any gate [laughter]

and the—flop [laughs]

cc   And he turned black 'cause it—stopped his circulation, you know,

dd   And I thought it was a Negro man,

ee   and boy, that was an *eery* night for me
comin' home [laughs] in the dark with that . . . *man*

In part 2, the narrative of Ross Hawkins turns out to be quite different from the story projected at the outset. The morality play of big-city versus small-town values continues but shifts from the death of a stranger to the frightening experience of a fifteen-year-old boy, which he still remembers at the age of seventy-three. The assignment of praise or blame now shifts from the responsibility for the death of a stranger to the responsibility for an experience that may still return as a current nightmare.

The most reportable event e_0 is encapsulated in the final evaluative sentence (ee), *that was an eery night for me comin' home [laughs] in the dark with that . . . man*. How did this come about? Following the narrative theory backward, it appears that e_0 happened because e_{-1} Ross had to lie in the back of the buckboard when they picked up the body because e_{-2} there were two men in the front, and Ross was with them because e_{-3} his father let him go with them. However, nothing in the preceding material accounts for his father's decision.

The actors in this second half are *They* (the people who called up), Mr. Hawkins Sr., Mr. Drury, Ross, and the chauffeur.

(8)   Participant analysis table for part 2 of "The first man killed by a car in this town"

	r	u	v	y	z	aa	aa	bb	cc	dd
	called	told	let	went	picked	sat	lay	feet	turned	thought
	him	him	me	out	up	front	back	flopped	black	Negro
They	y	y								
Mr. Hawkins	z	z	y	x	y	x				
Mr. Drury				x	y	x				
Ross Hawkins			z	x			x			x
Chauffeur					z			x	x	x

The responsibility for the actions rests with the active agents denoted by y in the participant table (8): first with the people who placed the phone call, then with Mr. Hawkins, who permitted Ross to come. Ross himself participates actively only in his final perception of the corpse as a Negro man. The question remains, why would a justice of the peace bring his fifteen-year-old son on such a grim expedition?

This inexplicable situation can be resolved by a close examination of the text. Ross reports that his father received a phone call and tells us the whole contents of the message. Because there were no speaker phones in those days, we must conclude that Ross learned about the message from his father by asking him, "What did they say, Dad?"

From (u) we know that Ross knew what had been said to his father, so (9) follows:

(9)   They said, (u) "Mr. Hawkins, we want you to get t' the livery barn, get Mr. Drury to get you a buckboard and a livery st—and have you drive it out there and get that man 'n' bring him t'town

A third deleted event follows necessarily from the main verb of v, *He let me come with him*. The expression X *let* Y *do* Z presupposes several conditions. One is that X was aware that Y wanted to do Z. One does not let someone do something unless there is evidence that they want to do it. Second, some persons (possibly including X) would have not wanted Y to do Z or prohibited him from doing it. Given these two conditions, the verb *let* asserts that X removed any such obstacle to Y performing the action Z.

The most likely way in which Mr. Hawkins could have become aware of Ross's desire to go with him was a third utterance in the deleted series,

(10)   I said, "Can I go with you?"

It is possible that Mr. Hawkins simply said "Yes," in spite of the presupposed prohibition introduced by *let*. But what follows in (w–x) strongly indicates that Mr. Hawkins's first response was negative. In fact, given (w), we can plausibly reconstruct (11):

(11)   My dad said, "No, that's no job for a twelve-year-old boy."

Furthermore, the most likely response of the son is prefigured by (x):

(12)   I said, "I'm more than twelve—I'm almost fifteen!"

At this point, the original form of (v) follows logically:

(13)   So my dad said it was all right for me to go with him.

The speech events (8–12) do not replace any of the narrative clauses in the original; they must be inserted after (u) and before (v), as shown in the amplified participant analysis table in (14).

(14)   Amplified participant analysis table for part 2 of "The first man killed by a car in this town"

	r	u	u1	u2	u3	u4	u5	v
	called	told	asked	told me	asked	answered	answered	let
		him	(8)	(9)	(10)	(11)	(12)	me
They	y	y						
Mr. Hawkins	z	z	z	y	z	y	z	y
Mr. Drury								
Ross Hawkins			y	z	y	z	y	z
Chauffeur								

The deletion of these events from Ross Hawkins' narrative is not unexpected. Like most family narratives, this is an integrative and not a polarizing transformation. Ross deletes the events that would assign blame to his father, as well as those that would assign blame to him. Such deletions frequently leave their traces behind, however, in the particular form of the lexical choices that had been made in the original. Thus, Ross could have transformed (v) to "So I went out there with them," but he did not, leaving the *let* that allows us to reconstruct the absent events and, in his quotations from the argument that followed, even the most probable shape of the linguistic forms.

The two key elements in the analysis of this narrative involve the linguistic signaling of voice—the linguistic category that relates the participants to the action. The zero causative *drove* assigned blame to the passenger, and the permissive *let* would have assigned blame to Ross' father if its implied constituents had been realized.

Testimony in the Truth and Reconciliation Hearings

On a recent visit to South Africa, I became acquainted with the work of Bock, McCormick, and Raffray (2001), who applied the narrative analysis of Labov and Waletzky (1967) to the hearings of the Truth and Reconciliation Commission (TRC).[8] The TRC implements the unique program of the South African government for avoiding a new cycle of retribution on the part of newly liberated South Africans against their former oppressors. The objectives of the TRC are "to promote national unity and reconciliation in a spirit of understanding which transcends the conflicts and divisions of the past" (TRC Report 2001, vol. 1: 55). Under the TRC, the Human Rights Violation Committee held hearings from 1995 to 1999, reviewing the conflicts and divisions that dominated the country in the period of apartheid from 1960 to 1994.[9]

The goals and achievements of the TRC have been widely reviewed, defended, and criticized. The concept of *truth* has been examined and discussed from many points of view. As summarized by Bock, McCormick, and Raffray (2001), the TRC addresses the factual questions "What happened? to whom? by whose agency?" Because most of the testimony is in the form of narrative as here defined, the questions of the TRC coincide with the undertaking of this paper: to locate the underlying event structure of narrative.[10] The TRC did not minimize the difficulties involved. It endorsed the position of Ignatieff that "All that a truth commission can achieve is to reduce the number of lies that can be circulated unchallenged in public discourse" (TRC 2001, vol. 1: 111). The first section of this essay puts forward the idea that much of the narrative work can be illuminated by starting with the assumption that speakers transform reality by techniques more subtle and effective than lying. I hope that the techniques of narrative analysis developed here can be used to promote the aims of the TRC in achieving a better understanding of the testimony it has accumulated.

The Human Rights Violations Committee hearings include much testimony from the perpetrators of heinous acts, as well as their victims. Bock, McCormick, and Raffray (2001) apply the analytical concepts of Labov and Waletzky (1967) to the testimony of victims. My analysis here deals with the testimony of one of the perpetrators, applying the further steps of narrative analysis of Labov (1997) as developed in the first part of this essay. The testimony to be examined involved Case 1050/96; this testimony was given before the TRC by Cornelius Johannes Van Wyk, an Afrikaner member of a racist group with a genocidal program.[11]

My purpose in examining these narratives is to see if the techniques used in the first section of this essay can be useful in revealing the relationship between what is said in the narrative and what is likely to have been done—that is, to locate the underlying structure of events. Van Wyk has been charged with three charges of murder; robbery; attempted robbery with aggravating circumstances; housebreaking with intent to steal; and illegal possession of firearms and explosives. He is now in prison, serving sentences following conviction on these charges. His testimony shows many indications of efforts to mitigate responsibility for these crimes, and we must assume that he believes that his testimony might be relevant to possible amnesty or reduction of his sentences.

I examine some of Van Wyk's testimony to see what linguistic devices he used to transform the events in his narrative in a way that minimizes his participation in a series of killings. In the first section of this essay, I cite the value of beginning with the assumption that narrators do not lie. In this case, the assumption has more support than usual because Van Wyk's testimony can presumably be compared with court records available to members of the commission.

Van Wyk's actions were motivated by a deep-seated hatred of blacks, Jews, and other minorities. In (15), attorney Gimsbeek interrogates Van Wyk to reveal his early prejudices:

(15)   MR. GIMSBEEK: Mr. van Wyk . . . start right at the beginning and tell us a little about your childhood and your personal background and the various influences which led you to commit these offences. . . .

MR. VAN WYK: Yes. I think it will be suitable if I start during my puberty. I was about twelve, thirteen years old and at that stage—well I grew up in a very strict, conservative, and rightwing home. . . .

Perhaps I should refer to the most important chapter in the tenets of the White Men's Bible. It's an organization which was found in America, I think in the early 1900s. To refer to the White Man's Bible this is the basis of the tenets of this particular group . . . and in the document they relate how the Jewish slave traders rule the entire world as a result of their financial muscle and that they use people as political puppets, and this also means that they want to use the white man as a slave by plunging him into debt.

The particular killings involved here took place when Van Wyk and his associate White broke into a house belonging to two black people, Mr. and Mrs. Dubane, to steal guns. I have lettered the independent clauses and indented subordinated clauses, following the technique used to analyze oral narratives of personal experience.

(16)   a   Later at about seven o'clock we then proceeded to the house.
             b   There was a bushy area in front of the house
             c   and we took up our position there.
             d   Mrs. Dubane at that stage was outside busy sweeping the step,
             e   and we waited for her to leave the premises so that we could enter the house.
             f   At some point she came to the front of the house
             g   and she was standing right in front of us
             h   and virtually looking straight into White's face without actually noticing him because we were camouflaged,
             i   but I think she became suspicious at some point
             j   and that's when White told her in her own language
             k   he greeted her,
             l   he said hello,
             m   and she turned around
             n   and he then shot her from behind.
             o   He then proceeded to cut her throat.

To this point, Van Wyk's narrative shows him only as a spectator and White as the sole agent of the actions. Van Wyk waited while White greeted Mrs. Dubane, shot her from behind, and cut her throat.

(17)   p   At that stage I thought we should withdraw because the opera-
               tion was not going according to plan and it was planned that we
               would withdraw under those circumstances.

         q   But at that stage Mr. Dubane came around the corner,

         r   saw Mrs. Dubane lying on the ground,

         s   and fled down the path.

         t   White shot at him,

         u   he missed him

         v   and told me to shoot.

         w   I then followed Mr. Dubane down the road

         x   and fired a shot at him.

         y   White came around

         z   and passed me.

         aa   At that stage Mr. Dubane was lying on the ground;

         bb   he then slit Mr. Dubane's throat.

The calm and seemingly objective character of this grim story is typical of the TRC hearings of this class. Clause (p) is an overt evaluation section that exhibits no emotion, but rather practical reasoning. Van Wyk portrays himself as a moderate person who wanted to abstain from further killing, laying the chief responsibility on White. This is, however, easily recognized as special pleading of self-interest, since it is a subjective statement of the speaker's thoughts without any possibility of corroboration.

A closer look at the event structure of the narrative shows objective adjustments that operate to minimize the guilt of the speaker. The most reportable events are clearly (o) in (16) and (bb) in (17)—the two criminal acts of White that effectively ended the lives of Mr. and Mrs. Dubane. A participant analysis table of (17) is given as (18) below, showing the causal sequence leading to (bb). The active agent who initiates events (t), (v), and (bb)—entered as y—is White. White shot at Mr. Dubane, then told Van Wyk to shoot. The only action taken by Van Wyk in the narrative is (x), to *fire at* Mr. Dubane. Following this action, White again is the active agent who slits Mr. Dubane's throat.

(18)   Participant analysis table for Van Wyk's testimony (17)

	p thinks to withdraw	q came around	r saw Mrs. D.	s fled	t shot at him	u missed	v told me
White		x			y	x	y
Van Wyk	x						z
Mr. Dubane			x	x	z		
Mrs. Dubane			x				

	w followed Mr. D.	x fired at him	y came around	z passed me	aa lying on ground	bb slit his throat
White			x	x		y
Van Wyk	x	y				
Mr. Dubane	x	z			x	z
Mrs. Dubane						

The question that this part of the testimony has to deal with is, "Who killed Mr. Dubane?" Was it Van Wyk or White? The expression *fire at* presupposes, on Gricean principles, that Van Wyk missed the target. If one asks the question, "Did you shoot him?" an answer might be, "I fired at him but missed." One would not expect "I fired at him and hit him" since *firing at* someone is a necessary and expected prerequisite to shooting someone. The use of *fire at* in (x), then, would lead the listener to believe that White is completely responsible for the death of Mr. Dubane. Nevertheless, we find that incomplete deletion, as in the second half of the South Lyons account. In clause (aa) Dubane is lying on the ground. He may have tripped and fallen on his own momentum, but given the fact that White fired at him, the most likely explanation is that Van Wyk's bullet did hit him. Van Wyk's bullet may well have been the main cause of Mr. Dubane's death before White slit his throat.

The amended participant analysis table (18') restores two events deleted from the causal sequence in which Van Wyk was the active agent: *I hit him* and *he fell*. Left behind, however, are two traces that would undoubtedly be picked up by attorneys if this testimony were introduced into a court of law. To delete the two events effectively, Van Wyk would have had to delete the *at* of *fired at* or add the lie *but I missed*. He would also have to add the lie that White shot Dubane before he slit his throat. It seems likely that this would conflict with testimony already given by White. Deletion of the two events is simpler than deliberate fabrication, even though it may not be completely effective on detailed examination.

(18')   Amended participant analysis table (18) (additions in italics)

	x fired at him	*hit* *him*	*fell*	y came around	z passed me	aa lying on ground	bb slit his throat
White				x	x		y
Van Wyk	y	*y*					
Mr. Dubane	z	*z*	*x*	x	z		

The narrative continues to deal with the murder of a white, Afrikaner woman.

(19)   cc   At that stage once again I thought we would withdraw
                  because we were heading in the direction of where our
                  clothes and equipment had been left.
            dd   But White said no, we should continue with the operation.
            ee   We then entered the house,
            ff   I can't remember which door we used to enter the premises
            gg   but we did enter the premises.
            hh   We proceeded down the passage where we expected to find
                  the particular arms we were looking for.
            ii   White said we should search the cupboards
            jj   and we didn't immediately find the guns.
            kk   There was a separate change room to one side
            ll   and it contained a lot of built-in cupboards.

The special pleading of (cc) and the effort to blame White overtly is again a transparent device that needs little comment. Here I focus on the objective statements depicting the activities of the two men. The view presented in (ii) to (kk) is that the two men are searching cupboards in different parts of the room, probably back to back.

(20)   mm   then started searching through these cupboards
            nn   and he did likewise.
            oo   At some point I heard him slamming a cupboard door
            pp   and he then fired a shot into one of the doors
            qq   and I did exactly the same purely on instinct
            rr   and it was only later that I realized that Mrs. Roux had
                  been inside the cupboard.
            ss   I didn't know that beforehand.
            MR. GIMSBEEK: But you did suspect that there was somebody
                  inside the cupboard?
            MR. VAN WYK: Yes, but I didn't know it.

tt   White then opened the cupboard,
uu   slit Mrs. Roux's throat.

After (ss), the attorney points to a weakness in Van Wyk's self-serving testimony, and his response is the unconvincing excuse that he was not sure that Mrs. Roux was in the cupboard. Van Wyk goes on to express his regrets in two forms. The first is a plainly racist statement.

(21)   **Evaluation**

vv At that stage that action had a great impact on me.
uu You know we espoused the cause of the Afrikaner people
vv and now we had killed one of our own people.
ww At that stage it wasn't a great sadness for me to see two black people dying,
xx but to see Mrs. Roux dying was a terrible thing for me to have to witness.

The second apology is a statement that—taken at face value—would imply that Van Wyk is a profoundly changed person.

(22)   I think without detracting from what I said the way I feel now, the experience I have now gained, I would like to say to Mr. and Mrs. Dubane's family and all their friends, I would like to say to them I am really sorry for what happened. And I would like to say to Mrs. Roux's family and friends I am truly sorry for the error which we committed there. I am really, really sorry. I have no words to express how I feel and nothing can undo, no words can undo what we actually did, but I am very sorry.

The only appropriate response to these ritual apologies is made by the TRC chair: He adjourned the meeting. The apologies are all the more suspect because they show Van Wyk's continued efforts to transform the events in a way that assigns guilt to White and excuses himself. In (22) Van Wyk says, *we had killed one of our own people*—not *I had killed*. In (21) he portrays himself as a witness of Mrs. Roux's death, not the agent, and avoids the direct expression *It was a terrible thing for me to have killed Mrs. Roux*. Returning to the narrative proper, one finds other evidence of an underlying structure of events in which Van Wyk has the main responsibility for the killings.

In (qq) we can recognize another special pleading. Van Wyk argues that he did not intentionally fire into the cabinet but merely duplicated White's action *purely by instinct*. This subjective claim has no probative value in testimony and can easily be set aside. The factual question that remains is, Who killed Mrs.

Roux—White or Van Wyk? One possibility is that Van Wyk fired into the same cabinet that White fired into and that this second shot was not necessarily the cause of death. The other is that Van Wyk fired into a different cabinet, which White did not fire into, and that Van Wyk therefore was the agent of Mrs. Roux's death. Thus, two disparate readings of the narrative are possible, depending on the interpretation of the ambiguous construction much discussed by linguists: *exactly the same*.

If I say, "John scratched his nose and I did exactly the same," the expression "same action" is not usually understood to mean that I scratched John's nose but that I scratched my own. Yet both interpretations are possible. In this case, one can interpret the expression *did exactly the same* in (qq) to mean that White opened the cabinet door, saw Mrs. Roux in the cabinet, and deliberately fired into the cabinet to kill her, and Van Wyk, standing alongside him, fired by instinct into the same cabinet and perhaps did not actually hit her. On the other hand, if we are dealing with two different cabinets, the question remains, in which cabinet was Mrs. Roux and who killed her?

The use of the definite article *the* in (rr), coupled with the *the* in (tt), shows that Mrs. Roux was in the cabinet that Van Wyk fired into. The open question is whether White had fired into a different cabinet—the one designated originally with the indefinite article *a* in clause (oo). Thus, we have two different causal sequences.

In (23a), both men fire into the same cabinet—first White and then Van Wyk. White then reopens the door of the cabinet and slits Mrs. Roux's throat. In this scenario, White is the effective executioner of Mrs. Roux with gun and knife. In (23b), there are two cupboards. White fires into the empty one and then Van Wyk fires into the second, which contains Mrs. Roux. White then opens the door of the second cabinet and slits the throat of Mrs. Roux, who very likely already is dead from the bullet fired by Van Wyk.

(23a) Participant analysis table of (20)

	mm started searching	nn started searching	oo heard slam	pp fired shot	qq fired shot	tt opened cupboard	uu slit her throat
White	y		x	y		y	y
Van Wyk		y	x		y		
Mrs. Roux				z	z		z
cupboard			x	z	z	z	

(23b)   Alternate participant analysis table of (20)

	mm started searching	nn started searching	oo heard slam	pp fired shot	qq fired shot	tt opened cupboard	uu slit her throat
White	y		x	y		y	y
Van Wyk		y	x		y		
Mrs. Roux					z		z
cupboard₁			x	z		z	
cupboard₂	z						

Which is correct, (23a) or (23b)? Van Wyk has created this ambiguity by the use of the ambiguous expression *did exactly the same*. He has left evidence, however, that the true scenario is the second—in which he is the sole person who has shot Mrs. Roux. This assessment depends on the Gricean implicature of the verb *heard*.

If Van Wyk had said in (oo), "I saw him slam the door," that would be consistent with the two men standing side by side firing into the same cabinet. But *heard* is not consistent with this interpretation. *I saw him slam the door* has the conversational implicature *I heard him slam the door* (unless it is specified that the shooter is far away, or the speaker is deaf). On the other hand, *I heard him slam the door* has the conversational implicature *I didn't see it*.

The conclusion must be that White was standing so that Van Wyk could not see what he was firing at and that White's shot was into a different, empty cupboard. If Van Wyk had altered the verb of (oo) from *heard* to *saw,* the result would have been consistent with the ambiguity introduced by the expression *exactly the same*; because the verb is left as *heard*, however, there is no ambiguity.[12] The interpretation of (23b) is most likely.

I hope that this study of the Van Wyk testimony helps to accomplish the initial goals of the Truth and Reconciliation Commission: to discover what was done and who was responsible. The analysis of underlying event structure shows that Van Wyk has consistently transformed his account of events to minimize his own assignment of guilt for the actions involved. The transformation is accomplished through the same two basic techniques that were found in the narrative of the first man killed by a car in South Lyons: deletion of events and exploitation of ambiguous constructions. We have found that neither of these techniques produces a clean result. The interlocking and overlapping of linguistic structures across sentence boundaries leaves traces that point to the nature of the deleted material. With some care, we can use these traces to reconstruct the underlying events on which the narrative was formed.

There is no reason to regard the speakers' operations on the original event sequences as Machiavellian manipulations of the truth. On the basis of observations of a wide range of narrators, I believe that such transformations are automatic features of the organization of narrative. The narrator is unconsciously directed by a normative ideology that assigns praise and blame for actions involved in ways that are sensitive to the social relations of the narrator, his or her immediate addressees, and the wider potential audience. It is also clear that listeners normally do not engage in the analytic processes I have conducted here. They show no evidence of being aware of the gaps and minor inconsistencies in the narrator's construction; instead, they accept or reject the narrative as true or false as a whole on the basis of their overall impressions.

The procedures of this essay are therefore not a reconstruction of the listener's understanding. They represent an attempt to stand behind the narrators, from the moment of their first motivation to project a story that has entered into their biography, and follow the logic of narrative construction. I have tried to reconstruct what is involved in putting together a linear sequence of narrative clauses that correspond more or less to what happened and to what the narrators would like to have understood about what happened.

Clearly these reconstructions are far from certain. We have no measures of the degree of confidence in the correctness of the result. Nevertheless, the undertaking promises to illuminate the process by which narratives are created, transmitted, and understood.

NOTES

1. This paper was first delivered at a meeting of the advanced discourse seminar taught by Professor Heidi Hamilton at Georgetown University in February 2001. I am grateful to members of the seminar for the fruitful discussion that contributed to the form of the paper presented at GURT in March 2001 and the present version: Anne Berry, Sylvia Chou, Elisa Everts, Philip LeVine, Heidi Hamilton, Karen Murph, Aida Premilovac, Anne Schmidt, Nicole Watanabe, Alla Yeliseyeva, and Najma Al Zidjaly.
2. In rare cases, several of those present provide narratives of the same events. Longitudinal studies of the same speaker focus on retellings of the same narrative (Labov and Auger 1998). These limited data sets provide a different approach to the problem of this essay, which focuses on the normal case in which no independent information can be found.
3. Though the most reportable event often is mentioned in the abstract, if there is one.
4. We are dealing here with serious accounts of everyday life told by ordinary people with the purpose of conveying information about real events. The success or failure of such narratives, and the status of the narrator, is intimately involved with their credibility. These considerations do not extend to the special genre of "tall tales," which are told by skilled narrators for the purpose of entertainment, with no investment in the truth-conditional status of the events (Bauman 1986).

5. Not every clause preceding (m) is locked into the causal chain. Clauses (i) and (f) locate the path of the actions without themselves being causes of what follows or precedes.
6. One does not drive an airplane or balloon, which move vertically as well as horizontally.
7. Thus, a child who was driven to school by her mother may answer the question, "How did you get here?" with "I drove with my mom."
8. The discussion of the history and aims of the TRC is based directly on Bock, McCormick, and Raffray (2001).
9. The reports of the TRC are available at www.doj.gov/za/trc/index.html.
10. The present analysis does not deal with the deeper questions of reconciliation faced by the TRC: How could such things have happened? What were the effects of what happened? What kind of resolution can be achieved?
11. The narratives of interest can be found on the TRC website at www.doj.gov/za.trc/amntrans/pta1/vanwyk.htm.
12. It is possible, of course, that Van Wyk heard the shot fired and moved to where White was firing before he fired, but this scenario is not entirely consistent with firing "purely by instinct"—a more immediate reaction.

REFERENCES

Bauman, Richard. 1986. *Story, performance, and event.* Cambridge: Cambridge University Press.

Bock, Mary, Kay McCormick, and Claudine Raffray. 2001. *Fractured truths: discourse in South Africa's truth and reconciliation hearings.* Unpublished manuscript.

Labov, William. 1972. The transformation of reality in narrative syntax. In William Labov, *Language in the inner city.* Philadelphia: University of Pennsylvania Press. 354–96.

———. 1997. Some further steps in narrative analysis. *Journal of Narrative and Life History* 7: 395–415.

Labov, William, and Julie Auger. 1998. The effect of normal aging on discourse: A sociolinguistic approach. In *Narrative discourse in neurologically impaired and normal aging adults,* edited by Hiram H. Brownell and Yves Joanette. San Diego: Singular Publishing Group, 115–34.

Labov, William, and Joshua Waletzky. 1967. Narrative analysis. In *Essays on the verbal and visual arts,* edited by June Helm. Seattle: University of Washington Press, 12–44. Reprinted in *Journal of Narrative and Life History* 7 (1997): 3–38.

Sacks, Harvey. 1992. *Lectures on conversation,* vol. 1 and 2. Edited by Gail Jefferson. Cambridge: Blackwell.

Truth and Reconciliation Commission (TRC). 2001. *Truth: the road to reconciliation.* Available at www.truth.org.za.

Linquistics and history: Oral history as discourse[1]

Deborah Schiffrin
Georgetown University

In sharp contrast to the long and fruitful collaborations that have developed between linguists and anthropologists, sociologists, and psychologists, there has been surprisingly little reciprocity between linguists and historians. Yet just as the study of language intersects with the synchronic study of culture, society, and human beings, so too does it intersect with the diachronic study—the history—of these domains.

The general site of possible convergence between linguists and historians that I explore in this essay is *text*. Discourse analyses of one type of text—*oral histories*—offer an excellent opportunity to bring together a joint concern of historians and linguists: how individuals, societies, and cultures use texts to represent the past. My general goals are to apply linguistics to the concerns of people who are interested in oral history and to demonstrate the usefulness of oral histories as "data" for discourse analysts. I address these goals by drawing from a research project analyzing life stories of Holocaust survivors within and across oral histories (Schiffrin 2000a, 2000b, 2002)—which, in turn, is part of my more general research on Holocaust discourse (Schiffrin 2001a, 2001b). The specific data that I use are two different versions of one episode from a Holocaust survivor's oral history—one transcribed from an oral history interview, another excerpted on a website.

After describing some functions and features of oral histories, I present the two texts and discuss some key parameters of their contexts. I then summarize a more extensive analysis (which I am in the process of developing) to show how features of the texts are related to the contexts that underlie their production and influence their interpretation. My conclusion suggests the mutual benefits for linguists and historians of analyzing the language of oral histories.

Oral Histories: More (and Less?) than History

Oral histories are audio or video recordings of personal and communal memories that are collected during face-to-face interviews with people who were witnesses to events that are likely to have lasting legacies. Despite a dearth of linguistic analysis of oral histories, numerous scholars have offered important insights about the language of oral histories that can motivate and inform linguistic analysis. In this section, I draw on this scholarship to review the functions and central features of oral histories.

Holocaust oral histories are concerned with history in three different senses: They recount personal and collective "history" (the past), they provide data for historical research, and they contribute to History.[2] They also have commemorative and autobiographical functions, however, and thus aim to accomplish a variety of goals for a variety of audiences (Schiffrin 2002).

Let us begin with history/History. Along with diaries, personal letters, and memoirs, Holocaust oral histories provide insights into how macro-level social, cultural, economic, and political changes were experienced by everyday people. They complement scholarship on who helped set those changes into motion by adding personal details about the lives of those who suffered the consequences of those changes. In this sense, analysis of oral histories is comparable to the Italian microhistory perspective developed in the 1970s (Iggers 1997: chapter 9) and Bartaux's (1981) use of personal biography as a means by which to study society.

Although many Holocaust scholars quote freely and extensively from oral histories, others treat oral histories with caution and skepticism. The stories within them are about events experienced at least forty years prior to their telling. Many of the stories have been told many times, in many settings, to many people. Some scholars worry that they no longer represent an authentic and unmediated voice.

To assuage these worries, sets of guidelines have developed that propose solutions for a range of questions concerning the use of oral histories as factual documents. The *Oral History Interview Guidelines* (Ringelheim, Donahue, and Rubin 1998) published by the United States Holocaust Memorial Museum, for example, includes general guidelines (Chapter III) for learning about the basic historical facts of the Holocaust prior to an interview, as well as specific guidelines (appendix 9) for authenticating information (i.e., identifying places, names, dates, and so on) after an interview. Tec (1993) advocates checking basic dates and events, comparing different sources, and conducting multiple interviews with the same person, asking "the same questions again and again" (Tec 1993: 273; see also Greenspan 1998). Gurewitsch (1998: xx) supplements her collection of oral histories with extensive footnotes that reveal the extent to which she was "able to verify and corroborate the information in the interviews." She suggests that "although not all material is verifiable, an interview that is generally factual and consistent with other accounts should be read as reliable testimony" (Gurewitsch 1998: xx).

In addition to the effects of time and memory on the representation of "what happened in the past," the processes of transcribing and then publishing material from oral histories introduces additional levels of mediation—this time, between a spoken voice and graphic representations of that voice (Edwards 2001). Portelli

(1997: 15) observes, for example, that "there is no all-purpose transcript" and that "the same applies to editing: Is it intended to reproduce as carefully as possible the actual sounds of the spoken word or to make the spoken word accessible to readers through the written medium?"

When oral histories are integrated into the product of research—publications—they are mediated yet again. Although some are published in full form on their own, others appear as excerpts combined with excerpts from other oral histories or with different types of data that address a common analytical theme or problem. Publication usually is accompanied by grammatical and textual changes that shift the material to more conventional written styles; for example, editors remove nonfluencies and repetitions and often restore temporal order. As necessary as these changes may be to increase the readability of an oral transcript, editorial modification can make it difficult to uncover the nuances of an original voice. Likewise, as revealed by comparisons of multiple interviews with the same speaker, excision (or rearrangement) of segments from their original texts can lead to incomplete or misleading understandings of what happened (Schiffrin 2000a).

In addition to providing data for historians, oral histories serve commemorative purposes. Edited segments from oral histories of the Holocaust, for example, are replayed in museums, on television, and in movies; they are condensed, edited, and reproduced in printed media (e.g., books and magazines), on interactive media (e.g., computerized learning centers), and on websites. Holocaust oral histories have complemented the many other material and symbolic resources (e.g., museums, monuments, memoirs, films, paintings, sculptures, fiction, poetry, drama) commemorating the Holocaust and added the voices of survivors to the multitude of others (e.g., historians, theologians, journalists, fiction writers, literary theorists) who also have spoken of the Holocaust.

The role of oral histories in public commemoration reflects—and adds to— the important symbolic role that the Holocaust has come to play in American life (Flanzbaum 1999; Linenthal 1995; Novick 1999) and its firm niche within American collective memory. Learning about the wide range of persecution and extermination provides an important testament to the enormity of the Holocaust. Similarly, public memorials often embody the sheer vastness of the Holocaust by collecting and displaying six million items to help people grasp the fact that six million Jews were murdered by Nazis. A recent example is the efforts by students and teachers in a small midwestern school in the United States to collect six million paper clips; according to a radio report on the effort, their worldwide effort had resulted in two million in three years. Yet a variety of people also believe that subjective involvement in the details of individual lives (e.g., Hammer 1998; Miller 1990; Strassfeld 1985) offers a more accessible route toward understanding the devastating effects of the Holocaust on individual, family, communal, and cultural life by personalizing the otherwise numbing horror of the Holocaust.

The two relatively public roles of oral histories discussed thus far—historical inquiry and public commemoration—are supplemented by a third, more private, role: Oral histories provide survivors with a venue in which to tell their life stories. Little public attention was given to the Holocaust in the decade following World War II. Although Holocaust survivors themselves sometimes were vocal about their experiences within their own communities, they maintained a relative silence in relation to the outside world. Silence characterized institutional, as well as personal, realms of discourse. Publishers, for example, saw almost no market potential for books about the Holocaust. Although *The Diary of Anne Frank* has now been read by millions of people worldwide, its publication initially was turned down. The few stories that were told publicly were reconfigured into culturally acceptable American themes (e.g., "people move on from their past") or concluded with happy endings (e.g., "lovers/family members are reunited") (e.g., Shandler 1999: chapter 2).

When oral histories entered American memory culture, they not only helped to shift attention from the voices of Holocaust perpetrators whose actions already had been indelibly recorded through their consequences.[3] Oral histories also validated survivors' experiences by providing a site for co-construction of a life story: autobiographical discourse comprising stories, descriptions, explanations, and chronicles that recapitulate critical points about the speaker and reportable events in his or her life (Linde 1993). This is not to say, of course, that all Holocaust life stories are coherent (Hartman 1996; LaCapra 2001; Langer 1991). As Wieviorka (1994: 25) notes, however, "Victims are certainly beyond words, and yet, dispossessed of everything, words are all they have left. Words which will be the sole trace of an existence."

Despite limited attention to oral histories from linguists, other scholars have provided important reflections on the language of oral histories. Portelli (1997: 6), for example, comments that oral history as a genre "depends to a large extent on the shifting balance between the personal and the social, between biography and history." Efforts to strike such a balance can result in the appearance of recurrent narrative themes. Portelli (1997: 7) observes, for example, that stories with very different topics (e.g., war stories from men, hospital stories from women) similarly reenact personal confrontations with representatives of a public "other."

The shifting balance between individual and collective also creates an inherent multivocality of oral histories at concrete and abstract levels (Portelli 1997: chapter 2). At a concrete level, multiple voices emerge in oral histories simply because interviewers ask questions and make comments; likewise, interviewees typically respond to what interviewers say. Multiple voices also appear more abstractly through the confluence of different narrative modes and the influx of different sources of information over time. The combination of different narrative modes—personal, institutional, communal—into recurrent and meaningful patterns within a single oral history (Portelli 1997: 27), for example, can arise from the incorporation of *ex post facto* voices that reflect survivor myths in addition to historical facts (Wieviorka 1994) or are based in others' experiences rather than one's own experience (Allen and Montell 1981; Schiff, Noy, and Cohler 2000).

My observations to this point suggest that Holocaust oral histories are mediated by their functions and their multivocality: Efforts to serve historical, commemorative, and autobiographical functions produce a variety of blended voices directed toward multiple audiences and goals. Added to these mediating pressures is the inherent fluidity between past and present. In his seminal analysis of how survivors recount the Holocaust, Langer (1991: 40) finds that the language used in what he calls *testimonies* embeds memories and reflects experiences in ways that are "concerned less with a past than with a sense of that past in the present." On a psychological level, survivors may be unable to convey the details of the past because of the enduring trauma of the Holocaust (LaCapra 2001). The physical and symbolic "present" is introduced on an interactional level by the interview setting and situation—a condition shared with all oral history interviews (McMahan 1989). On more macro levels of social, cultural, and political meanings, "the world in which we live . . . changes the meaning [of the Holocaust] as time passes before our eyes" (Hilberg 1991: 19).

In sum, the telling of an oral history faces fundamental (and unavoidable) pressures imposed by language, context, and the simple passage of time. The use of oral history in History and in memory culture requires further transformations through processes of transcription and publication. These characteristics suggest that linguistic analyses of oral histories—perhaps even more than analyses of other discourse—must attend to a multiplicity of functions, voices, and text/context relationships.

In the following section, I turn to a sample from my more extensive project on life stories in Holocaust oral histories to focus on excerpts from two texts from one survivor, Susan Beer. In both excerpts, Beer tells about meeting Hannah Szenes in a Gestapo prison in Budapest in 1944.[4] Szenes was a parachutist on a rescue mission who had been captured, was executed, and fairly quickly became an important public symbol of Jewish idealism, courage, heroism, and resistance. The lives of Susan Beer and Hannah Szenes offer a contrast between private person and public figure that casts their own individual life stories into different functional realms. Thus, texts that report their encounter are an ideal site in which to illustrate how we can use discourse analysis to examine discourse that is mediated by time and situation, oriented to multiple functions (history, commemoration, autobiography), and blends individual and collective meanings.

Text and Context

In this section, I present two versions of Susan Beer's story about Hannah Szenes and discuss the contexts that underlie the production—and influence the interpretation—of these two texts. The first text (the interview text) is from a 1984 oral history interview. The second text (the web text) is an adaptation from a 1982 interview that appeared on a website in 2000.[5] Notice that the web text is not excerpted from the 1984 interview. When I began to work on this essay, I had not yet been able to access the 1982 interview from which the web text was excerpted. Thus, I cannot use the interview and web texts as evidence of discursive change over time (from 1984 to 2000) or interpret the differences as an adaptation of the same information to different modalities. Therefore, my focus here is how the contexts of the two texts—broadly construed as their means of production, intended functions, audiences, and mode of access—have an impact on, and are reflected in, their form and content.

Before reading the two versions of Beer's story about her encounter with Szenes, it will be helpful to have an overview of Beer's and Szenes' lives. The former is briefly reconstructed through Beer's oral histories and written memoir, the latter through Szenes' diary and later reconstructions of her life.

Beer was the only child in an observant Jewish family; she grew up in Topolcany, a small town in what was then Slovakia. Her father was a doctor in the town. When the Germans seized control of Slovakia, discrimination against Jews in Topolcany escalated: Families had to give up their material possessions and their civil liberties; Beer's father was forbidden to practice medicine. As word of deportations began to spread—and when Beer herself received an order to report for a transport to a labor camp—Beer's parents arranged for her to go illegally to Hungary, a country that was then safer for Jews. Beer's parents eventually escaped to Hungary as well, and they all lived clandestinely with false identities. As anti-Semitic measures in Hungary increased, however, the family decided to take a chance on what they thought was a mission of rescue organized by a small contingent of disenchanted German *Wehrmacht* who wanted to return Jews (for a fee) to a small part of Slovakia that had supposedly been liberated by partisans. The mission was really a trap: The family was captured and spent three and a half weeks in a Budapest prison. They were then sent to Auschwitz. Despite the many hardships of Auschwitz, death marches, near starvation, and disease, Beer and her parents all survived. Beer married a young man who had spent most of the war years hiding with his family in the mountains. Beer and her husband immigrated to the United States; Beer's parents (because of restrictive immigration laws) immigrated to Canada.

Szenes was born in Budapest in 1921 to a relatively assimilated Jewish family. Her father (a well-known playwright) died when she was young; Hannah and her brother were raised by her mother. When Szenes became interested in emigrating to Palestine in 1937, she began to study Hebrew and immerse herself in Zionist literature. She left for Palestine in 1939, just as World War II was beginning. There she enrolled in a girls' agricultural school and then joined a kibbutz. In May 1942 she was chosen as a member of the *Haganah*, the underground military organization whose goal was to rescue prisoners of war and organize Jewish resistance in Europe to assist British forces. After special British training (to help British intelligence in occupied Europe) and Zionist instruction (to organize Jewish resistance and escape), Szenes was recruited as one of several parachutists for a mission. When the mission failed, Szenes was imprisoned in Budapest; she was executed several months later. In the years following World War II, Szenes became an important international symbol of Jewish idealism and courage (Baumel 1996, 1998). Her symbolic role in Israeli collective memory quickly eclipsed that of two men with whom she had shared the mission, as well as several other parachutists from Palestine who also had died in occupied Europe. Szenes has been memorialized through plays, films, statues, songs, names of kibbutzim, and books.

Interview Text

All texts are simultaneous products—and realizations—of the context in which they are created. Because the excerpt in (1) is from a videotaped interview, I begin by commenting on the speech acts and participation structure of the interview.

Interviews are speech events designed to elicit information: One person typically takes a questioning role; the other provides information through his/her answers. Despite this seeming asymmetry, the questions asked by Holocaust oral history interviewers end up co-constructing a life story. They do so by building two overarching, but interlocking, frameworks: the linear passage of time (personal life stages and historical phases) and the nonlinear distribution and recurrence of themes (e.g., discrimination, contact with family, emotional reaction). These frameworks help to co-construct a life story because they encourage not only temporally structured recountings of experiences (stories, chronicles) but also recurring themes that facilitate intertextual connections among nonadjacent parts of discourse (Schiffrin 2000b).

In the 1984 interview with Beer, the interviewer (who introduces himself as Dr. Donald Freidheim) uses a variety of question types (Schiffrin 2000a) that help to co-construct Beer's life story. In the initial portion of the interview, the interviewer asks basic demographic questions that orient Beer toward specific times and topics. As the interview progresses, his role becomes more reactive: He intermittently repeats or reformulates questions that probe particular facets of an experience that Beer did not mention or did not elaborate. Beer thus becomes—and remains—the main speaker throughout the interview: She exerts more topic control; provides extended descriptions, narratives, and chronicles of her experiences; and consistently returns to her own topics and themes after attending to the interviewer's questions. The interviewer becomes quiet during much of Beer's oral history. Other than posing follow-up questions, his main contribution is the use of backchannels (*yeh, umhmm*) or recognitionals (see (1) *Right, Hannah Szenes*) that support Beer's active speaking role. The verbal dominance of Beer is matched by her centrality in the video: Except for a view of both the interviewer and Beer in the introduction, the camera provides a frontal view of Beer throughout the interview.

The segment in (1) is the portion of the oral history interview that immediately precedes and follows Beer's recounting of her encounter with Szenes. Beer had been talking about the escalating measures against Jews in Budapest (the place in which she initially found sanctuary from anti-Semitism and persecution in her hometown in Slovakia). After being discovered in various hiding places and disguises, she and her family decide to follow her father's lead and put their trust in what is supposed to be a rescue mission. As noted above, however, the mission is a trap: The family is captured and spends three and a half weeks in a Budapest prison. The story recounted in (1) begins just before the family and those who accompanied them (i.e., the *we* in (1)) is captured.

On the left of each line, I note the function(s) of each clause. Event-clauses (akin to complicating action clauses) within the imprisonment scene ((e)–(s)) and the transition section ((q)–(aa)) are numbered to indicate temporal juncture. Other narrative functions are labeled: I use ORN for orientation and EVAL for evaluation. The encounter with Szenes is italicized in (t), (u), (w), (x), and (aa)–(qq). Szenes' experience itself (the Szenes story) is in lines (cc)–(ll). The use of → indicates that a clause has a dual function in both the imprisonment chronicle and the Szenes story.

(1) SUSAN BEER'S 1984 STORY

(a)   And uh we were supposed to meet, at sundown, in a little park,

(b)   and, we will be going back to Slovakia.

(c)   And the rabbi gave us . . . his blessing,

(d)   and uh we were coming to that park,

(e)   EVENT-1 and as soon as we approached that truck flashlights were lit into our eyes,

(f)   EVENT-2 and we were kicked into the truck,

(g)   EVENT-3 and we knew right away that we were . . . .

(h)   Y'know it was uh- a scheme, to get <u>us,</u>   to get the money,

IVER: Right

(i)   EVENT-4 and they took us straight to the Gestapo headquarters.

(j)   EVENT-5 And uh the men were taken to the . . . uh third floor,

(k)   EVENT-6   and we to the fifth floor,

(l)   EVENT-7   and we were beaten, terribly,

(m)   EVAL   my nose was bleeding all night,

(n)   ORN/   uh the pregnant women, the children, we were all in one
        EVAL   room, about eleven people,

(o)   EVAL   and we were in a real prison.

(p)   EVAL   I mean like Sing Sing.

(q)   ORN/   In the morning, they would open just a crack, the, door,
        EVAL

(r)   EVAL   and . . . give us our food, or our wash basin,

(s)   EVAL   There was one toilet for all of us.

(t)   *ORN*   *And uh . . . as I was looking, across the hall,*

(u)   EVENT-8 ➔ *EVENT-1*
                    I saw a young woman . . . showing things,

(v)   ORN ➔ *ORN y'know when they opened the door,*

(w)   ORN➔ *ORN   she was uh gesticulating with her hands.*

(x)   ORN ➔ *ORN   And everyday they would let us walk in the courtyard,*

(y)   EVAL   *like real prisoners,*

(z)   EVAL   *for half an hour around and around.*

(aa)   EVENT-9 ➔ *EVENT-2 and this woman joined me.*

(bb)   EVENT-10➔ *EVENT-3 And she told me her story,*

(cc)   *EVENT-3a   that she was a parachutist,*

(dd)   *ORN   who came from . . . Israel, Palestine,*

(ee)   *ORN   in Yugoslavia.*

(ff)   *EVENT-3b   And she was caught,*

(gg)   *EVENT-3c   and they- they probably will hang her.*

(hh)   *EVAL   She always made this- this hanging sign.*

(ii)   *EVAL   And she was using-*

(jj)   *ORN/EVAL   they used to take her on a truck, for interrogation,*

(kk)	EVAL	*and she found some coal, or little pieces of coal on the truck,*
(ll)	EVAL	*and she would make marks under her eyes, to e-evoke some pity.*
(mm)	EVENT-11➔	*CODA* *And it turned out to-*
(nn)		*she became very well known she was Hannah Szenes.*
(oo)	IVER:	Hannah Sze[nes].
(pp)	BEER:	[Yes.
(qq)		*CODA* *And eh of course, y'know what happened to her.*
(rr)		Uh we were in this prison for three and a half, weeks.
(ss)		And after that time, they told us to take, whatever we had,
(tt)		and they took us downstairs,
(uu)		they- we stood in line,
(vv)		and, then we are going to the railroad station.
(ww)		Uh I saw my father.
(xx)		After three and a half weeks,
(yy)		and his hands were handcuffed, one hand to another man's hand.

Because the text in (1) was excerpted and transcribed from a videotaped interview, it is important to note some ways that I have transformed it from a spoken speech event to a written transcript. Exclusions and inclusions help construct "the data" and frame the direction of its analysis.

Present in the transcript are various graphic conventions that help create a representation of events. Although space prevents detailed analysis of how these conventions enter into analysis of (1), the following points are suggestive. Separation into lines, use of letters to identify lines, and punctuation (commas, periods), along with attention to syntactic boundaries, all work together to segment events and cluster events into larger situations. Pauses within intonation units, restarts, and repetitions suggest further segmentation; they also reveal an interplay among different discursive demands on word choice, semantic formulation, and the organization of information within text. The labels of events and functions serve a more overt analytical function: They facilitate discussion of different parts of the text, but they also reify the categories through which my analysis views the language of the text.

Although not included in the transcript, the excerpt contains traces of the longer life story that precedes and follows it. Background knowledge of the life story suggests that the text in (1) is thematically framed by—and reflects—a blend of personal and collective, of autobiography and history. The relevance of two specific themes—Beer's relationship with her father and the trajectory of persecution over time—is indexed by Beer through the people she mentions and the way she describes her experience. Because these themes intertextually link (1) to different surface topics across nonadjacent segments, I consider them here as part of the context that mediates the meanings of the interview text.

Consider, first, Beer's relationship with her father. In early parts of her life story, Beer recounts numerous pivotal interactions with her father, showing how deep an influence his personality and character had on her own intellectual and personal development. Later in Beer's life story, the generous actions and altruistic behavior of her father toward his patients develops a subtheme of reciprocity that provides some concrete help for Beer during the war. Beer's separation from her father frames the episode in (1). Not only does Beer mention that the men are separated from the women in the prison ((j), (k)); she also notes that she sees her father again on the train platform (ww) en route to Auschwitz after *three and a half weeks* (xx) have elapsed since their previous contact. The detail that her father's *hands were handcuffed, one hand to another man's hand* (yy) also provides an intertextual link to early times when she had witnessed—and been disturbed by—his subjugation in their hometown.

A second theme in Beer's life story is the Nazi persecution of Jews. Elsewhere in her life story, Beer develops this theme in several ways. In addition to dramatizing the Nazi regime by revoicing orders in German, Beer uses list-like recitations as an iconic reflection of the coldness and impersonal nature with which increasing restrictions are put on her and her family. Beer also uses details and metaphors to capture horrific scenes (e.g., in the camps, on death marches) and tells stories of close calls and escapes, small victories and failures, survival and death. Several stories recount incidents during which she (either alone or with her parents) just barely manages to escape from capture; narrowly avoids disclosure of her/their true identities as Jews from Slovakia; or, by sheer luck, survives disease, starvation, or placement in the wrong line during selection for a transport or within Auschwitz.

Whereas Beer's separation from her father in (1) connects with an intertextual theme that is personally salient, the family's capture and imprisonment connects with an intertextual theme that also is historically salient. In 1941 Hungary enacted laws comparable to the restrictive 1935 Nuremburg Laws in Germany (e.g., prohibiting intermarriage, depriving Jews of citizenship). Also in 1941, thousands of Jews were deported to German-occupied Ukraine; most were massacred. Yet not until 1944, under the leadership of Adolph Eichmann (head of the Gestapo section dealing with Jewish affairs), was fulfillment of the Final Solution for Jews in Hungary fully under way. Ghettoization was extended throughout the country by April 1944, and deportations proceeded geographically. By July 1944, almost 450,000 Jews from Hungary (220,000 Jews from Budapest alone—one-third of the population) had been sent to Auschwitz (Cesarani 1999; Rothkirchen 1986; Yahil 1990). Beer's imprisonment and subsequent deportation to Auschwitz in June 1944 was part of that general wave of persecution.

These historical details are important to the interview text: Imprisonment in the Gestapo jail is the first time that Beer and her family no longer are able to find an alternative that affords them any freedom. Thus, their capture, imprisonment, and subsequent train ride to Auschwitz in June 1944 combine to form a pivotal transition in the personal and historical trajectories of Beer's life story: The family will have no existence outside of the Nazi system of persecution and extermination until the end of the war.

In this section, I have presented the interview text and commented on two very different aspects of context—transcription conventions and intertextual themes—that provide frameworks of meaning that contextualize the text. In the following section, we see that the web text is embedded in a very different context.

Web Text

Beer's encounter with Szenes was rewritten by Bonnie Gurewitsch, an archivist and Holocaust scholar who had interviewed Beer at the Museum of Jewish Heritage in New York in 1982. Beer's story about Szenes reappeared in 2000 on the website *Women and the Holocaust*, under a topic titled *Women of Valor: Partisans and Resistance Fighters*, on a page titled *Susan Beer*. In reading and analyzing the web text, it is important to remember that this text is excerpted not from the 1984 interview but from an earlier 1982 interview to which I did not yet have access at the time of this research. Thus, what we are comparing represents neither a change over time (e.g., from 1984 to 2000) nor a transformation between an original source and an alteration of that source.

In (2), I replicate the layout of the Susan Beer page, alphabetizing the lines (as in (1)) for ease of reference and labeling of functions. Also appearing on the page is a list of links on the right. These links (added to the website by Judy Cohen, who originated and manages the site) initially were titles of other entries in the original journal publication in which Beer's excerpt first appeared. The entries to which the links point are more complete (auto)biographical summaries of the women's overall World War II experiences; they also are longer (as many as eight pages, compared to Beer's one page) and include footnotes.

(2) SUSAN BEER'S WEB TEXT

"Women of Valor: Partisans and Resistance Fighters"

Susan Beer

Susan Eisdorfer grew up in Topolcany, Czechoslovakia, in a traditionally Jewish home.

Her father was a physician, forbidden to practice medicine under Nazi law. In an effort to escape an order to report to a labour camp in 1942, she succeeded in crossing the border to Hungary, considered safer because it was not yet under German occupation. In Hungary, however, she lived illegally, in constant fear of detection and imprisonment. After the Germans occupied Hungary she was more vulnerable than ever, and tried to return to Slovakia, but was arrested and taken to Gestapo headquarters in Budapest. There she encountered Hannah Szenes, a fellow prisoner.

Historical Background

Aida Brybord

Zenia Malecki

Evelyn Kahn

Partisans: A Personal Memoir

Katherine Szenes

Susan Beer

Anna Heilman

Rose Meth

Biographical Sketches

Letters from the Holocaust

Halakha and the Holocaust

Glossary

Author: Dr. Yaffa Eliach

Someone special.

(a) In the morning, when they opened up the grills in our cell doors, (b) I saw that in a cell across the way there was one solitary woman. (c) She had dark circles under her eyes. (d) She smiled. (e) We saw her exercising, (f) standing on her head, (g) doing all sorts of vigorous exercises. (h) Her front teeth were missing. (i) I asked her, "Did they beat your teeth out of you?" (j) She was such a gentle person.

(k) She would pass little slips of paper through the grill of her cell, (l) hoping that someone would pick them up. (m) She was always cheerful, (n) even though she knew they were going to kill her.

(o) In the yard she would walk behind me (p) and carefully get closer to me when the guards didn't see. (q) Her mother walked in the same group, but far away. (r) The guards watched that the mother shouldn't get too close to the daughter.

(s) She told me that she was a parachutist. (t) That she really came to save her mother and maybe some other Jews. (u) She parachuted down on the Yugoslav border with two other men. (v) Someone betrayed her. (w) She was caught and brought to the prison. (x) She constantly showed me, with a smile, (y) that she knew she's going to be hung. (z) She did not really hope to live.

(aa) I saw her about ten times, in June 1944. (bb) I heard from others that she made gifts. (cc) When someone had a birthday she would put the gift up to a window and show it.

(dd) She was 23 years old at the time. (ee) I felt she was someone special. (ff) I didn't know exactly what she was, (gg) but I never forgot her. (hh) There was something special about her. (ii) She didn't behave like the others. (jj) She wasn't scared, thinking of herself. (kk) She was beyond that. (ll) She had an aura about her. (mm) To me she was very exotic; (nn) she was close to my age, (oo) and she came from Palestine. (pp) In that prison it was good to hear something like this, something beyond our misery.

Excerpts of the interview by Bonnie Gurewitsch, 5/25/82

The web text is mediated by very different contextual parameters than the interview text. First, the web text has a more direct presence in public discourse. Whereas the interview text is housed in the research archives of a museum and available primarily to scholars and students only through a reference librarian, the inclusion of the later version on the web makes it easily accessible to a wide variety of people.

Second, the web text provides very little connection to Beer's life story.[6] The only link to Beer's own life prior to her encounter with Szenes is through what I call "the synopsis," the summary of Beer's life in a single paragraph. In the synopsis, Beer's father, so thematically central to Beer's life story, is largely absent: He is mentioned only once, in the context of his professional status and Nazi restrictions. In sharp contrast to the experiences recounted in Beer's 1984 life story (and in other versions of her life story), Beer is presented as an individual who acts completely on her own. For example, although the synopsis states that Beer made *an effort to escape an order to report to a labour camp*, we know from Beer's interviews that her father arranged for this escape. Thus, the condensed and modified versions of events prior to Beer's imprisonment provide a sense of neither the collective nature of Beer's experiences nor the impact of imprisonment on her life. The synopsis ends once Beer is taken to Gestapo headquarters, where she encountered the only person, other than her father, mentioned in the synopsis: *Hannah Szenes, a fellow prisoner.*

Although there are minimal connections between the web text and Beer's life story, the Susan Beer page itself has numerous intertextual links. The title of the section in which the page was included—*Women of Valor: Partisans and Resistance Fighters*—resounds with Judaic significance. The phrase *women of valor* is used not only in the Bible (Proverbs 31) but also in a weekly Jewish Sabbath blessing for the women in the family; in the latter case, the phrase praises the heroism of women's ordinary domestic tasks. In addition to the intertextual connection with religious themes, other connections are within the website itself: We find connections to Holocaust scholarship through three links (*Scholarly Essays, Reviews, Bibliography*), as well as connections to Holocaust commemoration (*Poetry, Personal Reflections*).

Still another contextual parameter arises from the fact that the web text is *Excerpts of the interview by Bonnie Gurewitsch, 5/25/82*. Not only was material reduced and possibly rearranged (as implied by the term *excerpted*); because the source of the material was an interview, the modality changed from spoken to written.[7] Published versions of oral histories never appear in the transcription format to which linguists are accustomed. Instead, they look more like written discourse: They follow conventions of punctuation (e.g., periods, commas, quotation marks), grammar (no sentence fragments), and paragraph structure; they have no false starts and few indications of pauses. Beer's web text is consistent with these conventions.

Visual and graphic conventions associated with written modalities (e.g., color, size, font, page layout, titles, headings) also appear on the Susan Beer web page. The page opens with the section title *Women of Valor: Partisans and Resistance Fighters* and the name *Susan Beer* under the title. Color provides a functional contrast: Whereas the heading (title and name) is brown, black letters are used on the rest of the page. Page layout and format separate sections of the text. The brief synopsis of Beer's life is separated from Beer's encounter with Szenes not only grammatically (the former is in the third person, the latter in the first person) but spatially by a title (**Someone special**), a different format (paragraphs), and a shift in layout (instead of being in two columns, the text goes from margin to margin).

Summary: Texts in Context

In this section, I have presented two different versions of Susan Beer's encounter with Hannah Szenes. First was a transcript of a section of an interview. I observed that details of spoken language were conveyed in ways that made the transcript readable as a text that is useful for discourse analysis. I also noted that two intertextual themes connected the interview text to broader domains of meanings from Beer's life story, thus indexing the autobiographical function of her oral history. Next was a page from a website. The web text was excerpted from a different oral history interview and appeared on a publicly accessible Internet site. The conventions of written discourse that it follows make it familiar to purveyors of the web and comprehensible as a written text: A topic is identified, sentences are grammatical, sentences are grouped into paragraphs. The text itself is linked to themes that likewise bridge the personal and collective, biographical and historical. The difference is that these themes do not appear in relation to Beer's own life. Instead, they appear through links to the biographies of other people and to histories written by scholars that are posted on other parts of the website.

Comparing Interview and Web Texts

The interview and web texts ostensibly are about the same experience: Susan Beer's 1944 encounter with Hannah Szenes in a Gestapo prison in Budapest. Although the basic facts about Szenes are very similar, the distribution and type of information presented about each character are quite different. In this section, I discuss referring terms, event types, style, and use of boundary/bridging devices in the two texts as a way to highlight their different styles, emphases, and characterizations. I then turn to their similarities.

References to Beer and Szenes provide an initial glimpse of their different portrayals in the texts. Table 5.1 compares singular to plural referring terms in subject position. The former includes *I*, proper name, and definite/indefinite singular nouns; the latter includes *we* (inclusive, exclusive), *they*, and definite/indefinite plural nouns.

Beer's first-person references in the interview text are primarily collective: "We" are planning to return to Slovakia, and "we" are in prison. The inclusion of self in a collectivity changes dramatically in the web text. The only first-person plural reference that includes Beer is during her view of Szenes: *We saw her exercising, standing on her head, doing all sorts of vigorous exercises* ((e)–(g)). In sharp contrast, references to Szenes in the interview and web texts are overwhelmingly individual—prefigured, in the latter text, by the initial mention of her as *one solitary woman* (b).[8]

It is important to note that the individual/collective dichotomy is not necessarily dictated by "the facts." Studies of the use of second-person plural pronouns (e.g., deFina 1999: chapter 3) show that speakers use the collective *we* even when other information establishes that they acted independently. Similarly, in my

Table 5.1. Personal References

	Interview	Web	Total
Beer alone	6	8	14
Beer with other	25	1	26
Szenes alone	13	31	44
Szenes with other	1	0	1
Total	45	40	85

study of family and friendship discourse in the oral history of another Holocaust survivor (Schiffrin 2002), the use of plural references was related not only to "what happened" in the real world but also to how characters (at interpersonal, archetypal, and historical levels) fit into overall themes of solidarity and distance. Thus, Beer could have displayed her autonomy from a group: She could have said *I was beaten* or *I was in a room with ten other people.* Likewise, because Szenes was one of three parachutists on the Haganah mission—all of whom were captured and briefly held in the same prison (Baumel 1996: 523)—Beer could have displayed Szenes as a member of a group.

The referential patterns in Table 5.1 also index Beer and Szenes to strikingly different functions of oral histories. The collective focus of Beer's experience is consistent with intertextual themes of group solidarity and reciprocity in her own life story. Whereas collectivity in Beer's story thus indexes the more personal, autobiographical functions of Beer's oral history, individuality in the representation of Szenes indexes the more commemorative functions of Szenes' life within memory culture. Although Hannah Szenes was one of six Jewish parachutists who perished in Europe (including two other women), she had "become the standard against which her fellow parachutists were being measured" as early as 1945 (Baumel 1996: 527). Thus, Szenes' role as *one solitary woman* (web text (b)) who represented Jewish idealism, courage, resistance, and heroism during the Holocaust soon eclipsed that of the other parachutists who also died in occupied Europe. Later commemorations and public memorials (e.g., renaming locales, dramatizations, statues, educational programs, films, poetry, songs), intensified the position of Hannah Szenes *herself* within Jewish (especially Israeli) history (Baumel 1996, 1998).

A comparison of event-types shows a slightly different perspective on the textual characterization of the two women. The verbs used to convey "events" in the texts can be categorized in one of three ways: as internal (mental) states (e.g., "know," "realize"), physical attributes (e.g., "be gentle"), or physical actions (e.g., "smile," "ask").[9] Table 5.2 compares the types of events that Beer portrays for herself and Szenes in the interview and web texts.

In both versions, the single largest category of Beer-events and Szenes-events is physical actions. The decrease in physical actions for both Beer and Szenes in the web text is related to the addition of other event types: an increase in Beer's internal states (from 8 percent to 38 percent), Szenes' internal states (from zero to 18 percent), and Szenes' physical attributes (from 22 percent to 35 percent).

Clauses that report physical attributes and internal states have different roles in narrative than physical action clauses: They are descriptive (nonnarrative) clauses that contribute primarily to evaluation.[10] Thus, the increase in physical attributes and internal states is a crucial part of a shift away from the referential style of reporting "what happened" (with evaluative devices embedded within narrative clauses) in the interview text to an evaluative style that depends more on descriptive clauses distributed among action clauses in the web text.

A subtle contrast within the physical attributes themselves shows the same shift toward descriptive evaluation. In the interview text, the verbs implicate activity (*she was a parachutist* (cc)) or presuppose change over time (*she became very well known* (nn)). In the web text, the verbs *have* and *be* predicate qualities (e.g., *had dark circles under her eyes* (c), *was such a gentle person* (j)) that may endure indefinitely. Thus, the frequency of internal states and physical attributes, and the qualities of these verbs themselves, indicate the shift to a descriptive means of evaluation.

We can get a clearer picture of how this stylistic shift works in the characterization of Beer if we turn from what unites physical attributes and internal states—their descriptive roles in narrative—to what differentiates them. Physical attributes and internal states reflect different modes of evidence and

Table 5.2. Who Does What?

	Interview (%)	Web (%)	Total
Susan Beer			
Internal states	1 (8)	3 (38)	4
Physical attributes	1 (8)	0 (0)	1
Physical actions	10 (83)	5 (62)	15
Subtotal	12	8	20
Hannah Szenes			
Internal states	0 (0)	6 (18)	6
Physical attributes	2 (22)	12 (35)	14
Physical actions	7 (77)	16 (44)	23
Subtotal	9	34	43
TOTAL	21	42	63

Table 5.3. Beer's Source of Information about Szenes

	Interview (%)	Web (%)	Total
Observation	9 (100)	28 (82)	37
Inference	0	6	6
Total	9	34	43

knowing about another. Like physical actions, physical attributes can be observed. Another's internal state (e.g., thoughts, feelings), however, can only be inferred. Notice, then, that Beer's statements about Szenes' internal state are what Labov and Fanshel (1977: 10, 227) call B-events: They are statements about events about which the "other" (B)—but not the "self" (A)—has knowledge. In other words, they require Beer to make inferences about the mind (knowledge, perceptions) and the emotions (feelings) of Szenes.

Table 5.3 groups physical activities and attributes as "observations" and internal states as "inferences."

As Table 5.3 shows, the only means by which Beer obtains information about Szenes in the interview text is by observation. In the web text, however, Beer also reports internal states that depend on inference.

As suggested above, the addition of inferential modes of knowing is a shift in style and characterization. Along with a shift from referential/evaluative to descriptive/evaluative, then, comes a repositioning of Beer into a role that adds reflection and inference to a minimized level of agency. This new stance is reflected even more strikingly if we reexamine the clauses from the web text that report Beer's physical actions (from Table 5.2):

(3)   **BEER'S PHYSICAL ACTION CLAUSES (WEB TEXT)**

"see"   *I saw . . . there was one solitary woman* (b)

we saw her exercising (e)

I saw her about ten times (aa)

"ask"   *I asked her, "Did they beat your teeth out of you?"* (i)

"hear"   *I heard from others that she made gifts* (bb)

Physical action clauses are exactly those clauses that typically serve to move the narrative forward. As we see in (3), however, Beer's physical actions actually link Beer to Szenes through her own senses ("see," "hear") and speech acts ("ask"). In this sense, they are similar to the three internal states from Beer (also from Table 5.2) that also link Beer to Szenes: *I felt she was someone special* (ee), *I didn't **know** exactly what she was,* (ff) *but I never **forgot** her* (gg). Thus, virtually all of the clauses in the web text in which Beer is engaged in physical action position her only as someone reacting (through sight, hearing, feeling) to Szenes or eliciting information from Szenes. Thus, Beer's inferences and actions are both immersed within and subordinated to her encounter with Szenes.

Structuring devices in the interview and web texts also show that Beer's experience in the web text is centered less around her own experience and more around her reaction to, and encounter with, Szenes. In (4), I reproduce the clauses from the interview text that facilitate a transition from Beer's own imprisonment to her encounter with Szenes. We see that evaluation of imprisonment (grammatical voice, details, and descriptive clauses, (e)–(p) in the interview text) continues in the transition, where it combines with time/space/activity to facilitate a transition from imprisonment per se to an encounter with Szenes. I use different fonts to indicate **time**, *activity*, and ***space*** in (4); evaluative material is underlined.

(4)   **TRANSITION TO SZENES STORY**

(q)   **In the morning,** *they would open* just ***a crack, the, door***,

(r)   and . . . give us our food, or our wash basin,

(s)   There was one toilet for all of us.

(t)   And uh . . . **as** *I was looking,* ***across the hall***,

(u)   *I saw* a young woman . . . showing things,

(v)   y'know **when they** *opened the door*,

(w)   she was uh gesticulating with her hands.

(x)   And **everyday** they would let us walk ***in the courtyard***,

(y)   like real prisoners,

(z)   for half an hour around and around,

(aa)   and this woman joined me.

Although space does not permit extensive discussion of this sequence, it is important to note that the confluence of information in (4) weaves Beer's encounter with Szenes into her imprisonment without overtly marking a change in topic. For example, each sequence is opened with a preposed temporal expression: a phrase (*in the morning* (q)), clause (*as I was looking* (t)), or word (*everyday* (x)). Consistent with research on the informational and textual functions of preposing (Ward and Birner 2001), these temporal markers form a referential bridge that reaches back to prior text and extends into subsequent text.

Turning to the evaluative clauses, we see that the habitual activities ((q), (x)) transform a restrictive space (*the door, the courtyard*) into a portal to a previously denied locale. This spatial configuration has a dual function. In addition to facilitating evaluation of imprisonment (((r), (s), (y), (z)), it alters Beer's visual/physical confinement and thus allows the transition to the story about Szenes: It is *as* [she] *was looking, across the hall* (o)) that Beer *saw a young woman* (p). Likewise, confinement to place and activity within the courtyard evaluates a more public arena that also makes Beer available for interaction with other prisoners. Thus, it is during Beer's walk that Szenes *joined* her ((aa)) and, in the very next clause, that Szenes proceeds *to tell her story* (bb).

The multiple functions of clauses in (4), then, embed the Szenes-story so deeply within the imprisonment episode that the incremental contact between Beer and Szenes—seeing (u), joining (aa), telling (bb)—is seamlessly textualized as event clauses within both the imprisonment episode and the embedded Szenes story:

> EVENT- 8 → *EVENT - 1*   *I saw a young woman . . . showing things,* (u)
>
> EVENT- 9 → *EVENT- 2*   *and this woman joined me.* (aa)
>
> EVENT- 10→ *EVENT-3*   *And she told me her story,* (bb)

Thus, the actions in lines (u), (aa), and (bb) serve a dual role in the event structure of the text: They are part of Beer's imprisonment and Beer's telling of Szenes' story.

Like the interview text, the web text also establishes a connection between Beer's encounter with Szenes in prison and prior events in Beer's life. Yet in keeping with the different context, structure, format, and themes of the text, a slightly different set of textual devices, as well as a different distribution of information, intensify the importance of Szenes in the web text.

For example, at the end of the one-paragraph synopsis of Beer's life on the web page, we learn that Beer is taken to Gestapo headquarters, and *There she encountered Hannah Szenes, a fellow prisoner*. This clause functions as both coda to the synopsis and abstract for the Szenes story. The coda role is enabled through spatial anaphora: *There* locates the encounter in the previously mentioned location—Gestapo headquarters in Budapest (e). Both coda and abstract are created by the preposed position of *there* (like temporal preposing, spatial preposing has a bridging function) and by the introduction of a new character, *Hannah Szenes,* who will be the focus of the next segment. The use of the verb *encounter* and the description of Szenes as *a fellow prisoner* also contribute to the role of (6) as an abstract by connecting Beer and Szenes: *Encountered* is a symmetric predicate requiring the joint mention of Beer and Szenes; *a fellow prisoner* implicates a shared identity.

Once the web text switches to a first-person narration from Beer, headed by the ***Someone special*** title, we see some of the same phrases used to convey Beer's first view of Szenes and to mark a transition to the place where Beer and Szenes have direct contact: the preposed temporal *in the morning*, the vague *they*, the spatial preposition *across* (*the hall/the way*), and Szenes as a *woman (a young woman/one solitary woman)*. The interview and web texts both place Szenes at the very end of the sentence—the position designed for new focal information. In *I saw that in a cell across the way there was one solitary woman* ((b)), however, Szenes is doubly positioned (through "see" and "there") as new and important information. Furthermore, whereas the interview text immerses Beer's view of Szenes within her more general activity of *looking* (t) at a general view *across the hall* (t), what Beer is represented as having seen in the web text—*one solitary woman*—encompasses her entire visual field.

The distribution of information about Szenes in the interview and web texts also shows the centrality of Szenes to the web text. Whereas the interview text follows the introduction of Szenes with Beer's recounting of Szenes' story itself, the web text provides a great deal more information about Szenes even before her story is told. After her introduction as *one solitary woman* (b), Szenes remains a focus of attention for twelve clauses that describe (largely from Beer's point of view) Szenes' demeanor, physical state, and activity, all of which indicate cheerfulness (d) and strength ((e), (f), (g)) despite fatigue (c) and abuse (h). We also find inferences about Szenes' personality ((j), (m)) and internal state ((l), (n)). Also present are direct contact between Beer and Szenes (i) and observations of behavior ((k)) that is assumed to be communicatively driven (l). This early dispersion of information is in sharp contrast to Beer's withholding of information about Szenes until she hears Szenes' story in the prison yard.

The most comparable section of the interview and web texts is Szenes' story itself. In both texts, Szenes' story is presented (indirectly) in Szenes' voice. Both stories follow a referential style: a sequence of events with minimal background. (5) compares TYPES of information (noted in CAPS on the left) in the two versions and details of information; similar information from the two versions is underlined.

(5) WHAT HAPPENED TO HANNAH SZENES?

	INTERVIEW TEXT	WEB TEXT
	She told me her story that	She told me that
ROLE	<u>She was a parachutist</u>	<u>She was a parachutist</u>
GOAL		She really came to save her mother
		and maybe some other Jews.

ORIGIN	who came from . . . Israel, Palestine	
DESTINATION	in <u>Yugoslavia</u>	She parachuted down on the <u>Yugoslav border</u>
PARTICIPANTS		with two other men.
OUTCOME		Someone betrayed her.
	And <u>she was caught</u>	<u>She was caught</u>
		And brought to the prison.
FORECAST		She constantly showed me, with a smile,
	and they- they probably	that she knew
	<u>will hang her</u>.	she's <u>going to be hung.</u>
	She always made this-	She did not really hope to live.
	this hanging sign.	
STANCE	they used to take her on a truck,	
	for interrogation	
	she found some coal	
	she would make marks under her eyes	
	to evoke some pity	

Four types of information appear in both versions: ROLE, DESTINATION, OUTCOME, and FORECAST. The only information presented in exactly the same words is Szenes' ROLE (*she was a parachutist*) and (in part) the OUTCOME of the mission (*she was caught*). Differences concern the amount of detail in DESTINATION and OUTCOME, as well as the quality of evidence in Szenes' FORECAST of her future. Each version of Szenes' experience also contains information that the other does not. Appearing only in the interview text are Szenes' ORIGIN, presented parenthetically as a relative clause (*who came from . . . Israel, Palestine*), and STANCE. Appearing only in the web text are GOAL and PARTICIPANTS.

These divergences across the two stories are related to the larger texts in which the story about Szenes is embedded. In the interview text, Beer presents virtually everything that she says about Szenes when they are together in the prison yard. The web text, however, already has presented similar information in Beer's report of their initial contact ((a) to (n)), and it continues to do so after the reported encounter ((aa) to (pp)). For example, Beer's development of Szenes' STANCE in the interview text portrays Szenes not only as victimized but also as agentive, as resisting subjugation. A comparable characterization appears in the web text, but earlier: When Beer first sees Szenes *in a cell across the way* (b), she notices that *she had dark circles under her eyes* (c) and that *her front teeth were missing* (h). Beer herself implies an interrogation, when she asks, *"Did they beat your teeth out of you?"* (i). An agentive and resistant characterization also is embellished later in the web text when Beer supports her evaluation (*I felt*) that *she was someone special* (ff) with *She wasn't scared* (kk), *she had an aura about her* (mm). Also included in Beer's evaluative coda is Szenes' ORIGIN (*she came from Palestine* (pp)): When conjoined to her age (*she was close to my age* (oo)), it is part of what makes Szenes seem *very exotic* (nn) to Beer. Thus, comparable evaluative themes appear in both the interview and web texts. They are woven into the two texts differently, however, so that they appear in locations that are consistent with the overall development and organization of each text.

The patterns described for the beginnings and middles of the interview and web texts continue as they end. The interview text blends Beer's voice with the experiences of the people with whom she was captured and imprisoned. Beer's encounter with Szenes was one aspect of that experience. Thus, after ending the Szenes story and securing recognition of the identity of her fellow prisoner ((mm)–(qq)), Beer returns to the chronicle of imprisonment ((rr)–(ss)):

Beer:	And it turned out to- she became very well known she was Hannah Szenes.
Interviewer:	Hannah=
Beer:	=[Yes.] And eh-
Interviewer:	=Sze[nes.]
Beer:	of course, y'know what happened to her.=
Beer:	=Uh we were in this prison for three and a half, weeks. And after that time, they told us to take, whatever we had, [continues]

Beer's oral history then tells us—in approximately another 10,000 words—what happened *after that time*.

When we turn to the end of the web text, however, we learn no more about Beer's own fate. Instead, we find a repetition of the title *someone special* within an evaluative coda—first individual, and then collective (*our misery*)—that high-lights the positive effect of Szenes on Beer's feelings:

> She was twenty-three years old at the time. I felt she was someone special. I didn't know exactly what she was, but I never forgot her. There was something special about her. She didn't behave like the others. She wasn't scared, thinking of herself. She was beyond that. She had an aura about her. To me she was very exotic; she was close to my age, and she came from Palestine. In that prison it was good to hear something like this, something beyond our misery.

In sum, the interview and web texts ostensibly are about the same experience: an encounter between Susan Beer and Hannah Szenes in 1944 in a Gestapo prison in Budapest. Although the "facts" of the two texts are basically the same, the "stories" differ in style, emphasis, and characterization. In the concluding section of this essay, I turn to the sometimes troubling relationship between facts and story to embed my analysis in some recent concerns of historians—thus suggesting the value of discourse analysis not only for the study of oral history but also for the study of History.

Conclusion

One of the first scholars to undertake the collection of Holocaust oral histories, Geoffrey Hartman, has argued that "the conviction has grown that local knowledge, which speaks from inside a situation rather than from the outside in an objectifying manner, can provide a texture of truth that eludes those who adopt a prematurely unified voice" (Hartman 1996: 135). Both versions of Susan Beer's story about Hannah Szenes are representations about the past that speak from "inside a situation." Yet the "texture of truth" they offer differs, in part, because of the different contexts in which they appear. The two texts also speak in different voices—certainly not a "prematurely unified voice"—that adopt observational or inferential stances, dwell in different domains (autobiography, commemoration), and are directed to different audiences.

A discourse perspective on oral history has shown how these differences occur and, in so doing, has raised issues of interest to linguists: the impact of transcription and other modes of presenting texts, the intertextual relevance of personal and historical themes, the display of identity through referring terms and event-types, referential and evaluative styles in narrative, transitions between episodes. The question of how this perspective and these issues can be of interest to historians is not one that I can fully answer here. Instead, I try to clarify the question by embedding it in recent concerns of historians that bear on the intermingling of story and facts in History.

Historians have observed that the same multiple voices and mediation that are endemic to oral history also appear in other textual data and in History itself.

Evans (1999: 90), for example, observes that "the language of historical documents is never transparent." Because History itself is permeated with ambiguities and mediated through various factors, it involves listening to a "chorus of different voices sounding through the text" (Evans 1999: 92).

Certainly one voice that emerges in the textual chorus is that of the Historian. Is there one unified Historian's voice, however? In his discussion of two starkly different styles of historical writing, Lang (1999) suggests that Historians' representations of the past may converge stylistically with fictional renditions of the past.[11] Likewise, Young's (1988: 4) analysis of "writing and rewriting the Holocaust" ponders whether historical tracts on the Holocaust are "less mediated by imagination, less troped and figured, or ultimately less interpretive than the fictions of the Holocaust."

A more complex view of multiple voices has been suggested by White, who separates a factual voice from a literary voice but then argues for the primacy of the literary voice in History. In White's (1992: 49) view, the goal of writing History requires one to "prefigure as a possible object of knowledge the whole set of events reported in the documents." The actual act of writing History itself is a poetic act, however, best understood in terms of metaphor, metonymy, synecdoche, and irony and their corresponding modes of emplotment. Because these choices are not completely dictated by empirical evidence, History can be "put together in a number of different and equally plausible narrative accounts of 'what happened in the past'" (White 1992: 50). The consequence of this *modus operandi* is that "one must face the fact that, when it comes to the historical record, there are no grounds to be found in the record itself for preferring one way of construing its meaning rather than another" (White 1973, quoted in Evans 1999: 86).

An even more radical separation of History from "what happened" has been brought about by what has been called the "linguistic turn" in history (Rorty 1967). The linguistic turn basically is the adoption of a postmodernist perspective on language. Stemming from de Saussure's separation of signifier from signified (and apparently ignoring the crucial role of convention in reconnecting these two aspects of the sign), the postmodern perspective was developed through Derrida's claim that language was an "infinite play of significations" (quoted in Evans 1999: 82) and Barthes' claim that History was "a parade of signifiers masquerading as a collection of facts" (quoted in Evans 1999: 81). Thus, postmodernism shifts a well-known and accepted assumption—that meaning can be relative to context—to a level of hyper-relativity: Meaning is indeterminate and ever-changing. The consequence is that language can never tell us what happened in the past.

I have come far from the initial observation of a textual connection between Linguists and Historians. After reviewing the functions and features of oral histories and comparing two versions of one woman's story about an encounter in a Gestapo prison in 1944, I have ended with more theoretical questions about the language of History. I hope that the path I have followed in this essay has suggested the potential of the linguistic turn for History. What I envision, however, is not the postmodern turn adopted by narrative theorists, literary critics/theorists, and philosophers but a turn that is based more on the strong empirical tradition of socially constituted linguistic perspectives (to borrow Hymes' (1974) term) such as sociolinguistics, discourse analysis, and pragmatics.

Socially constituted linguistic perspectives have had much to say about the same aspects of language that postmodernists have addressed. In contrast to the theoretical hyperrelativism of postmodern approaches, however, socially constituted linguistic perspectives offer a situated relativism that not only imbues methodology and theory but also motivates analysis of crucial interfaces between language and "reality." This enables them to address questions that arise within that interface: How are representations of events (the "facts") and people immersed within texts (the "story")? How are texts immersed within their contexts of use? How do contexts both inform and restrict the vast (but not infinite) web of potential interpretations and meanings? How does the coherence of text emerge from linguistic, social, and cultural factors? Answers to all of these questions can help address the controversies incumbent in oral histories—and in History itself—that seek to represent the past but are produced and interpreted in the present.

NOTES

1.   I am grateful for discussion of the ideas in this paper to Deborah Tannen, Teun van Dijk, Gayle Weiss, and the students in my fall 2001 Georgetown University class on "Life Stories": Daniel Beckett, Linda Isaacs, Andrew Jocuns, Philip LeVine, Kristen Mulrooney, Meghan Nelson, and Aida Premilovac. The Center for Advanced Holocaust Study (at the United States Holocaust Memorial Museum) and a Senior Faculty Research Fellowship (at Georgetown University) provided material and symbolic support for research leading to this work. I thank the Cleveland Alliance for Jewish Women and the United States Holocaust Memorial Museum for permission to cite excerpts from the 1984 interview with Susan Beer. I also am grateful to Bonnie Gurewitsch (Museum of Jewish Heritage, New York) for permission to reproduce the excerpt on Susan Beer (what I call the web text). It is important to note that this excerpt initially appeared in the *Newsletter for Holocaust Studies, Documentation and Research*, volume 4, no. 6 (spring 1990). The topic of this issue was "Women of Valor: Partisans and Resistance Fighters." The excerpt on Susan Beer was on page 34.

2.   See Veit-Brause (1996) on the polysemy of the word *history*. In keeping with Ankersmit (who applies formal linguistic philosophy to the writing of History; Ankersmit 1983: 8), I separate historical research from the writing of History, using uppercase "H" to denote the social and cultural status of the latter as received knowledge and an academic discipline. I also follow Ankersmit's observation that although it is impossible to draw an exact line between history and History, this blurring of boundaries does not mean that we should abandon the distinction.

3.   I follow Shandler's (1999: xiv) definition of memory culture as the range of practices a community uses to recall its past. These practices include broadcast media, written media, verbal practices, public memorials, formal education, family legends/stories, and so on.

4. The spelling "Szenes" alternates with "Senesh."

5. Susan Beer's excerpt appeared on the website "Women and the Holocaust" as part of an (unauthorized) reproduction of the spring 1990 newsletter cited in note 1. Its first known appearance on this website was in 1998. Despite its original source, and without intending to disregard its initial site of public appearance, I refer to Susan Beer's excerpt as the "web text." I do so for several reasons: Its location on the web is what accounts for its current presence in public discourse; it is this public appearance in which I am interested; the web is where I found it in 2000; and it is where other members of a general public are also likely to find it.

6. As Bonnie Gurewitsch explained (personal communication), the relatively shorter text about Susan Beer reflects the fact that although Beer had spoken for more than two hours during their interview, at that point Beer felt too tired to continue, even though she had not completed her life story.

7. How to extract a short text from a longer text is an issue that faces virtually all reproductions of oral histories (and, indeed, all segments of discourse); it is impossible to include the most complete record available—audio/video recordings—every time one wants to display, discuss, or analyze a segment. Even websites whose inclusion of brief audio and video clips of selected segments give a very vibrant sense of "being there" with the survivor (e.g., the Yale University Library Fortunoff Archives of Holocaust Testimonies) cannot possibly manage to do so for entire interviews. Thus, as potentially disruptive as extracting excerpts can be, it is necessary: One cannot reproduce an entire life story/oral history every time one quotes or analyzes it.

8. The one collective reference to Szenes in 1984 includes Beer: *And everyday they would let us walk in the courtyard* (x). The major exception is the individuated view of Beer presented in the synopsis: As we saw, Beer is presented as acting alone, despite evidence through other oral history interviews that the actions recounted were group actions. This information does not appear in Table 5.1 because the synopsis was written by someone other than Beer.

9. As Deborah Tannen points out, "be gentle" can be differently categorized—as a physical action (it can be a way of doing something). It also can convey a more enduring quality or demeanor, however (reflected through its encoding as a stative predicate), and thus be categorized as a physical attribute. Although I count it here as a physical attribute, we should keep in mind that "be gentle" may differ from other attributes (e.g., "have dark circles under her eyes") because of its emergence through action. The quantitative comparisons here do not include actions or references from the synopsis of Beer's life. Not only does the synopsis not deal with a comparable topic (i.e., imprisonment), but (as indicated through the use of third person) it was not Beer's own "voice."

10. Stative descriptive clauses can have a role in the complicating action of a narrative when they are inferred by readers/hearers as inceptive (e.g., a character's discovery, realization, view of what had been an ongoing state).

11. Here are Lang's (1999: 24) two examples. First is from Hilberg (1985: 411); it is a description of the fare system for deportees to concentration camps: "The basic charge was the third-class fare: 4 pfennig per track kilometer. Children under 10 were transported for half this amount; those under four went free . . . . For the deportees one-way fare was payable; for the guards a round trip ticket had to be purchased." The second example is from Daniel Goldhagen's (1996) description of Germans in his book *Hitler's Willing Executioners*: "The Germans made love in barracks next to enormous privation and incessant cruelty. What did they talk about when their heads rested quietly on their pillows, when they were smoking their cigarettes in those relaxing moments after their physical needs had been met? Did one relate to another accounts of a particularly amusing beating that she or he had administered or observed . . . ?"

REFERENCES

Allen, Barbara, and William L. Montell. 1981. *From memory to history*. Nashville, Tenn.: American Association for State and Local History.

Ankersmit, Frank. 1983. *Narrative logic: A semantic analysis of the historian's language*. The Hague: Martinus Nijhoff Publishers.

Bartaux, Daniel. 1981. *Biography and society*. Beverly Hills, Calif.: Sage Publications.

Baumel, Judith. 1996. The heroism of Hannah Szenes: An exercise in creating collective national memory in the state of Israel. *Journal of Contemporary History* 31: 521–46.

———. 1998. The "parachutists' mission" from a gender perspective. In *Resisting the Holocaust*, edited by Ruby Rohrlich. Oxford/New York: Berg, 95–114.

Cesarani, David. 1999. Introduction. In Steven Spielberg and Survivors of the Shoah Visual History Foundation, *The last days*. New York: St. Martin's Press, 14–57.

DeFina, Anna. 1999. *Immigrant identities*. Ph.D. diss., Georgetown University.

Edwards, Jane. 2001. The transorption of discourse. In *Handbook of discourse analysis*, edited by Deborah Schiffrin, Deborah Tannen, and Heidi Hamilton. Oxford: Basil Blackwell, 321–47.

Evans, Richard. 1999. *In defense of history*. New York: W. W. Norton and Co.

Flanzbaum, Hilene, ed. 1999. *The Americanization of the Holocaust*. Baltimore: Johns Hopkins University Press.

Goldhagen, Daniel. 1997. *Hitler's willing executioners*. New York: Random House.

Greenspan, Henry. 1998. *On listening to Holocaust survivors*. Westport, Conn.: Praeger.

———. 1999. Imagining survivors: Testimony and the rise of Holocaust consciousness. In *The Americanization of the Holocaust*, edited by Hilene Flanzbaum. Baltimore: Johns Hopkins University Press, 45–67.

Gurewitsch, Bonnie. 1998. *Mothers, sisters, resisters: Oral histories of women who survived the Holocaust*. Tuscaloosa and London: University of Alabama Press.

Hammer, Reuben. 1998. Commemorations and the Holocaust. In *Lessons and legacies: Teaching the Holocaust in a changing world*, edited by Peter Hayes. Evanston, Ill.: Northwestern University Press.

Hartman, Geoffrey. 1996. *The longest shadow: In the aftermath of the Holocaust*. Bloomington: University of Indiana Press.

Hilberg, Raul. 1985. *The destruction of the European Jews*. New York: Holmes and Meier.

———. 1991. Introduction. In *Lessons and legacies: Teaching the Holocaust in a changing world*, edited by Peter Hayes. Evanston, Ill.: Northwestern University Press.

Hymes, Dell. 1974. *Foundations in sociolinguistics: An ethnographic approach*. Philadelphia: University of Pennsylvania Press.

Iggers, Georg G. 1997. *Historiography in the twentieth century*. Hanover, N.H.: Wesleyan University Press.

Labov, William, and David Fanshel. 1977. *Therapeutic discourse*. New York: Academic Press.

LaCapra, Dominick. 2001. *Writing history, writing trauma*. Baltimore: Johns Hopkins University Press.

Lang, Berel. 1999. Holocaust genres and the turn to history. In *The Holocaust and the text*, edited by Andrew Leak and G. Paizis. Durham, N.C.: Duke University Press.

Langer, Lawrence. 1991. *Holocaust testimonies*. New Haven, Conn.: Yale University Press.

Linde, Charlotte. 1993. *Life stories*. Oxford: Oxford University Press.

Linenthal, Edward T. 1995. *Preserving memory*. New York: Penguin Books.

McMahan, Eva M. 1989. *Elite oral history discourse*. Tuscaloosa and London: University of Alabama Press.

Miller, Judith. 1990. *One, by one, by one*. New York: Simon and Schuster.

Novick, Peter. 1999. *The Holocaust in American life*. New York: Houghton Mifflin.

Portelli, Alessandro. 1997. *The battle of Valle Giulia: Oral history and the art of dialogue.* Madison: University of Wisconsin Press.

Ringelheim, Joan, Arwen Donahue, and Amy Rubin. 1998. *Oral history interview guidelines.* Washington, D.C.: United States Holocaust Memorial Museum.

Rorty, Richard. 1967. *The linguistic turn.* Chicago: Chicago University Press.

Rothkirchen, Livia. 1986. The historical background. In Ruth Whitman, *The testing of Hanna Senesh.* Detroit: Wayne State University Press, 13–23.

Schiff, Brian, Chaim Noy, and B. Cohler. 2000. Collected stories in the life narratives of Holocaust Survivors. Unpublished ms.

Schiffrin, Deborah. 2000a. Multiple interviews with Holocaust survivors. Fellows' Seminar, Center for Advanced Holocaust Study, United States Holocaust Memorial Museum, November.

———. 2000b. Mother/daughter discourse in a Holocaust oral history. *Narrative Inquiry* 10 (1): 1–44.

———. 2001a. Language, experience and history: "What happened" in World War II. *Journal of Sociolinguistics* 5 (3): 323–52.

———. 2001b. Language and public memorial: "America's concentration camps." *Discourse and Society* 12: 505–34.

———. 2002. Mother and friends in a Holocaust life story. *Language in Society* 31: 309–53.

Shandler, Jeffrey. 1999. *While America watches.* New York: Oxford University Press.

Strassfeld, Michael. 1985. *The Jewish holidays.* New York: Harper and Row.

Tec, Nechama. 1993. Diaries and oral history. In *Individualizing the Holocaust through diaries and other contemporaneous personal accounts,* edited by Robert Shapiro. Hoboken, N.J.: Ktav, 267–75.

Veit-Brause, Irmline. 1996. The disciplining of history. In *History-making,* edited by Rolf Torstendah and Irmline Veit-Brause (proceedings of international conference, Uppsala, Sweden). Stockholm: Kungl Vitterhets Historie och Antikvitets Akademien, 7–29.

Ward, Gregory, and Betty Birner. 2001. Discourse and information structure. In *Handbook of discourse analysis,* edited by Deborah Schiffrin, Deborah Tannen, and Heidi Hamilton. Oxford: Basil Blackwell, 119–37.

White, Hayden. 1973. *Metahistory: The historical imagination in nineteenth-century Europe.* Baltimore: Johns Hopkins University Press.

———. 1992. Historical emplotment and the problem of truth. In *Probing the limits of representation,* edited by Saul Friedlander. Cambridge, Mass.: Harvard University Press, 37–53.

Wieviorka, Anna. 1994. On testimony. In *Holocaust remembrance,* edited by Geoffrey Hartman. Oxford: Basil Blackwell, 23–32.

Yahil, Leni. 1990. *The Holocaust.* New York: Oxford University Press.

Young, James. 1988. *Writing and rewriting the Holocaust.* Bloomington: Indiana University Press.

The voice of the audience in contemporary American political discourse[1]

Alessandro Duranti
University of California, Los Angeles

In the past two decades, terms such as "co-construction," "intersubjectivity," and "negotiation of meaning" have become very popular in discourse analysis, sociolinguistics, and linguistic anthropology. The basic assumption has been that it is always the case that a person's words are not simply the expression of privately owned ideas and individually controlled thoughts; they also are a by-product of interactions and contextual conditions that must be documented for any researcher to be able to say how a given stretch of talk came to be the way it is and how it is interpreted by its recipients. Some of the best cases of co-construction have been documented by conversation analysts, who also coined the term "recipient design" to convey the idea that speakers' formulation of referents and events must always take the addressee into consideration. Because of this requirement, talk also can be used to get a sense of speakers' own understanding of their audience's knowledge (e.g., Schegloff 1972; Goodwin 1979, 1981).

To date, however, there has been very limited documentation of spontaneous events in which the same speaker addresses different audiences with roughly the same communicative goals (e.g., to tell the same story, make the same promise, give the same advice, tell the same joke). Whereas analysis of variation-on-a-theme is common in musicology and ethnomusicology, whereby different performances of the same song or the same harmonic structure are routinely compared (e.g., Lord 1960; Berliner 1994), analysts of talk rarely have the data, let alone the interest, to analyze how the same narrative or speech act changes over time and space (for some exceptions, see Bauman 1986; Tannen and Wallat 1986; and Philips 1992 for spontaneous discourse and Chafe 1980 for a semi-experimental situation). Given the pervasiveness and importance of repetition within the same conversation (Tannen 1987, 1989) and the belief—at least among some linguists—that much of what appears spontaneous invention in language use in fact might be repetition of already heard speech (Bolinger 1961: 381), the lack of interest and documentation of repetition across speech events is quite puzzling. Possible explanations for this gap include the tendency to focus on "language," "speaking," or "talk" and, more frequently, on specific forms rather than individual speakers' performance across time and space (Johnstone 1996); the practical and ethical problems associated with recording the same individual speaker throughout the continuous and sufficiently lengthy span of time that would allow researchers to find examples of the same linguistic material recycled in different contexts; the low statistical likelihood of recording spontaneous repetition of the same linguistic material across events, with the exception of phonological segments deprived of denotative meaning, as quantitative sociolinguists have done; and doubts about whether variation analysis can be extended to denotative meaning at all (Lavandera 1978; Romaine 1984).

As I show in this essay, documentation of the speeches by the same political candidate over the course of a campaign can offer a solution to some of these problems. As a candidate moves through a district or state, we can assess changes in his or her slogans, analyses, stories, and jokes across time and space. This type of variation not only gives us a sense of how speakers adapt or "design" their speech for particular audiences, it also gives us a glimpse of the role played by members of the audience in shaping the form and content of a person's talk. By comparing different versions of what can be considered as the same stories, assessments, promises, attacks, questions, answers, and introductions, we have a chance to evaluate the extent to which candidates adapt to or resist the audience's wishes. More important, we also get a glimpse of a struggle that all speakers must face, yet becomes particularly conspicuous in political arenas—namely, the struggle to maintain control of one's goals and values while trying to win the favor of the widest range of people.

For political candidates who are seeking approval, it is quite easy to move closer and closer toward the ideal projected by their audience responses and to lose touch with their own original plans and aspirations. The issue of authorship (e.g., who is the author of this message, its premises, its implications, its consequences?) becomes, in very concrete ways, the issue of the coherence of the self.

I approach the topic of intersubjectivity with this particular issue in mind. In the anthropological tradition of person-centered ethnography, I take a sympathetic rather than an adversarial or critical view of a political candidate's (in this case, Walter Capps') struggle over the meaning of his words, and I use the tools of my trade (ethnographically informed discourse analysis) to identify the methods he used in dealing with some of the dilemmas encountered by anyone seeking public office.

The Capps-for-Congress Campaign

In 1995–96 I had the opportunity to document the political campaign of Walter Capps, a professor of religious studies at the University of California at Santa Barbara (UCSB), for the U.S. Congress. I first met Capps in the summer of 1994 through his daughter Lisa, then a graduate student in psychology at UCLA who was interested in ethnographic methods. At the time of our first meeting, Walter Capps was running his first campaign for Congress. I met him again in

January 1995. By then he had lost to Republican Andrea Seastrand (a former California Assemblywoman) by less than 1 percent of the vote. I asked him whether he would run again, given that, I confessed, I would love to follow him around with my video camera. He said that if he decided to run again, he would call me. A few months later he did. He told me then that, although some of the people on his staff were a bit apprehensive about my project, he saw no problems having a video camera record his interactions throughout the campaign. If anything, he seemed intrigued by the idea of documenting the political process and comforted by the prospect of having a fellow academic next to him while he engaged in this new adventure, toward which he had complex feelings—which I would not hesitate to characterize as a mixture of fascination and aversion, depending on the situation.

Over a period of twelve months (November 1995 to November 1996), I spent as much time as I could driving up and down the central coast of California, recording Capps at debates, rallies, and fundraising events, as well as in more intimate moments, in the car or at home. By November 6, 1996, I had collected a thick notebook of field notes and more than fifty hours of videotapes that showed Capps interacting with staff members, family members, journalists, opponents, and government officials (including George Stephanopolous, Bill Clinton, and Hillary Rodham Clinton). Throughout the campaign, Capps continued to be a strong supporter of my project and never asked me to turn off the camera even during the most private conversations. (The only times I was not allowed to record were related to the foreseen or actual reactions of other participants involved in the interaction, not Capps' own concern for privacy.) After a close and nationally monitored race, Capps won the 1996 election and served in Congress until October 28, 1997, when he suffered a fatal heart attack at Dulles Airport on his way to Capitol Hill. His wife Lois, who had provided continuous emotional support and political advice throughout both campaigns and had followed him in Washington, ran for the same seat and won. She was reelected in 1998 and 2000.

Among the large corpus of transcriptions that this documentation produced, I concentrate on a small subset of the verbal interactions recorded during the first official day of the campaign—November 14, 1995—when Capps announced his candidacy to groups of supporters and potential voters at several places in the 22nd District of California (Santa Barbara-San Luis Obispo).

Designing a Joke for Different Audiences
I start from what we already know: Speakers fashion their speech in ways that make it interpretable by their listeners, and in so doing they display their understanding of audience needs and wishes while activating situationally signif-icant frames (e.g., private versus public identities). The most important work in this area has been done by conversation analysts, who introduced and employed the notion of "recipient design" to highlight in particular the fact that speakers, in

choosing among several alternative descriptions (e.g., here, my office, my house, Los Angeles, California, the United States) display their knowledge of and sensitivity to specific interlocutors (recipients) (Schegloff 1972; Sacks and Schegloff 1979; Sacks 1992). In some cases, as shown by Goodwin (1979, 1981), speakers can even change the meaning of their utterances in midstream to make it relevant to the particular individual who is actively listening (e.g., the individual who is gazing at the speaker at the moment).

I often was reminded of this sensitivity to the audience in designing one's talk while following Walter Capps around during his campaign. He was constantly editing his speeches, adding some phrases and paragraphs, deleting others, making some new connections, and adjusting transitions from one point to the next. Between stops—especially in the privacy afforded by the car rides with his wife Lois and some of his closest associates—Capps often discussed the logic and content of his verbal performance, showing a keen interest in whether he was reaching out to the audience. In going from one stop to the next he made small but potentially consequential modifications around the same theme or point. His ability to adjust and revise his speech must have been nurtured by a very successful teaching career at UCSB. (His "Religion and Politics" course enrolled more than 1,000 students, and his course on the Vietnam War—the first of its kind in the United States—had reached enrollment of as many as 860.) As I had a chance to see again and again throughout the campaign, Capps was quite receptive to the pulse of his audience, and he knew not only how to build an argument but also how to tell a story that would make the argument come alive for his listeners. He was not always right in his expressive choices or his timing, but he was constantly engaged in predicting and assessing audience responses. From my experience in watching Capps deliver his speeches and then reflecting on them, there is no question in my mind that he tried to learn as much as possible from each performance and tried to put what he learned into practice in the next appearance on the campaign trail.

One of the most revealing examples of Capps' ability to assess his audience's knowledge and evaluate their preferences is provided by the different versions of an account of his itinerary that he offered on the first official day of his second campaign. The first version of the itinerary-narrative is delivered in Paso Robles—the northern tip of the 22nd district—after he has concluded his speech, thanked the audience, and asked first his wife Lois and then the rest of the Capps-for-Congress team (consisting of his brother Doug, his nephew Lindsey, and two campaign staff members, Bryant Winnecke and Thu Fong) to stand next to him before they leave for the next stop of the day. In this context, the itinerary-narrative is delivered as an afterthought or coda to his speech, a way of closing the event. As is common in these situations, the information about the places he is going to next also works as an excuse for having to leave. The itinerary-narrative employs repetition as well as syntactic and semantic parallelism, which includes the temporal conjunction *then* and four tense/aspect formats that project future actions: the future form *we're gonna go*, the present progressive *we're goin'*, the present form *we go*, and the future *we'll. . .go*. In each case, the verb is followed by the name of a location. As shown in (1), as Capps finishes the list of places where he and his team will be going to make the announcement of his candidacy, he introduces a type of location that constitutes a violation of the implicit type defined by the previous locations. The breaking of the frame, i.e. the adding of an item of the list that is incongruent with the previous items (Beeman 2001), produces a well-timed joke that evokes a good laughter from the audience.[2]

(1)   (November 14, 1995, Paso Robles, CD1.51m:54s)

W. Capps: (well) we're gonna get in the car here in a minute

             because- uh because we're gonna go now to uh-

             we're gonna go to: San Luis Obispo, . . .

             then we're goin' to Santa Maria,   . . .

             then we go to Santa Barbara,   . . .

             then we go to Lompoc,   . . .

             then we go to Buelton,   . . .

             then we go to:- Solvang.   . . .

             and then I think- uh after ((fast ->)) we'll probably go to bed.

Audience: ((loud laughter)) HA!! HEHEHE!

There are two properties of the punch line that I want to focus on briefly. The first is that the punch line is audience-designed, and the second is that it is spontaneous. By *audience-designed*, I mean to say that the joke is produced to be understood and approved by this particular audience, which is made up mostly of senior citizens. The breaking of the frame is accomplished by mentioning an activity ("going to bed") that maintains the syntactic and semantic frame "go to + NOUN" of the last four clauses while contrasting in several ways: "bed" is not like the other locations—that is, instead of being the name of a city or town, it is a common noun that is part of an idiom "(to) go to bed," which requires a different type of "going"; it describes an ordinary as opposed to special activity; it introduces a private as opposed to a public space; and, as such, it implies a different set of activities (resting and sleeping are the most obvious, but also—for at least some listeners—other, more intimate, acts are suggested). The resounding laughter that the joke receives suggests that the audience gets some pleasure out of the breaking of expectations constituted by the "go to bed" punch line. This response, I believe, is the strongest evidence of the hypothesis that the joke is appropriately designed for this particular crowd: mostly older and retired people, who certainly can sympathize with the fact that one might be tired after having to go to all the places Capps mentioned and for whom the connotation of intimate contact, if perceived, would not be regarded as problematic.

The second property I want to discuss briefly is the degree of spontaneity of the joke. I suspect that this joke had not been planned with the rest of the speech but was inspired by the long and repetitive structure that Capps himself had just produced. The evidence for this claim is circumstantial. At the second stop, in San Luis Obispo, when Capps had his written speech in front of him, the itinerary-narrative showed up again—but this time it was placed at the very beginning of the speech and did not have a humorous resolution. Instead, Capps inserted a con-clusion-summary at the end of the list of places ("we'll be doing this the entire day") and then quickly moved into his (first) two announcements.

(2)   (November 14, 1995, San Luis Obispo,
            CD2.14m:50s)

W. Capps: Thi- this is the uh- the third stop of a: .. of a-a <u>full</u> day.

            of making- of making this announcement.=

            =we started in San Miguel this morning. uh,

            we've just come from Paso Robles. uh

            after this we'll go to. Santa Maria

            and on to Santa Barbara.

            then we go into Lompoc

            and back to Buelton

            and Solvang=

            =we'll be doing this the entire day=but I came here-

            I came here actually to make <u>two</u> announcements. [. . .]

The humorous punch line returns, however, in Santa Maria, at Hancock College, and at UCSB—two situations in which Capps addresses audiences that are made up mostly of students. The punch line changes each time, however, and is aptly formulated to display an understanding of the cultural preferences of the audience.

First, let us analyze the other two versions of the itinerary-narrative joke. Here is the version delivered at Hancock College, near Santa Maria, where Capps has been invited to speak in a political science course.

(3)   (November 14, 1995, Hancock College, Santa Maria, CD2.53m:47s)

W. Capps: We're in the middle of a::- . . . a: very very full day. . . . uhm

we started the day at- San Miguel Mission. . . . uh,

we did that for uh . . . spiritual. liturgical reasons to become . . . (you know) rightly .. rooted and oriented . . . uhm in . . . this life. which is:: sacred life to me.

and then we went . . . from there. to Paso Robles and met some

people . . . um- on the street corner and- . . . talked with them for a while and uh-

we've just come from San Luis Obispo

and we'll go next . . . back to our own campus, UCSB,

then on to .. Lompoc

and- .. Buelton

and .. Solvang,

and then -hh it will probably be time for dinner. // uhm.

Audience: ((sparse laughter)) he-he-he.

Inside the classroom, the audience comprises staff, supporters, at least one representative of the media, and the students in the political science course whose instructor invited Capps to speak. The punch line changes from going to bed to having dinner. This change makes sense given that college students are notorious for not going to sleep until late, and mentioning bedtime might make Capps sound "lame" or "old" whereas the desire to have some food ("time for dinner") is a more safe activity with a young crowd. It also is possible that the "going to bed" activity is not used because its possible sexual connotations would not be appropriate in a classroom context.

Finally, at UCSB, the itinerary is not quite at the start but certainly within the first part of Capps' speech. Here the list of places also ends with a joke, this time about going to a bar in downtown Santa Barbara that features live music—an unlikely place for Walter and Lois Capps to attend but one that is quite popular among UCSB undergraduates (Capps also inserts a deadpan joke in the midst of the list of places that is more difficult to appreciate out of context).

(4)   (November 14, 1995, UCSB Campus, CD3—15:45)

W. Capps: you know- we-we-we <u>sta</u>rted the day in San Miguel. uh,

             north of here. uh-

             we went all the way to the- to the Monterey County line. . . .

             we started the day there=.

             =we went to Paso Robles next. . . .

             we've been to San Luis Obispo=

             =we've been to Santa Maria. . . .

             we- we- we're here now of course.

             I'm standing here.

             we go //next to uh I mean it's clear.

Audience: ((sparse laughter)) haha- haha

W. Capps: //it's clear that I'm standing here.

Audience: ((laughter)) haha- hahaha- hahah

W. Capps: ((clears throat))

             uh, and we go next to:- .. to Lompoc, . . .

             and then we go to Buelton, . . .

             and then we go to Solvang,=

             =and then uh- . . . if-

             if my wife agrees we're gonna go to Matty's Tavern //after that.

Audience: ((Laughter, cheers)) hehehe-heheheheheh

There are other variations in these four excerpts that are equally interesting. I briefly mention the changes in the grammatical subject of the utterance constituting the punch line. It is an undifferentiated "we" in excerpt (1) ("we'll probably go to bed")—which could be interpreted as the whole group that is at that moment standing in front of the supporters (Capps, his wife Lois, his brother Doug, his nephew Lindsey, and the two staff members Thu Fong and Bryant Winnecke) or as just Capps and his wife Lois. In excerpt (3), the change of the punch line is done with an impersonal construction ("it will be time for dinner"), which does not commit the speaker to any particular referent but carries the conversational implicature that the people who have been going to all the listed places will be the ones wanting to have dinner. Finally, in excerpt (4) there is the introduction of "my wife" in "if my wife agrees," which pushes the following "we" of "we're gonna go to Matty's Tavern" toward the more restricted interpretation of Walter and Lois.

I chose these examples of conscious efforts to elicit laughter from the audience by displaying an understanding of their habits and potential wishes in order to establish an appropriate contrast with my next point which will be based on situations in which it is the audience who decides that something is humorous.

When the Audience Has a Different Take

The audience is important not only in the designing of the talk (e.g., referential expressions, use of humor, types of jokes). Audience members also actively participate in guiding the direction of talk, even in a formal event in which they are expected to give minimal responses at largely predictable points.

Previous analyses of audience responses in political arenas have identified specific ways in which speakers design their speech to elicit approval or support from the audience at predictable moments (e.g., Atkinson 1984a, 1984b; Heritage and Greatbatch 1986), as well as the most common conditions under which the audience disaffiliates, such as with boos or derisive laughter (Clayman 1992, 1993). Although these studies are programmatically interested in political oratory "as an emergent interactional process in which the audience plays an active role" (Clayman 1992: 34), the authors' ability to see more fully the outcome of such an interactional process is restricted by the paucity of data that can show what happened the next time the same speaker used or was about to use the same expression, promise, joke, or story. The longitudinal data collected during Walter Capps' 1995–96 campaign provide us with an opportunity to analyze some of the consequences or effects of audience responses.

In addition to expressing their approval or disapproval of a candidate's position, audiences have ways of imposing a particular interpretation on what is being said to them, and speakers may find themselves struggling to retain control of the meaning of their own words. Clayman (1992, 1993), for example, showed that audiences may use laughter to display their disbelief of a particular claim that has just been made by a candidate. In those cases, the audience usually is considered to be taking a stance that is clearly in opposition to that of the candidate (e.g., refusing to believe the candidate's claim to be a strong supporter of a particular policy). In the data that I analyze here, however, the audience is manifestly approving and sympathetic. In other words, the laughter produced is meant to be affiliative, not disaffiliative. Yet it seems to be taking the meaning of the candidate's words in a direction that he does not intend.

To illustrate this situation, I return to a particular point in Capps' first speech of the day in Paso Robles, where he makes two consecutive statements that are taken to be humorous by his audience despite the fact that, as I claim below, no humor seemed to be intended by the speaker.

(5)   (November 14, 1995, Paso Robles, CD1—41m)

W. Capps: but the second announcement is just as important. . . .

                and that is we- that- that we <u>will</u> win this time.

                //we will win this time.

Audience: ((clapping)) yeah:::

                //((more intense clapping, cheers))

W. Capps: ((smiles visibly pleased by the audience reaction))

W. Capps: and how do- how do- how do I know that?

                how do I know // we're gonna win?

Audience: ((laughter starts)) hehe ((increases)) HEHEHE!

W. Capps: ((smiles at the audience)) well, you know, I can see it in your faces. (I mean-)

Audience: ((laughter)) haha//ha

W. Capps: and- and- and I- and I- and I mean that <u>totally</u> because-

                because . . . uh, ((points to his wife Lois))

                Lois and I . . . have lived. here,

                in fact the <u>first</u> time we came in here in- August. of 1964 [. . .]

I argue that the rhetorical question "and how do I know that?" and the statement "I can see it in your faces" were not originally meant to be funny by Capps, despite the fact that he had purposely injected humor earlier in his talk. The humorous interpretation is imposed by the audience and only partly endorsed by Capps himself; while still smiling with satisfaction at their support—the clapping and cheers that greet his fake second announcement ("we will win this time")— he finds himself endorsing a humorous reading that does not quite go along with his next point: namely, that he knows the people of the 22nd district. In fact, when we examine the next stretch of talk, we find a narrative of personal experience that is full of old memories and ends in an emotionally charged coda that might have been produced exactly to move away from the light mood established by the laughter ("You are. . .the people with whom we've lived our lives"). One sign of the fact that Capps wants to reduce the force and potential implications of the audience response is his metanarrative statement (Babcock 1977) "I mean that totally," which he produces just before transitioning to the personal narrative. "I mean that totally" makes sense only if we assume that he is not fully (i.e., "totally") satisfied with how the audience thinks he means it. Here is the passage again, all the way to the climactic end of the personal narrative:

(6)   (November 14, 1995, Paso Robles, cont., CD1.41:59)

W. Capps: that I- and I- and I mean that totally because- because . . . uh, Lois and I . . . have lived here, in fact the first time we came in here in- August of 1964, we stayed across the street. we- we came out from- from uh, Yale University, uh to teach uh at UC Santa Barbara. and we came down from Oregon. we stopped across the street, had a- . . . had a- .. we were carrying a- trailer with uh, our belongings. we didn't have any children then=that was in nineteensixtyfour.   . . . we've been here a:ll this time. .. we've lived here a:ll these years. we know the people. .. of the twenty-second district. . . . you know- . . . our . children were born. in the twenty-second district. they've all gone to school here. . . . uh so what I'm suggesting is, . . . not only suggesting I know this to be the case: that I represent . . . majority. opinion. in the twenty-second district. I mean=I know what people in the twenty-second district believe in because- these are our people. . . . you are- . . . the people with whom we've lived our lives.

The narrative of belonging is anything but humorous. It is constructed to create a sense of solidarity and trust through the recounting of key points in Capps' life in California (hence the added importance of the mentions of "Yale" and "Oregon"). One might even argue that in Paso Robles the personal narrative is particularly charged with emotions precisely to counteract or cancel the humorous reading of Capps' earlier question.

In his second stop, in San Luis Obispo, Capps delivers a speech that is closest to his prepared written speech (this was the only time he had his written speech in front of him). In this speech, the rhetorical question "how do I know that?" reappears—suggesting that it had been planned—but is delayed. It is presented only after its variant "how do we know we will- how do we know we're gonna win?" has been answered by Capps himself while maintaining a straight face, with no hint of a smile.

(7)   (November 14, 1995, San Luis Obispo, CD2.15m:30s)

W. Capps: and then the:: um- and the second announcement I think is probably even more important. . . . the second announcement is. that we. will. win. we will win.// in November.

Audience: ((clapping, cheers))

W. Capps: how do we uh- how- how do we know we will- how do we know we're gonna win? .. uhm- I- I- I can tell you. the reason we're going to win is that- uhm- that I have. every confidence. that I represent . . . majority. .. opinion- the majority (of) viewpoint .. of the people in the 22nd. district. of California. . . .
how do I know // I do that?=

Audience: ((sparse clapping))

W. Capps: thank you. how do I know that? because we've lived here for <u>thir</u>ty-<u>two</u> years. we've, ou::- our children were <u>born</u> here, I've <u>taught</u> here uh <u>a:ll</u> that time. we've lived among you. we know what you think about things. ((looks at notes)) uh ((looks up)) we- we know your points of view, we know your attitudes, we know your beliefs, we know your convictions.

The restrained, serious "key" of the San Luis Obispo speech is particularly striking given that after the Paso Robles speech, while Capps was going around shaking hands with members of the audience, at least two of them encouraged him to "keep up the humor" in his speeches. One possible explanation of such a switch of interpretive "key" (Hymes 1972) is that Capps had learned from the Paso Robles performance that if he did not want the audience to decide for him what was funny and what was serious, he ought to keep his own joking under control. In San Luis Obispo, he never smiled throughout any of his statements or rhetorical questions, and the audience did not interject any laughter.

One might argue, however, that the San Luis Obispo speech is not a good indicator of how Capps conceptualized the rhetorical question "how do I know that (I'm gonna win)?" precisely because of the overall lack of humor throughout the speech. (The audience eventually produces some laughter after the speech is over—when Capps, prompted by his wife, speaks again to acknowledge some of the people in the audience.) Given this possible objection to what to make of the San Luis Obispo speech, the version delivered at his third stop, at Hancock College, is potentially more revealing. On this occasion, inside a classroom, Capps returns to a more informal tone, starting the speech in a nonserious "key" with what will become one of his favorite jokes throughout the campaign—the "seventy-five minutes joke":

(8)   (November 14, 1995: Hancock College, CD2.53m:26s)

W. Capps: I'm- uh- I'm very happy to be here today and:- . . . uh- see the problem with this is that I'm- I'm so used to this <u>format</u> . . . that I ma- I may go on here for- . . . you know seventy five <u>minutes</u> because-

Woman: ((laughter)) ha-ha-ha!

W. Capps: because the classes in Santa Barbara are an hour and fifteen min-
              utes. but, ((clears throat)) [. . .]

Capps then continues with the itinerary-narrative joke, as shown in (3). This
time, however, despite the earlier introduction of humor, when he uses the line
about his confidence in a victory ("we're gonna win . . . we('ll) win") he leaves
out the "how do I know that?" question, thus removing the piece of talk that had
been followed by laughter in Paso Robles.

(9)   (November 14, 1996: Hancock College, Santa Maria,
              CD2.54:46s)

W. Capps: the second announcement is- . . . and I- I have total confidence on
              this one, we're gonna win. .. // we('ll) win.

Audience: ((clapping))

W. Capps: and: uh, I think the reason we're going to win is- .. becau::se I under-
              stand the people. of the twenty-second district, .. uh I know their
              views, .. I know what they want . . . uh- a representative to do. in
              Washington. and I'm committed to doing that because I've- we
              have-.. lived our- lives with-.. these people- I've been here for- thir-
              ty one years as a professor at- UCSB,   . . . our children were born
              and raised here- so um- .. you know- we-uh, we belong here ((CL))
              and we- and uhm- . . . and-uh. . . we- we know the people. so well
              that I know I can represent. their views in- in Washington.

The skipping of the planned question suggests that by the third speech of the
day, Capps had learned how to have some control over the potential implications of
his words. The insertion of humor earlier in the speech had to be balanced by the
removal of verbal material that could be interpreted as a continuation of that humor.

Can One Attack without "Being Mean"?
In presenting his political persona, Walter Capps faced problems—often
leading to paradoxes—that are not uncommon for candidates in the United States.
One was having to explain why he wanted to leave a respectable profession and
a successful, thirty-two-year career at the University of California to embrace a
political career that was not equally respected in the public's eyes. Another problem was created by the pressure he felt to attack his main opponent, the incumbent Rep. Andrea Seastrand, while wanting to remain faithful to the image of fair-
ness and compassion that he had acquired in his teaching—especially through the
highly popular and highly publicized course on the Vietnam War.
On the first day of his new campaign, we find Capps working hard to try to
deal with both of these problems. He dealt with the first by presenting himself as

following a call—inspired, in his own words, by the Jeffersonian model of the citizen-representative who goes to Washington as a form of duty to his country rather than for personal ambition. He approached the second problem by framing his negative assessment of Seastrand as something unfortunate but necessary in politics. Capps seemed to be convinced that he could do "attacking" in some straightforward fashion, without having to sound too critical or mean-spirited. But he had not taken into consideration his audience's expectations, grounded in contemporary American political discourse.

Whatever image Capps was trying to project through his words was going against deeply rooted assumptions about political speeches and political criticism. Contrary to his own anticipation, his audience did not always allow him to be "Mr. Nice Guy." On the contrary, they read "meanness" in his words, regardless of his framing and his disclaimers. Here is an example of how Capps' criticism of Seastrand is interpreted in a way that seems contrary to his intentions. His attempt to reframe his own words ("I'm not being mean here") is greeted with even more laughter, confirming the audience's reading of his earlier words as purposely critical and his added disclaimer as sarcastic.

(10)   (November 14, 1995, Paso Robles, CD1.42m:55s)

W. Capps: now, you know when you run for office, . . . it isn't just like applying for a job=I mean you have to- you've gotta beat the uh- . . . you've gotta beat the other candidate. . . . and this is what I say about her. .. she doesn't represent . . . // the majority

Woman: no. she doesn't.

W. Capps: she does not represent the majority .. viewpoint. of the people of the 22nd district. . . .

in fact, I don't think she represents anybody. // in the 22nd district.

Audience: ((laughs)) hehehe! hahaha!

W. Capps: (???) I'm not- . . . I'm not being mean here,

//I'm not at all being mean.

Audience: ((laughter)) hehehe. //haha

We can easily speculate that the audience is led to laughter by the rhetorical effect produced by the contrastive pair shown in (11)—a well-known technique that also is used to evoke applause (Atkinson 1984a: chapter 3):

(11)

A.   she does not represent the majority .. viewpoint. of the people of
                the 22nd District.   . . .

B.   in fact, I don't think she represents anybody. // in the 22nd District.

The second part of the contrast violates what is a reasonable inference from the
first part—namely, that she represents the minority viewpoint.

The laughter, however, must make Capps realize that this group of supporters is not buying into the innocence of his criticism. Before continuing with his
attack, Capps tries again to regain the high moral ground by claiming restraint
during the first year of Seastrand's tenure in the House. The addition of the hypothetical "whether anyone believes this or not" and the emphasized repetition "I
mean I really wanted her to do well," however, give away his fear of not sounding sincere even to a group of supporters.

(12)   (November 14, 1995, Paso Robles, CD1.44m:08s)

W. Capps: but now, I have not critiqued her in a- in a full year because,   . . .
                whether anyone believes this or not, .. you know she's my repre-
                sentative too, .. and I wanted her to do well, I mean I really want-
                ed her to do well because I want- people in our district, .. to be
                well represented. in Washington.

When we examine his speech at the next stop, in San Luis Obispo, we see a different framing. Capps leaves out the line about Seastrand not representing anyone and
goes straight into the planned series of rhetorical questions about her performance,
framed in a call-and-response format. This time the punchline is different.
Furthermore, there is a metapragmatic cue that lets the audience know that they are
expected to participate in a question-answer drill ("I'll just have to ask you").

(13)   (November 14, 1995, San Luis Obispo, CD2.16m:35s)

W. Capps: the reason I know we can beat my opponent is because our oppo-
                nent next fall does not represent the people of the twenty second
                district. of California.

                I'll just have to ask you,

                does our representative represent the seniors of the twenty-second
                district?

Audience: NO::!

W. Capps: does she represent. . . the students of the twenty-second district?

Audience:	NO::!
W. Capps:	does she represent the <u>chil</u>dren, of the twenty-second district?
Audience:	NO::!
W. Capps:	does she represent the <u>wo</u>men, of the twenty-second district?
Audience:	NO::!
W. Capps:	does she represent the people who care for the environment of the twenty-second district?
Audience:	NO::!
W. Capps:	does she represent the people who believe in local government of the twenty-second district?
Audience:	NO::!
W. Capps:	who does she represent? she- she campaigned- I heard it. I heard it. she campaigned- she campaigned on the theme a leadership-leadership that listens. well I can tell you the voice to which she pays the most attention. and the voice- to which she pays the most attention is the voice of Newt Gingrich.
Audience:	YEAH!
W. Capps:	and we didn't elect-
Audience:	boo:::!
W. Capps:	we didn't elect Newt Gingrich. We didn't elect Newt Gingrich. We elected a representative
Audience:	(b)oo::!
W. Capps:	and we need to hold the representative to the charge that the representative has been given.

Capps' strategy here is to stay closer to his prepared speech and perform the attack on Seastrand in a straightforward way, letting the audience co-author the criticism all the way through. He follows the same strategy on the campus of his own university (UCSB) but changes it at Hancock College, where the audience includes people who could not be counted on as supporters. In this context, instead of inviting the audience to answer the rhetorical questions about who Seastrand represents, Capps takes off from Seastrand's slogan "Leadership that listens" to ask a series of questions that he answers himself, simultaneously avoiding a test of the audience's loyalty and reducing the effect of the former drill:

(14)   (November 14, 1995: Hancock College, Santa Maria, CD2.01h:02m:30s)

W. Capps: I've been asking myself, has she listened to the seniors . . . in our community? I don't think so. . . .

              has she listened to the people who want to protect the environment, . . . in our community?

              I don't think so. . . .

              has she listened to the people who are advocates of education?

              that one kills me because- [. . .]

This excerpt is a much more mitigated form of criticism, with the personalized "I don't think so" instead of the well-timed collective shout "NO!!!" Capps obtained in San Luis Obispo. Furthermore, Seastrand's actions with respect to certain initiatives, such as her alleged record on education, are presented as having a direct impact on Capps himself as a believer in education ("that one kills me because-. . ."). By presenting himself as a victim of Seastrand's voting record and beliefs, Capps puts himself in the same category as the students he is trying to attract to his side.

Capps uses different form of mitigation of the attack at UCSB, where the audience—which includes some of his own students—is very supportive, making him seem more at ease and willing to insert new parts into his speech. In this context, standing at a microphone on a platform (where a rock band has just finished performing) and without the help of any notes, Capps launches into a new story about his own inability to be "critical," which ends with Seastrand becoming the butt of an obviously planned joke.

(15)   (November 14, 1995: University of California, Santa Barbara, CD3.16m:20s)

W. Capps: uh, uh but what I've been telling people is that running for- running for office is not . . . quite like just applying for a job=you know, not, just that- that you're qualified . . . and you get the job. I mean it- to run for office really means . . . that you have to beat your opponents. and the only way that this can become successful, . . . is if I beat Andrea Seastrand in November.

Audience: ((clapping, // cheers))

W. Capps: well, . . . people who- . . . people who know me well . . . know that . . . I have had some difficulty in the past in being critical of other people=because it goes against my nature. uh- ((clears

throat)) uhm last time around I would say things like- . . . you
know=I've heard it said that- . . . that Andrea Seastrand is a: . . .
very warm- . . . human being, . . . but I looked up warm . . . in the
dictionary . . . and it said "not too hot." . . .

Audience: ((laughter)) haha//hahaha!

W. Capps: now- see- that's about- that's about as far as- . . . as I can go with-
. . . critique because . . . I think one of the things we want to <u>fight</u>
in our- resist in our culture is this- this invective- this- . . . this
super- charged political rhetoric that- [. . .]

This excerpt and those preceding it provide a glimpse of what I saw as a
recurring pattern—namely, Capps' hard work at finding a way of attacking his
main opponent in ways that could be approved by his audience without making
him feel uncomfortable with the implications that such attacks would have on his
own persona. Although Capps, perhaps because of his academic background,
tended to verbalize some of the challenges he was facing, I believe that his
dilemmas and struggles were the same as the ones faced by any candidate for
public office.

Conclusions
In examining the speeches recorded during the first day of the 1995–96 campaign for the U.S. Congress by Democratic candidate Walter Capps, I have iso-
lated several sequences in which we can see Capps' work at designing his speech
for the particular audience he was speaking to. I also have identified sequences in
which the audience seemed to have interpreted Capps' words in ways that he did
not intend. Analysis of subsequent versions of the same points and the different
rhetorical strategies employed by Capps throughout the speeches I was able to
record during the same day suggest several lessons. The first is that to be a good
political orator it is not sufficient to have a good script. For one thing, there are
many situations in which candidates might not be able to have access to that script
(e.g., if there is no podium on which to place one's notes). Furthermore, speakers
must be able to evaluate their audience—its knowledge, its likes and dislikes—to
design their speech in ways that display their intimate knowledge of the audience,
including its habits and preferences.

We also have learned that there are situations when the audience, instead of
acting as a passive recipient of made-up slogans or jokes, may impose an interpretation that diverges from whatever the speaker had in mind. This type of situation creates a difficult moral dilemma for candidates, especially when the
audience reaction suggests that they approve what they are hearing the candidate say. Speakers must decide whether to go along with the audience and cap-

italize on its unexpected reaction or try to keep control of the meaning of their own words.

In this case, we have seen how one candidate edited his own speech and reformulated his stances with respect to several key issues in his speech to retain some control over his own message and present himself as a person who could be critical without sounding "mean." This type of struggle between the speaker's voice and the audience's voice is fought at many different levels at once, involving specific sequences of acts; specific grammatical and narrative frames; and, in this case, specific cultural expectations about what it meant to be a political candidate for the U.S. Congress in the last decade of the twentieth century. Above all, however, this struggle over the right balance between pleasing others and asserting oneself reminds us of the centrality of morality in the construction of human agency through talk.

NOTES

1. This article is based on audiovisual recordings and participant observation of events centered around the 1995–96 race for the 22nd Congressional District in California (Santa Barbara-San Luis Obispo). The recordings and transcriptions of those recordings were partly supported by several Senate Grants at the University of California at Los Angeles. Some of the ideas presented here were developed during the 1999–2000 academic year, while the author enjoyed a sabbatical with the support of the John Simon Guggenheim Foundation and the University of California at Los Angeles. The project on the Walter-Capps-for-Congress campaign could not have been possible without the support of the candidate, Walter Capps; his wife, Lois; and many of the people involved in the campaign, especially Walter's brother Doug Capps, his son Lindsey, and campaign staff members Steve Boyd, Thu Fong, and Bryant Winnecke. The original idea of following Walter Capps around during the campaign was born out of conversations in 1994–95 with Walter Capps' daughter Lisa, while she was a graduate student at UCLA. After accepting a position in the department of psychology at The University of California, Berkeley in 1996, Lisa continued to be a fervent supporter of my project and a source of insights on the impact of her father's campaigning on herself and the other members of the extended Capps family. Our conversations about the campaign, my project, and how to make something valuable out of it continued even during her last year of life, while she was fighting cancer. This article is a continuation of those conversations.
2. I thank Carmi Bleviss for our discussions of this and other examples of humor in Capps' speeches.

REFERENCES

Atkinson, J. Maxwell. 1984a. *Our masters' voices: The language and body language of politics.* London: Methuen.
———. 1984b. Public speaking and audience responses: Some techniques for inviting applause. In *Structures of social action,* edited by J. Maxwell Atkinson and John Heritage. Cambridge: Cambridge University Press, 370–410.

Babcock, Barbara A. 1977. The story in the story: Metanarration in folk narrative. In *Verbal art as performance,* edited by Richard Bauman. Rowley, Mass.: Newbury House, 61–79.

Bauman, Richard. 1986. *Story, performance, and event.* Cambridge: Cambridge University Press.

Beeman, William. 2001. Humor. In *Key terms in language and culture,* edited by Alessandro Duranti. Malden, Mass.: Blackwell, 98–101.

Berliner, Paul F. 1994. *Thinking in jazz: The infinite art of improvisation.* Chicago: Chicago University Press.

Bolinger, Dwight. 1961. Syntactic blends and other matters. *Language* 37: 366–81.

Chafe, Wallace (ed.). 1980. *The pear stories: Cognitive, cultural, and linguistic aspects of narrative production.* Advances in discourse processes. Norwood, N.J.: Ablex.

Clayman, Steven E. 1992. Caveat orator: Audience disaffiliation in the 1988 presidential debates. *Quarterly Journal of Speech* 78: 33–60.

———. 1993. Booing: The anatomy of a disaffiliative response. *American Sociological Review* 58: 110–30.

Goodwin, Charles. 1979. The interactive construction of a sentence in natural conversation. In *Everyday language: Studies in ethnomethodology,* edited by George Psathas. New York: Irvington Publishers, 97–121.

———. 1981. *Conversational organization: Interaction between speakers and hearers.* New York: Academic Press.

Heritage, John, and David Greatbatch. 1986. Generating applause: A study of rhetoric and response at party political conferences. *American Journal of Sociology* 92 (1): 110–57.

Hymes, Dell. 1972. Models of the interaction of language and social life. In *Directions in sociolinguistics: The ethnography of communication,* edited by John Gumperz and Dell Hymes. New York: Holt, Rinehart and Winston, 35–71.

Johnstone, Barbara. 1996. *The linguistic individual: Self-expression in language and linguistics.* New York: Oxford University Press.

Lavandera, Beatriz. 1978. Where does the sociolinguistic variable stop? *Language in Society* 7: 171–82.

Lord, Albert B. 1960. *The singer of tales.* Cambridge, Mass.: Harvard University Press.

Philips, Susan U. 1992. The routinization of repair in courtroom discourse. In *Rethinking context: Language as an interactive phenomenon,* edited by Alessandro Duranti and Charles Goodwin. Cambridge: Cambridge University Press, 311–22.

Romaine, Suzanne. 1984. On the problem of syntactic variation and pragmatic meaning in sociolinguistic theory. *Folia Linguistica* 18: 409–39.

Sacks, Harvey. 1992. *Lectures on conversation: Volume II.* Cambridge, Mass.: Blackwell.

Sacks, Harvey, and Emanuel A. Schegloff. 1979. Two preferences in the organization of reference to persons and their interaction. In *Everyday language: Studies in ethnomethodology,* edited by George Psathas. New York: Irvington Publishers, 15–21.

Sacks, Harvey, Emanuel A. Schegloff, and Gail Jefferson. 1974. A simplest systematics for the organization of turn-taking for conversation. *Language* 50: 696–735.

Schegloff, Emanuel A. 1972. Notes on a conversational practice: Formulating place. In *Studies in social interaction,* edited by David Sudnow. New York: Free Press, 75–119.

Tannen, Deborah. 1987. Repetition in conversation: Toward a poetics of talk. *Language* 63 (3): 574–605.

———. 1989. *Talking voices: Repetition, dialogue, and imagery in conversational discourse.* Cambridge: Cambridge University Press.

Tannen, Deborah, and Cynthia Wallat. 1986. Medical professionals and parents: A linguistic analysis of communication across contexts. *Language in Society* 15: 295–312.

Appendix: Transcription Conventions

The excerpts presented in this article are transcribed according to a modified version of the conventions originally established by Gail Jefferson for the analysis of conversation (Sacks, Schegloff, and Jefferson 1974: 731–34).

W. Capps:	name of speaker is separated from the rest by a colon (:) and one or more spaces.
anybody	underlining represents emphasis or contrastive stress.
NO!!	capital letters indicate high volume.
job=I mean	equal sign (=) stands for "latching" (i.e., no hearable interval between two turns or between two utterances by the same speaker).
becau::se	colon (:) stands for lengthening of sound.
go //next	point in a party's turn where overlap by other speaker(s) starts.
((laughter))	double parentheses frame contextual information about the following talk.
(??)	a portion of talk that could not be heard accurately.
. . .	untimed pause.
[. . .]	a portion of the transcript was left out.
.	a period stands for a falling intonation that suggests the end of a turn.
the women,	a comma represents a slightly rising intonation.

Narrative in the construction of social and political identity

Robin Tolmach Lakoff
University of California, Berkeley

Let me begin[1] by proposing a working definition of the terms I will be using here—"narrative" or "story" (for my purposes, the two are synonymous). Much of it is borrowed from Labov (1972a) and Schiffrin (1994). A narrative is a linked series of utterances constructed by one person or several persons acting together, consisting of five main parts (not all of which need be explicitly present)—usually in the following order: abstract, orientation, complications, evaluation, coda—told in a linear order, and having a point that is recognizable by participants (e.g., persuasion, entertainment, uplift, or education).

In many fields within the humanities and social sciences, "narrative" has been a very productive area of interest for the past decade or two. While the study of narrative has been around for a very long time, especially in the realm of literary analysis, the proliferation of areas of study in which the idea of narrativity has been fruitful is relatively recent. Some of these fields are discourse analysis, pragmatics, and sociolinguistics; psychology (cognitive psychology and psychotherapy and, within the latter, psychoanalysis); the law; literary theory; history; and anthropology. To support such breadth of interest, the notion of narrative must be rich indeed.

Perspectives on Narrative Analysis

Narratives can be examined from more than one perspective. Labov (1972b) was the first to suggest a *structural* analysis of narrative, analogous to the structural analysis of sentences pioneered by Chomsky within the theoretical framework of transformational generative grammar. In work in this genre, the analyst must discover the necessary components of the sample under investigation, the order in which they occur, and the constraints on co-occurrence of the items in the sample; the analyst determines how changes in the order of components affect the meaning of the whole. To use Schiffrin's (1994: 284) summary:

> Narratives have a linear structure in which different sections present different kinds of information.... Narratives are opened by an abstract...[followed by] orientation clauses.... The main part of the narrative is comprised of complicating action clauses....

> Evaluation pervades the narrative.... Finally, the story is closed by a coda.

As transformational grammar allows for the inclusion of ungrammatical sentences among the data, as a way of determining the limits on the applicability of syntactic rules, structural analyses of narrative must include the consideration of aberrant examples, in which elements may occur in a different order from that given above, or one or more of them is missing or not what it purports to be. One might treat certain kinds of detective stories or postmodern fiction as aberrant examples capable of being "parsed" by sophisticated readers. Evaluations are not fixed, but may shift: "Good guys" and "bad guys," "right" and "wrong," "now" and "then" may switch places with each other. The plot may unfold in nonlinear order, with flashbacks and interpolations or actions interpreted and then reinterpreted by successive narrators. Yet just as a fluent speaker with sufficient linguistic and conversational contextualization can make sense of aberrant sentences (which might be unintelligible in isolation), with sufficient "contextualization" in the form of prior experience with the literary genre (or the individual telling the story: "Max always starts his stories in the middle"), a reader or hearer can salvage an otherwise uninterpretable narrative. This structural treatment of narratives offers us a deep understanding of narrativity and allows us to examine the similarities and differences between stories and other kinds of connected discourse, as well as similarities and differences between oral and written, spontaneous and constructed, and other narrative types. It also implicitly makes the important point that narratives are products of a linguistic grammar and work by principles that are basically similar to those of sentences or other more self-evidently "linguistic" units: Narrative structures are rule governed and predictable.

One should be wary, however, of pushing the sentence-narrative analogy too far. Sentences, in an autonomous-syntax framework such as transformational generative grammar, are strictly formal entities. The understanding of narrative entails a significant functional aspect. That is, within autonomous-syntax theories, sentences can be considered fully analyzed (i.e., understood) in *purely* structural terms: word-order, word-choice, co-occurrence and distribution constraints.[2] But even if it were possible to define narratives in structural terms, doing so would not tell us all we needed to know to understand why the object of our investigation can be called a "narrative" or whether that example is prototypical, atypical but interpretable as narrative, or altogether anomalous. The full analysis or understanding of a narrative must include a functional component: Why did the teller tell this story, in this form, under these real-world conditions, to this audience? What were the social and cognitive aims of the speech event? Who tells what stories to whom?

Narrative as Culture-Creating

Just as purely linguistic grammar forms a significant part of our cultural knowledge, so the shared rules of storytelling bind a culture together. Two hundred years ago, the ability to tell, and understand, a fairy tale identified people to themselves and each other as members of a culture. This form of knowledge may be less critical for us today; many of us may not recognize fairy-tale motifs (unless we have been exposed to their Disney versions), and still less are we expected to know how to tell them. Yet a legitimate twenty-first century American is expected to have the same kind of active and passive familiarity with sitcom characters and plot lines. Woe betide the contemporary party guest (outside of rarefied academic circles) who is not conversant with the doings on the current episode of "Friends"! Stories about the real world—we call them *news*—have a similar function. Sharing opinions of the *dramatis personae* in the news and evaluations of their actions makes a group cohesive. On the other hand, discovering that a supposedly shared tale has different endings, or different moral evaluations, for subgroups other than one's own can engender suspicion, bewilderment, anger, and fear. People lose their sense of cohesion; *we* don't know who "we" are any more.

News Stories as Narratives

Most narratives that have been studied have the prototypical form of stories told by one person to one or a group of people, with a specific and explicit structure. While some stories are passed from one teller to another—typically changing in the process—usually the telling of a story has been studied as a unique event.

In this age of mass electronic media, however, news stories are not typically constructed in this way. We can think of a host of contemporary stories that Americans (and, often, people all over the world) share.[3] These stories have the general form of typical individually constructed narratives, but while the basic characters and events may be consistent among tellers, other parts of the narrative—details, interpretations, evaluations—may differ strikingly. Such stories involve a diverse set of active and passive participants in a wide variety of media: television and radio news programs and magazine shows; newspaper news stories, opinion pieces, and gossip columns; radio call-in shows. From those options, each of us, in turn, constructs our own story that we trade with friends, cutting and pasting, and our remade narratives then circulate back into the public domain, perhaps via the Internet, to the electronic media, from where... (and so on).

Because these stories are constructed both formally and informally, explicitly and implicitly, responsibly and irresponsibly, it is impossible to assign to them a specific form or format. As individuals and as a culture, however, we still can recognize the story and its details in all of its forms, long after the events themselves have occurred. Suppose you encounter the following list:

- Judge Ito
- "If it doesn't fit, you must acquit"
- Slow-speed car chase
- Kato the Akita
- Ron and Nicole

You immediately will be able to provide not only the name of the only narrative of which all of these elements are parts,[4] but also—even years later—the "plot" of the story. And the fact that you can do so, and that everyone expects that you can do so, brings us together as Americans of the early twenty-first century, as much as we may differ in other ways (and as much as the specifics of our individual narratives may differ).

Two Examples

But here I am less interested in examining how shared narrative creates cohesion than in how its absence brings about the opposite: What happens when narrative-based cohesion based on participants' assumptions of shared narrative is cast into doubt? I use two stories that attracted great attention during the 1990s: the O.J. Simpson story and the story of the relationship between Bill and Hillary Clinton. They are different kinds of stories: One is predominantly social, the other mainly political, though neither is exclusively one or the other. One has a precipitating action that can be located at a moment in time, the other continued, shifting and changing, for eight years. The two stories share certain traits; perhaps the most striking is that both move somewhat uneasily in the shadow area between hard "news" and soft "gossip"—an ambiguity that only intensifies their irresistibility for us all—and both have well outlasted the normal limits of the American attention span.

Most stories retain interest for only a few news cycles. Even the 2000 election—beyond doubt a story of high drama and importance—faded away almost as soon as the Supreme Court announced its decision. By contrast, the O.J. Simpson saga continued to attract public and private attention well beyond the conclusion of his civil trial in late 1996. Even after leaving office, the Clintons (unlike most former presidential couples) are fodder for both the front page and the gossip column. Stories like these that last are marked and require explanation. They pass what I have called (Lakoff 2000) the Undue Attention Test.

Like any compelling group narrative, both of these stories call their culture's important beliefs into question: the role of celebrity and money in the administration of justice; racial tension in America; the meaning of marriage; the roles of the sexes; the corruption that seems to come inevitably with power. On one level (deplored by the intelligentsia) these stories are tawdry dirt about sex, lies, violence, or infidelity; on another, they are veritable morality stories about how human beings should not be but are—and therefore about sex, lies, violence, and infidelity. These stories are not the ephemera or effluvia of our trivial dailiness, even as they are; stories like these, with their unusual staying power, define us and change us as individuals and as a society.

Public stories like these have a major effect on the group as a whole (although individuals transmit them and individuals interpret them). But their function is related to that of the stories that individuals tell themselves (in the same semi-coherent way), which work in similar fashion to create or destroy an individual's sense of identity and self-cohesion. Psychotherapists have for many years been using the analysis of patients' or clients' narratives to explain the distress that brings them into therapy.

Dysfunctional Private and Public Narratives

Classical Freudian psychoanalysts saw psychic unhappiness—what they called "neurosis"—as the result of disturbed communication between an individual's conscious and unconscious mind. Family and couples therapy has traditionally attributed similar distress to poor communication between or among individuals in a family. Both methodologies locate the distress at the level of the speech act, in units not much larger than sentences; to take the stereotypical case, "I want to kill my father and marry my mother." With an intuitive therapist, this sort of interpretation can often be effective. After an initial period of optimism in the first half of the twentieth century, however, analyses lengthened and frequently got stuck. Analysts and other psychotherapists therefore began to concentrate less on the obvious, often florid, symptoms that corresponded to speech acts and to focus instead on the symptoms that were bringing more and more of their clients into therapy in the late twentieth century: feelings of *anomie*, pointlessness, and emptiness. As narratology was becoming a focal point in many academic disciplines in the late 1970s and early 1980s, therapists borrowed those ideas in order to consider *the story* as an aspect of psychic structure that, if deformed, could lead to the kinds of symptoms that brought their clients to them. These symptoms were experienced as *bad stories* rather than *infelicitous speech acts*: They rambled, events in them were disordered, there were gaps in them, they eluded understanding; they were incoherent and noncohesive. Analysts such as Roy Schafer (1992) and Donald Spence (1982) suggested that the basic etiology of neurosis had not changed since Freud's time: a psychically traumatic event suffered in childhood. For Schafer and Spence, however, the route by which traumatic events precipitated psychological distress was that, because they were intolerable to contemplate, they forced a reorganization of the sufferer's narrative. To avoid confronting, recognizing, or reexperiencing the trauma, the individual remakes the narrative in distorted form, with events omitted, reordered, or changed in relationship to others or otherwise rendered unrecognizable. While this process allows individuals to function more or less well, it leaves their story incoherent—which in turn creates a sense of unreality, nonexistence, and meaninglessness, since personal narratives tell us who we are, link us to reality, and give meaning to our lives (see Aftel 1996).

The analyst's job becomes less that of making unilateral interpretations than of collaborating with the patient to re-create—or even create in the first place—a cohesive narrative the patient can live with and through.

Societies experience analogous traumas when their stories become incoherent or noncohesive. There are signs that this is happening to us now. Social critics speak derogatorily, and nostalgically, about the fall of our public and private discourse from some putative standard in a hypothetical Golden Age. But I think these complaints are analogous to those of prescriptive grammarians who agonize over the use of "hopefully" as a speech act adverb or "like" as a discourse marker. If we understand why our culture is changing and how these changes are connected to current shifts in the kinds of narratives we produce and who is allowed to produce them, we may get through this period of uncomfortable flux with a bit more grace.

The O.J. and Clinton Narratives as Aporias

Consider a set of possible stories about the O.J. Simpson episode. Choose the version you prefer:

(1)   O.J. Simpson killed Nicole Simpson and Ron Goldman. He was tried in a spectacular, televised trial that, because of defense manipulation, prosecutorial incompetence, judicial malfeasance, and the antiwhite bias of the jury, resulted in a "not guilty" verdict.

(2)   O.J. Simpson was accused of the murders of Nicole Simpson and Ron Goldman. The evidence presented was convoluted and, for a nonscientifically specialized jury, hard to follow but quite probably involved one or more frame-ups by the police. But thanks to the investigative efforts and rhetorical skill of Simpson's "dream team" and the jury's courage in rejecting the verdict clearly desired by the majority community, a "not guilty" verdict was returned.

The first scenario represents the predominant postverdict narrative of the white community; the second, the predominant version of the black community. Both take unambiguous positions on the facts of the case and the role of the jury. Arguably the much-noted postverdict distress of the white community was due as much to their anguish and perplexity at the ability of the minority community to reject the majority's narrative (version 1) as to the verdict itself.

These stories create what postmodernists call an *aporia*: a break in the cohesion in the text, an impossibility of reconciliation of the two offers of meaning into one cohesive whole shared by all members of the community. This impossibility itself suggests a serious problem with using the word "community" to describe Americans as a group: The aporia tells us that "community" does not exist between whites—the majority group and the tellers of story (1)—and blacks, the minority and tellers of story (2).

A similar analysis is possible for another set of apparently unreconcilable stories:

(3) Bill and Hillary Clinton are sincere liberals whose dedication to the rights of minorities and women incurred the wrath of conservatives. As a result during their residence in the White House they were subjected to an unending series of inquisitions and persecutions, misreadings and character-assassinations, for alleged actions that were either fictional or trivial. This is the only way to understand (a) the impeachment, (b) the outcome of the presidential election of 2000, and (c) the outcry over presidential pardons, misappropriations of White House furniture, and so forth after Bill Clinton left office.

(4) Bill and Hillary Clinton are irresponsible political and social radicals who have committed blatant criminal acts and escaped due punishment by luck, charisma, or deceptiveness. Only the dogged efforts of people committed to traditional values and virtue in high places kept them in line even as far as they were kept in line and led to the events that culminated in (a), (b), and (c) above. The ultimate downfall of the Clintons is both richly deserved and utterly necessary as a moral lesson for the country, and the Republican victory in 2000 was both fair and a necessary corrective.

These narratives too are clear-cut, direct, and unambiguous. In these respects, each is satisfying to those who tell it, and both have been told, endlessly, since the early 1990s. For both the O.J. and the Clinton cases, though, the simple and satisfying narratives fail to account for the fact that these stories just won't go away. O.J. makes headlines if he does anything noticeable even many years after the crime. The same people who have complained for years about "Clinton fatigue" now fan the flames of new Clinton scandals, reportedly to the distress of the Bush administration. Clinton fatigue has to compete with, and take a back seat to, the need for a conclusion: a need, as with the O.J. story, for a narrative with no ambiguity, with tidy ends, that we can all agree on (in terms of what happened and what it means). For both of these stories—one "about" race, one "about" gender, the two explosive issues America currently can't deal with—there is no such calm end in sight, so the stories must continually be told and retold, retooled and recycled. Without a compromise, fighting over narrative rights and with them social and political clout must go on (see Lakoff 2000).

In both stories, attempts fail in a major function: to mark and create group cohesion—to define the "we" who agree on "our" story. In this way, they resemble the unsatisfactory, distorted stories that bring people into psychotherapy or force them to repeat and rework those stories endlessly, never quite getting their stories, or themselves, into coherent shape. In the individual cases, background presuppositions are intolerable and therefore discarded, leading to problems with framing and cohesion. In the group cases, subgroups are unable to agree on the frames and presuppositions to be used in constructing the stories. What is "justice"? What is "decency"? What is sex, and what, if anything, does "is" mean? Who among us has the right and the ability to frame these questions and provide the answers to them? As long as we cannot agree on these presuppositions, it is unlikely that we can achieve a single, coherent, narrative for such cases that all of us can agree on.

So we cannot agree on our most important stories because we disagree (often without acknowledging it) on

(a) the presuppositions and frames underlying and giving meaning to the stories (what "justice" is and how it is properly dispensed)

(b) the characterizations of the actors in the stories and assessments of their motives (the characters of the President and First Lady)

(c) the determination of what the stories "mean," why we tell them, and what the "morals" may be for all of us

(d) perhaps most significant, the allocation of the right to determine (a)–(c): who, if anyone, controls the rights to make the interpretations of events that underlie "our" narratives.

I have mentioned two types of narrative competition: within individuals and between groups. But since groups are made up of individuals, and group values contribute to individuals' sense of themselves and their worth, the two are not separable. If implicit agreement on shared narratives underlies that aspect of our self-definition that can be stated as, "I am an American," and "I am an American" is part of an individual's identity, then group incoherence is apt to affect individual feelings of status and belonging. So it is not surprising that when social forces create disruptions in public agreement over group narrative, therapists regard narrative incohesion as a common basis of individual psychic distress.

That confusion necessarily creates in the society experiencing it—or the individuals who compose that society—a sense of chaos, distress, and *anomie*. If our stories tell us who we are, individually and socially, then if we can't make stories that work for all of us, it becomes harder to assume identity of interests, shared language, or mutual trust.

Gregory Bateson (1972) discusses what happens when conflicting stories cannot be resolved—in his examples, within an individual. He speaks of this situation as one of "schismogenesis"—literally, the production of schizophrenia or a severe breakdown of communication between the affected individual and his or her society. An individual faced with an unresolvably paradoxical message is put into a double bind. According to Bateson, the only way out of the double bind, and communicative breakdown, is moving the discussion to a higher level—to another frame that incorporates both conflicting narratives and perceives each as rational and meaningful in its context.

In that spirit, (5) can be understood as a higher-level substitute for (1) and (2):

(5)   O.J. Simpson was accused of the murders of Nicole Simpson and Ron Goldman. The evidence was ambiguous and complex, and the defense used both of those characteristics to suggest, to a majority-black jury, the possibility of reasonable doubt. Moreover, evidence in the form of Mark Fuhrman's use of racist epithets suggested a pattern of racism in the Los Angeles Police Department. And a majority of the mostly black jury had themselves encountered evidence of police racism. On the basis of these claims and experiences, and encouraged by head defense attorney Johnnie Cochran's closing statement, the jury reframed the question before it from, "Did O.J. Simpson commit the murders?" to "Can a black person, such as O.J., receive justice in an American courtroom?" Their "not guilty" verdict was intended as a negative answer to that question.

Narrative (5) is a compromise—an ambiguous and complicated statement that attempts to view the outcome of the case from several perspectives at once, offering an answer (not necessarily the only one) to the question: Why did the black community see things so differently from the white majority? Therefore, it is a different kind of narrative—perhaps a metanarrative, attempting to explain the existence of the other narratives and the impossibility of resolving the story within either of them. If a society can accept such a metanarrative, it might escape the perils of schismogenesis. To date, by all the evidence, we have not done so.

Racial divides are not the only ones along which schismogenesis can occur. Splits along lines of gender and political affiliation are involved in the competition over the Clinton narratives. Again, it is possible to substitute a metanarrative, (6), for the unresolvably paradoxical (3)–(4).

(6)   Bill and Hillary Clinton are ambiguous, together and singly. They are politically liberal, but conservative; socially radical, but traditional; smart, but stupid; sincere, but corrupt; dedicated to

helping the less fortunate, but blindly ambitious for themselves; sexually ambiguous, together and singly, experimenting with gender roles in ways that make even some progressives uncomfortable, constituting a veritable referendum on postmodernism. Both the adulation and the hostility directed toward them are extreme, and both emotions can be understood as emanating from what the Clintons stand for or seem to stand for, or from what observers read into their reported actions, based on conflicts in these observers' own lives and psyches much more than anything the Clintons themselves have actually accomplished.

What if we, as a society, find it impossible to move above the schismatic narratives we have created? Bateson suggests that when this is the case for individuals, they literally go mad: They become schizophrenic. It is of course true that the psychiatric understanding of the etiology of schizophrenia has deepened—or rather changed radically—since Bateson did his original work in the 1940s and 1950s (*Steps to an Ecology of Mind* is a reprint of many of his papers). Researchers are now overwhelmingly likely to see this disease as the result of physical processes in the brain, rather than communicative anomalies in the mind. And while there is some justification for referring to current American societal behavior as "crazy," "schizophrenic," or "out of control," at least the first two should be taken figuratively. But even metaphorical schismogenesis can have literal effects.

Narrative Competition as Agonistic
For several years there has been a great deal of concern expressed by the punditry about a breakdown in American public civility. Different terms are used to describe this phenomenon: "coarsening," "incivility," "agonism" (Tannen 1998). All of these terms presuppose that discussants come together with no trust in a middle ground, no hope of finding a common language or common cause, no desire to compromise. Some of the complaints sound like mere whining over the fact that people other than white middle-class males are increasingly being allowed an active role in framing public discourse—and that these interlopers bring new perspectives and new public styles into the mix, illegitimate precisely because they are nontraditional. Yet even liberals—who might be expected to applaud such changes—express distress, and certainly it is impossible to ignore the fact that the public airwaves have become, often, very unpleasant places in which to spend any time.

I wonder if the breakdown of our former expectation (whether that expectation was accurate or not) of consistent and coherent shared group narrative is a contributory cause of the malaise many Americans feel is infecting the public discourse. If we suspect—as we have suspected for at least the past decade—that as individuals and as a group we don't tell the same stories and don't perceive important events similarly, then we have to fear that no one we speak to is likely to hear what we have to say as we intended it to be understood—unless we punch it up, or yell, or overenunciate just as we have always done with foreigners in the futile hope that by so doing, we can get them to understand us across a language barrier. Of course, it doesn't work with foreigners; it only makes them mad, and their inability, or unwillingness, to understand despite our exertions makes us mad back. So we shout louder. So they get more insulted.

As Watzlawick, Beavin, and Jackson (1967)—disciples of Bateson—note, when communication breaks down, couples or families move in the direction of "complementary schismogenesis": the tendency for each member to exacerbate the very traits of his or her own communicative style that created the difficulties in the first place. Those ways are comfortable because they are old, and when we are in distress, we reach for what is tried and true and comfortable. The discourse gets louder as each side fights to protect its own turf. The two sides grow at once more distinct and more desperate to merge—each on its own terms.

Conclusion

If narratives are one way we can reach out of our separate selves and construct ourselves as a group, then the failure of that language to bridge those boundaries any more could be a significant contributing cause to the increase in incivility. We can understand our increasingly obvious explicit inability to agree on narratives as a sign of social change—not necessarily, as is often argued, for the worse. If the dominant group can understand that its narratives will no longer automatically be privileged as *the* narratives that everyone must accept, and if all groups can contemplate narratives composed at the meta-level, the newly-explicit complexity[5] of American discourse will have a positive effect.

NOTES

1. I would like to thank Dean James Alatis and Professor Deborah Tannen for organizing the conference at which the original version of this essay was presented. As in previous years, GURT 2001 served as a reminder to all of us of the importance and centrality of sociolinguistics. As Labov remarked many years ago, the field might be better off if what we call "sociolinguistics" were recognized as, in fact, the central concern of the field, under the name of "linguistics," and if what is commonly referred to as "core linguistics," on the other hand, had been given a hyphenated or complex name like "autonomo-linguistics." So let us think of this and the other chapters in this volume as contributions to "linguistics" proper.

2. Whether those criteria really do allow for a full understanding of sentences—or whether the autonomous "sentence" is merely a fictitious convenience—is a question that cannot be exam-

ined within a theory of autonomous syntax and one that is thankfully beyond the scope of the present discussion.

3. For instance, in May 1996 I spent a few weeks giving lectures at several universities in Sweden and Finland. I was surprised at the great interest and thorough knowledge the Swedes in my audience had of American current events and the actors in them. Americans, on the other hand, typically have only the most superficial knowledge (at best) of current events in other countries.

4. In case I'm wrong about this premise, it's the O.J. Simpson story.

5. Of course, I am not suggesting here that American society is only now achieving complexity. We have been a complex society from the beginning. For most of our history, however, groups other than the politically dominant one might tell their stories privately, among themselves, but those stories could not compete in the public marketplace of ideas; one thing that made the "dominant" culture dominant was its ability to put its narratives out as the *only* ones available for "everyone." What has been happening, extraordinarily, since the 1960s is the opening of narrative competition to groups formerly out of the running—which, as I have suggested, creates confusion and fears of malaise and agonism but in the long run permits meaning-making for many people who formerly played no role in it.

REFERENCES

Aftel, Mandy. 1996. *The story of your life.* New York: Simon and Schuster.
Bateson, Gregory. 1972. *Steps to an ecology of mind.* New York: Chandler, 1972.
Labov, William. 1972a. The transformation of experience in narrative syntax. In *Language in the inner city.* Philadelphia: University of Pennsylvania Press, 354–96.
———. 1972b. Rules for ritual insults. In *Language in the inner city.* Philadelphia: University of Pennsylvania Press, 297–353.
Lakoff, Robin. 2000. *The language war.* Berkeley and Los Angeles: University of California Press.
Schafer, Roy. 1992. *Retelling a life: Narration and dialogue in psychoanalysis.* New York: Basic Books.
Schiffrin, Deborah. 1994. *Approaches to discourse.* Cambridge, Mass.: Blackwell.
Spence, Donald. 1982. *Narrative truth and historical truth.* New York: Norton.
Tannen, Deborah. 1998. *The argument culture.* New York: Random House.
Watzlawick, Paul, Janet Beavin, and Don Jackson. 1967. *The pragmatics of human communication.* New York: Norton.

Patient's voices in the medical world:
An exploration of accounts of noncompliance[1]

Heidi E. Hamilton
Georgetown University

Many scholars of language are drawn to the profound linguistic issues one finds in the study of medical discourse. Some of these researchers focus their efforts primarily on furthering our understanding of some aspects of discourse, such as frame-shifting (Tannen and Wallat 1982), questions (Ainsworth-Vaughn 1998), or giving of recommendations (Roberts 1999); others (Frankel 1994; Frankel and Beckman 1995) direct their work to the health care providers and consumers—the physicians and patients who talk to each other in doctors' offices and hospitals, far from university seminar rooms. Still others try to live in both worlds, shuttling between medical conferences and linguistics conferences and working hard to translate one set of disciplinary assumptions and frameworks into another.

Beginning with my study of conversation and Alzheimer's disease in the 1980s (Hamilton 1994a, 1994b, 1996), I have straddled both worlds: I have been involved in a variety of interdisciplinary projects examining aphasia (Hamilton 1994c); mental health delivery systems (e.g., the National Institute of Mental Health's "Healthy People 2000" initiative); genetic counseling (Benkendorf et al. 2001); physician-nurse communication (Larson et al. 1998); and Internet health support groups (Hamilton 1998). In 1999 I began to explore physician-patient communication as a linguistics consultant to a health care education project being conducted by a major health care communications company in the northeastern United States.

In this essay I discuss one facet of the project: patient compliance[2] in chronic or life-threatening illnesses, with a focus on diabetes. Specifically, I investigate verbal accounts offered by eighteen patients to excuse or justify noncompliant actions as related to the diabetes management plans recommended by their physicians. Based on analyses of the accounts' discourse structure, as well as personal attribute statements made within the accounts, I argue that these accounts contain information about the patients' lifeworld circumstances that is critical to the health of these patients and yet only rarely comes to light in interactions with their physicians. I close with specific recommendations on how to increase the exploration of such information in the patients' visits to their doctors.

Before I examine patient accounts, however, I step back for a moment to provide relevant background information in several areas. First I present the health care problem that motivated the analysis; second, I discuss relevant frameworks within the area of medical discourse analysis that guided my eventual focus on accounts and briefly describe the interactions I examine in this essay; third, I provide insights into the challenges of compliance related to diabetes.

The Health Care Problem
Why might it make sense for a linguist to study compliance in diabetes or other chronic illnesses? What makes me think that an investigation of the language used by patients and their physicians could have anything to do with compliance and health? To commit to such a project, I had to assume two things: Physicians have the best interests of their patients in mind and at heart, and patients *do* want to comply because they understand the link between such compliance and better health.

If these assumptions are correct, the following fact is startling and cries out for action: According to the U.S. Health Care Financing Administration, 50–60 percent of medical costs paid by insurers can be traced to only 3–5 percent of all patients in the United States.[3] Although some of these patients face high medical costs related to unpredictable and largely unavoidable circumstances such as serious accidents and cancer, most of these patients have serious chronic conditions such as high blood pressure, congestive heart failure, and diabetes that can be managed to minimize serious long-term complications. For example, uncontrolled diabetes—cases in which patients do not, will not, or cannot comply with what their physicians think will help them live healthier lives—is the leading cause of kidney failure, lower extremity amputation, and new cases of blindness in adults. Thus, there is strong evidence that noncompliant actions by patients are leading them into worse and worse health accompanied by higher and higher costs, pain, and suffering. In fact, the American Diabetes Association reports that total direct and indirect costs related to diabetes in the United States in 1997 were approximately $98 billion.

How Might Linguistics Help?
Research into physician-patient interactions undertaken by language scholars over the past twenty-five years or so has focused a good deal on the pervasive and readily apparent asymmetries displayed and (re)created within such interactions. When the discourse of physician-patient interactions is contrasted with everyday conversations, it is clear that institutional discourse is shaped by the specialized education, training, and experience of the physician, as well as the institutional work that needs to be accomplished in such interactions. Technical vocabularies and presuppositions that are based on expected professional knowledge combine with expertly managed control of the interactional agenda as effected by asking

questions, initiating topics, and deferring or ignoring topics introduced by patients. Not only are patients not usually privy to the specialized knowledge of the physician, they usually have less experience with the goal-oriented interactional agendas and discourse structures that are typical of physician-patient encounters. In a seminal article, ten Have (1991) made the point that such asymmetry, although prevalent, actually is constructed every time patients and their physicians get together. Patients must collude with physicians as the discourse unfolds if the asymmetries are to be upheld. This fact encourages us not only to look to language and the emergent discourse for clues to how this asymmetry is accomplished but also to think seriously about ways in which the discourse might change to allow patient voices to be heard more frequently within the medical encounter.

Alongside this thread of discussion runs another, somewhat connected, thread having to do with the patient lifeworld or patient perspective. Mishler's (1984) foundational work in this area identified the "voice of the lifeworld" and the "voice of medicine," whose collision can be used to describe some problematic interactions between physicians and their patients. For example, whereas a physician may understand a disease in terms of objective blood counts and cultures, a patient with that disease may understand it primarily in terms of its impact on his or her life's activities—such as being too tired to go to work or socialize with friends. In her examination of claims to power in medical encounters, Ainsworth-Vaughn (1998) argues that glimpses into the patient's lifeworld can be offered through personal experience narratives told by the patient as part of the physician-patient interaction. These narratives can be integral parts of the diagnostic process for physicians who allow them to be told and understand them to contain important insights regarding patient symptoms and experiences of the disease.

Shifting slightly from sharing aspects of the patient's lifeworld to the patient's perspective, Maynard (1991) characterizes the "perspective display series" that some physicians use strategically to encourage patients (or parents of patients) to display their understanding of their medical problem before the physician discusses his or her own diagnosis of the problem. The fact that the patient's perspective is "on the table" allows the physician to tailor delivery of the diagnostic news, emphasizing points of agreement between perspectives and carefully discussing points of difference. My own ongoing work within genetic counseling and hormone replacement therapy in menopause has highlighted the importance of such exploration of individual patients' perspectives as health care professionals and patients weigh potential risks and benefits of medical decisions in areas where recommendations are made against a backdrop of medical uncertainty.

All of this work revolving around the role of patients' voices as related to the accomplishment of various kinds of medical work made me wonder about the possible connection between patients' voices and the problem of patient noncompliance. I began to think that some clues to this connection very likely were waiting to be found deep within patients' and physicians' talk, so I gathered the project videotapes and transcriptions and embarked on my search for these clues. An examination of the project data set took me on a videotape-aided journey into physicians' offices in three locations: a group practice specializing in diabetes treatment in a small city in the northeastern United States; a family practice affiliated with a county hospital in a second small city in the northeastern United States; and an inner-city primary care practice in a large midwestern city. I watched and listened to twenty-four diabetic patients in routine check-ups with their physicians, aided by videotapes of open-ended interviews that were held with each patient immediately following the check-up. Videotapes of interviews with each of the six participating physicians regarding twenty-three of the twenty-four patients provided insight into the health care professional's perspective on these particular physician-patient interactions, as well as on diabetes issues in general.

I was immediately struck by the patients' account-giving within the larger discussion of noncompliance within their post-interviews. The insights into the patients' personal circumstances surrounding specific issues of noncompliance were obvious. I returned to the physician-patient videotapes to look for this type of information and found almost nothing. I had discovered my clue; a fuller investigation of patient accounts seemed to be a fruitful way to proceed.

Compliance Challenges in Diabetes

Before we examine the patients' talk about compliance, we must understand the many challenges these patients and their physicians face. To manage their diabetes effectively, patients typically must control or lose body weight; exercise regularly; take prescribed medications in the correct dosages at the prescribed times of day; monitor blood glucose (sugar) levels in the morning and evening; have regular examinations by a variety of medical specialists, including ophthalmologists and podiatrists, in an attempt to diagnose and treat physical changes caused by diabetes; and watch the kinds and amounts of food they eat, taking care not to eat foods that can raise their blood sugar levels. These foods include potatoes, rice, and pasta in addition to the more obvious candies and desserts that contain sugar. The patient speaking in excerpt 1 offers some insight into the often overwhelming nature of this compliance.

> *Excerpt 1*
>
> It's a strain on your lifestyle.
>
> I'll put it that way.
>
> If you're cooking at home,
>
> how you got to cook your food
>
> and then you take your medicine

and then you got to keep checking your sugar

and you're ripping and running,

you're going to work.

You got all the stuff to do

and it just seems like it's a hassle to life, you know.

There's just so much to do.

Most of these compliance areas are integrally connected to how patients live their lives, helping to make diabetes one of the most "psychologically and behaviorally demanding of the chronic medical illnesses" (Ciechanowski et al. 2001: 29). Anderson (1985) reports that 95 percent of diabetes management is conducted by the patient.

Many physicians understand how difficult it is for patients to be consistently compliant. One physician in our study expressed it as follows:

Excerpt 2

Well, I think it's a tough disease to work with in many of these people,

because a lot of, you know, many of these people are Type-2 diabetics

who are overweight,

who basically need lifestyle changes in order to control it,

and that's a difficult -

Anytime you're asking anyone to do . . . that they have to do something, you know, other than take pills,

then it becomes very difficult.

The compliance difficulties patients experience represent immense challenges to their physicians. Our taped physician-patient interactions were filled with frustration—first as patients admitted to not adhering to aspects of their treatment plan and then as their physicians tried to get them to change. Over and over in our post-interviews, physicians mentioned the strategies they use in an attempt to encourage patient compliance. Many rely on education, calmly reciting relevant facts and figures. Some add affect to the facts, sounding more like salespersons than physicians. Others fall into yelling and nagging; they admit that they feel like mothers trying to get their children to behave. Still others resort to instilling fear in their patients—highlighting the kidney failure, blindness, or amputation that may await the patients if they do not change their ways. As a last resort, some physicians try intimidation tactics, telling their patients that they will have to go elsewhere for treatment if they do not become more compliant. Out of desperation, many physicians report that they find themselves switching strategies from visit to visit or even over the course of a single visit in the hope that another approach might be more successful with a particular patient. Clearly the combination of low levels of compliance and high levels of interpersonal frustration points to a significant problem that cries out for solution. I propose that part of this solution may be found in patients' own accounts of their noncompliant behaviors.

Accounts

An individual with diabetes has a multi-faceted treatment plan with which he or she must comply to remain relatively healthy. The vast majority of this compliance takes place in the lifeworld of the patient, with compliance decisions being made virtually each and every hour of each and every day. *Should I have syrup on my pancakes at breakfast? Should I take the cookie being offered to me at the office? Should I have an extra helping of rice at dinner? Do I have the time to go to the gym after work? Do I have the energy to get on my treadmill during the baby's nap?* One patient put it this way: "Diabetes never takes a vacation."

In stark contrast to this big, real-life world of patient compliance, the physician has a very limited view of this context for compliance when he or she is sitting with the patient within the four walls of his or her office. The typical individual with diabetes visits his or her physician every three months or so; between these visits life goes on, full of temptations. The patient makes decisions to comply or not multiple times each day—for a quarter of a year.

How can a physician gain crucial insight into the patient's lifeworld—and the patient's decisions relating to compliance—in the intervening months between doctor's visits? For help I turned to work by sociologists Scott and Lyman (1968: 46) on "accounts," which they define in the following way:

> An account is a linguistic device employed whenever an action is subjected to valuative inquiry. Such devices are a crucial element in the social order since they prevent conflicts from arising by verbally bridging the gap between action and expectation . . . . By an account, then, we mean a statement made by a social actor to explain unanticipated or untoward behavior.

Accounts as Evidence

Such verbal bridges between a patient's noncompliant actions and the patient's self-expectations (or, alternatively, recognition of others' expectations of him or her) can provide windows on individual struggles with compliance, on the individual circumstances of living with diabetes that are so critical to a physician's understanding of his or her patient. According to Scott and Lyman, accounts can be of two basic types: excuses, when one admits the act in question is bad, wrong, or inappropriate but denies full responsibility; and justifications, when one accepts responsibility for the act in question but denies the pejorative quality associated with it.

Of the twenty-four patients in this study, eighteen gave accounts in their post-interviews for some type of noncompliant action. Of those eighteen, fifteen were accounting for noncompliant actions related to food.[4] Fourteen of these fifteen accounts were excuses, as illustrated in excerpt 3.

Excerpt 3

Oh you don't stay on your diet in Las Vegas.

We went to buffets,

which is the worst thing in the world to do for a person that overeats.

They got lots of delicious desserts right on the counter there,

where you can walk by and pick up anything you want, any amount you want. It's impossible.. [laughter]

I'm a chocolate lover..

It's impossible to walk by.

In this account, the speaker implies that her actions at Las Vegas buffets were wrong but sends a strong message that she cannot be held fully responsible for her eating behavior. The words she chooses in the design of this account indicate no possibility of compliance in these circumstances: "You don't stay on your diet in Las Vegas" and "It's impossible to walk by."

Account Components

Recall that Scott and Lyman (1968: 46) characterize accounts as "verbally bridging the gap between action and expectation." I now turn to an examination of each of these basic notions—addressing first expectation and then action.

Expectation

In the accounts examined in this study, patients talk about these expectations in terms of knowledge—knowledge about expected actions regarding the fundamental compliance areas of diet, exercise, and medication. In excerpts 4 and 5, speakers refer to such knowledge by stating "I know" followed by a negated action ("I'm not doing everything right"; "I just can't rest until I have it"), shedding light on what the speaker expects to be the "right" course of action: being able to do everything right or to "rest" (not act) in the face of an "awful urge" (see Tannen 1979 on the relationship between negation and expectation).

Excerpt 4

I <u>know</u> I'm <u>not</u> doing everything right.

I like my sweets.

I just love my sweets.

They shouldn't have given me this.

They should have given me something else.

Some other disease.

Not this one, you know?

Because I love my sweets.

And I do eat them now and then.

Excerpt 5

Once in a while I get this awful urge

and I just <u>can't</u> rest [laughs] until I have it.

And when I have it I kind of feel bad

because I <u>know</u> it's wrong . . . .

I feel guilty after I eat it.

But before, it's just like something I can't..live without.

If I don't have it, I don't know what's going to happen.

And well, after I eat it, I do feel guilty.

When we look at every instance of such knowledge statements by patients in their accounts of noncompliance, it is striking that not one patient produces one utterance that refers to *lack* of knowledge (such as "I just didn't know that I wasn't supposed to . . . ") as a way of denying full responsibility for the resultant noncompliant action. Indeed, these patients seem to know very well how to manage their disease and what the expectations of them are in this regard, and they readily admit this knowledge to their interviewers (e.g., "I know I'm not doing everything right"; "I know it's wrong"; "I know I just can't do it [eat cookies]").

This impression is supported by explicit comments made by patients in other parts of our interviews with them following their visits with the doctor. Many patients spoke of intense frustration surrounding issues of compliance. They know what they need to do, but they struggle with other parts of the compliance puzzle. One patient told us, "Oh I know it, and he [the physician] doesn't have to explain it to me. I know it already." Another said, "There's nothing to tell. I know the situation. I know what it is. I know what I have to do."

These statements provide strong evidence that attempts by physicians to encourage patient compliance through education often are less than effective. Many office visits include choral recitations of facts or pedantic series of questions and answers; in these parts of the visit, both parties seem to be operating on autopilot. Patients appear to have dutifully learned *what* they need to do to comply but not *how* to do it.

Action

I turn now to a discussion of action; I argue that careful consideration of the issues related to diabetes compliance compels us to deconstruct the notion before we can move ahead. Noncompliance related to food and diabetes is related to (at least) two different types of action: procurement and consumption. Although it seems clear that only the act of actually consuming the food (not merely procuring it) constitutes noncompliance, how the food became available is relevant to the evaluation the noncompliant action receives when it is "subjected to valuative inquiry," in Scott and Lyman's (1968) terms. For example, in one of our interactions, a patient admitted to her physician that she ate some glazed doughnuts late one evening; the physician's next move was to ask how the doughnuts came to be in the house in the first place. The subsequent discovery that the patient had actually gone out to the store and bought this "forbidden" food resulted in the physician judging the patient more harshly than he would have if someone else had brought them into the home.

As illustrated in Figure 8.1, a fuller understanding of the first action (procurement) must include information about the intended consumer of the food. In learning how a particular "forbidden" food became available to the patient, we note four possibilities: The patient procured the food for himself or herself; the patient procured the food for someone else; someone else procured the food for the patient; or someone else procured the food for someone else (and the patient just happened to be near it). I return to these distinctions in the discussion of discourse patterns below.

When we look at every action statement uttered in patient accounts of noncompliance, again it is striking (as it was with the knowledge utterances) that the speakers are so straightforward in admitting their noncompliant actions. We hear patients saying, "I do indulge," "I'll have a piece of cake," "I'll have dessert," "I go get something to eat like candy," and "I go overboard." Not one hedge or downgrading adverb is found in any of these utterances (e.g., "I might eat a little bit.").

Thus, the question remains: If patients have the relevant knowledge to comply, why don't they?

Action 1: PROCUREMENT

> Who procured "forbidden" food?
>
>> Patient
>>
>> Other(s)
>
> Who was the intended consumer?
>
>> Patient
>>
>> Other(s)

Action 2: CONSUMPTION

> Did the patient consume the food?
>
> (No matter who procured it or who the intended consumer was)

Figure 8.1. Two types of action related to noncompliance

Bridging Expectations and Actions

In an attempt to answer this question, I now look to insights provided by patients as they try to account for the mismatch between their knowledge of expectations and their actions, which they consistently and straightforwardly acknowledge. As noted above, eighteen of the twenty-four patients in this study gave accounts in our post-interviews for some type of noncompliant action. Of these eighteen, fifteen patients gave accounts for food-related actions. In what follows, I first address one marked type of utterance in these verbal bridges—what I call "personal attribute statements"—and then I discuss the two structural patterns in these accounts.

Personal Attribute Statements

As I began my examination of the accounts, I was immediately struck by the frequent mention of personal attributes by these patients. Closer examination of the accounts revealed that nine of the fifteen patients included at least one such statement in their accounts (for a total of fourteen). A quick glance at representative utterances should confirm the fact that these are not just any personal attributes (such as eye color or height) but exactly those that are directly incompatible with the kinds of compliance that go along with diabetes: "I'm a chocolate lover," "I'm an emotional eater," "I'm a big pasta eater," "I'm bad around candy," and "I love sweets. I always have. I love sweets."

Why would so many patients incorporate personal attribute statements into their accounts? For a possible explanation, I return to Scott and Lyman (1968).

Recall that fourteen of the fifteen accounts are excuses rather than justifications and that, in designing an account as an excuse, the speaker admits that the act in question is "bad, wrong, or inappropriate" but denies full responsibility for it. Scott and Lyman (1968: 49) mention that one typical way speakers can mitigate or relieve responsibility for their actions is to appeal to biological drive. They elaborate as follows:

> Precisely because the body and its biological behavior are always present but not always accounted for in science or society, invocation of the body and its processes is available as an excuse. The body and its inner workings enjoy something of a status of the sociological stranger as conceived by Simmel, namely, that they are ever with us but mysterious. Hence, biological drives may be credited with influencing or causing at least some of the behavior for which actors wish to relieve themselves of full responsibility.

It seems likely, therefore, that these personal attributes play a strategic role in the verbal bridge between noncompliant actions and expectations. That is, when the speaker states in a straightforward way that he or she performed a noncompliant act in spite of the fact that he or she knew better, inclusion of a relevant personal attribute can excuse that behavior by removing some of the speaker's agency (as if to imply, "I'm just that way. What can I do about it?").

Account Structure

To explore more fully the function of these mentions of personal attributes within patient accounts of noncompliance, I move now from an investigation of the individual clauses that constitute the accounts to an examination of accounts as whole texts. In this way, we can come to understand how patients portray how they came to perform noncompliant acts.

Two major structural patterns emerged in this analysis. Both patterns start and end the same way. In both patterns, the knowledge component remains relatively stable across tokens, as is expected from our earlier discussion of patient knowledge; that is, most patients in this study seem to (think they) know what they need to do to be compliant. Likewise, in both patterns, the account contains evidence that the patient carried out the action of consuming the "forbidden" food. What differentiates the two patterns is the constitution of the verbal bridge that connects these two components of knowledge and action.

To understand these differences, we need first to expand on the foregoing discussion about patient compliance. I have noted that one condition for such compliance is sufficient relevant knowledge about recommended diet, exercise, and medication. I also have noted, however, that in many cases knowledge is not enough. Fully informed patients still perform noncompliant actions. Motivation must be added to this knowledge. Patients must feel motivated to comply with the many difficult choices they must make in a life with diabetes. This motivation can be found in a variety of different sources—some extrinsic and others intrinsic to the individual. For example, some individuals tell us in their post-interviews that they are motivated by fear of kidney failure or amputation—common medical problems that accompany uncontrolled diabetes. Other individuals find motivation in their grandchildren.

Just as with knowledge, however, sometimes a person's motivation is not strong enough to ensure constant compliance. Patients are confronted with many roadblocks along the way that wear down their motivation. These barriers must be identified to be overcome. Examples of roadblocks mentioned in the patient post-interviews include unsupportive family members, friends, or co-workers who may tempt the patient to ignore his or her dietary restrictions; a hectic business travel schedule; or even a patient's own sense of self—as reflected, for example, in the foregoing personal attribute statements. The balance between a given patient's motivations and his or her roadblocks is delicate; for a patient to remain compliant, his or her motivations must be stronger than the roadblocks. In situations where the roadblocks overpower the motivations, the patient may be on the path to noncompliance.

With this understanding of motivation and roadblock added to the notions of knowledge and two action types, we can resume our characterization of the differences between the two account patterns. Pattern 1, as illustrated in Figure 8.2, is what I call the "give in and go get" account. This type of account begins with the identification of (or allusion to) a tension between a motivation and a roadblock, with the roadblock temporarily defeating the motivation. This unstable situation leads the patient to carry out the first action, procurement, which makes the "forbidden" food available to him or her. The patient then performs the second action, consumption.

Excerpt 6 illustrates an account of this type. Note that the roadblock in this account is characterized as a personal attribute ("I crave the sweets"). According to the account-giver, her (unspecified) motivation to comply usually keeps the

1. KNOWLEDGE

2. MOTIVATION<->ROADBLOCK tension

3. Action 1 (PROCUREMENT) by patient

4. Action 2 (CONSUMPTION) by patient

Figure 8.2. Patient accounts of noncompliance: Pattern 1 ("give in and go get")

roadblock in check. Here, however, the roadblock overcomes the motivation, and the patient goes to "get something to eat like candy."

> *Excerpt 6*
>
> Even though I stay away from them pretty much,
>
> **I crave the sweets.**
>
> And every once in a while
>
> **I go get something to eat like candy or something like that.**
>
> But then I know for the next couple of days
>
> I've got to really watch it and stuff like that.

The performance of the second action, consumption, is left unstated, although it is clear from the stated consequences ("for the next couple of days I've got to really watch it") that the action was indeed carried out.

Pattern 2, as illustrated in Figure 8.3, is what I call the "see and succumb" account. In this type of account, the "forbidden" food becomes available to the patient; that is, the patient has not procured it himself or herself. The availability of the food, then, is the destabilizing force as related to the tension between motivation and roadblock. Just as in pattern 1 above, the roadblock in pattern 2 temporarily overcomes the motivation, leading the patient to perform the second action, consumption.

Excerpt 7 illustrates an account of this type. In this situation, the speaker's children bring the "forbidden" food into his house in the form of candy collected door-to-door on Halloween.[5] The availability of the candy, then, destabilizes the precarious balance between the speaker's (unspecified) motivation to comply and his roadblocks to compliance, expressed (as in excerpt 6) as a personal attribute ("I'm an old Reese's Peanut Butter Cup freak").

1. KNOWLEDGE

2. Action 1 (PROCUREMENT) by other

3. MOTIVATION<->ROADBLOCK tension

4. Action 2 (CONSUMPTION) by patient

Figure 8.3. Patient accounts of noncompliance: Pattern ("see and succumb")

Excerpt 7

Let's see, the other night was what.

It was Sunday night.

The kids came home with big shopping bags full of -

I'm an old Reese's Peanut Butter Cup freak.

I used to..and all my kids,

I have three of them.

Before I had diabetes,

my two oldest ones,

I'd take them out,

I'd say

"You both owe me at least two Reese's.

Keep going until you get two Reese's

and the rest of it's yours."

That was kind of like a family joke.

So now it's just carried on with my stepson.

So, of course he..the first one he gets,

he's ready to win.

He's like "Here, Dad!"

"Hmmm.

I shouldn't,

but I guess I will."

So I.. I have a weakness there.

As in pattern 1, the roadblock temporarily overcomes the motivation, leading the patient to eat the candy. As in excerpt 6, the consumption action in excerpt 7 is not explicitly stated, although it can be confidently inferred through the speaker's reported conversational exchange with his stepson ("He's like, 'Here, Dad!' 'Hmmm. I shouldn't, but I guess I will.'").

Bringing Accounts into the Doctor's Office

Close examination of the language in and of the accounts has revealed just a hint of the array of varying circumstances that can lead a patient to perform noncompliant actions in the face of knowledge and motivations that would indicate otherwise. Patients themselves know that their individual sets of circumstances are different from other patients and call out for individual attention from their doctors, as seen in excerpts 8 and 9.

> *Excerpt 8*
>
> I don't want to be treated like all the other patients.
>
> I want to be treated as an individual.
>
> I have to be treated as me.

> *Excerpt 9*
>
> Sure, we all want to do it,
>
> but I'm Terry.
>
> You got to say,
>
> "Well, okay, you're a little chubby.
>
> Take five steps instead of ten."
>
> Do you know what I mean?
>
> He's [the physician] got to use his common sense for the person he's handling is what I believe.

These individual differences underlying noncompliant actions challenge physicians to (re)consider the strategies they employ to encourage patients to make choices that will lead to better health. In conversations with patients, one size does *not* fit all. Most doctors understand this point, but they often slip into what look like autopilot monologues regarding complications of uncontrolled diabetes or quick verbal slaps on the wrist, with no exploration of the reasons for patient noncompliance.

One of the greatest dangers of this kind of untailored talk on the part of physicians may be that it (unintentionally) blocks out the vast majority of information contained in accounts such as those discussed in this essay. One of the best ways to expand the domain of the physician-patient talk—to get it to include life outside of the physician's office—is for physicians to encourage account-giving by their patients. In some cases, this strategy may lead to more thorough understanding of an unsupportive family or a heavy business travel schedule that makes compliance difficult. In these cases, some creative solutions may be custom-designed to fit the problem. In other cases, the accounts might identify a personal attribute of the patient that is directly at odds with compliant actions. In such cases, practical solutions may be more difficult to come by, and the physician may need to help the patient "try on" a new identity (in the sense of Bruner 1990: 54) that is more compatible with compliant behavior.

To illustrate the interactional effect of physicians' moves on the patient discourse, I briefly refer now to three different physician-patient scenarios from our study. In each case, the issue of patient noncompliance came up within the first minute or so of the visit. That is where the similarity ends, however. I look at each in turn and focus on what the physician does immediately following the patient's admission of noncompliance.

In excerpt 10, the patient has had problems complying with her treatment because of a death in her family.

> *Excerpt 10*
>
> Patient: Everything was irregular. My whole life was upside down. I wasn't eating properly. I wasn't watching what I was eating.
>
> Physician: We've got to make progress on this, because we can't leave it the way it was. You can't tolerate that. It's totally out of whack. We've got to get things back under control.

In excerpt 10, the physician's utterances immediately following the confession of noncompliance by the patient address the present situation ("It's totally out of whack") as well as the future ("We've got to make progress on this," "We've got to get things back under control"). Note that the physician makes no move that allows exploration of the circumstances surrounding the noncompliance.

In excerpt 11, the patient has had trouble complying because of stress at work.

> *Excerpt 11*
>
> Physician: You haven't been losing lots of weight, I see.
>
> Patient: No, I'm about the same.
>
> Physician: Okay. How has your vision been? No double vision?

Following the inferrable admission of noncompliance by the patient ("No, I'm about the same") in response to the physician's observation that the patient has not lost any weight, the physician quickly acknowledges her statement and then abruptly changes the topic. As in excerpt 10, no move by the physician allows exploration of the circumstances underlying the patient's difficulty with compliance.

In excerpt 12, the patient was having problems complying because she was ambivalent about starting a medication that might have problematic gastrointestinal side effects.

Excerpt 12

Patient: Well, I haven't done anything that I said I was going to do.

Physician: Were you worried about side effects?

Here the physician immediately responds to the patient's statement of noncompliance with a question about the past. Although this question is a yes-no question rather than a more open-ended "wh-" question—such as "Why not?" or "What happened to stop you?"—the fact that the physician gave the patient a possible reason for not having complied with her treatment plan opens the door to a discussion of other reasons the patient might have had (e.g., "No, I wasn't, but . . . ").

If physicians wish to increase patient compliance with their recommendations and are convinced of the potential value of patient accounts in shedding light on individual circumstances surrounding noncompliance, it seems obvious that their contributions to the discourse of the physician-patient interaction must encourage the giving of such accounts. Neither the future orientation of excerpt 10 nor the abrupt topic change of excerpt 11 will facilitate the type of exploration of the circumstances leading to noncompliance that is necessary for a change in action that leads to a change in health. The discourse of excerpt 12, with its opening to the past, offers a step in the right direction.

Conclusion

Patient noncompliance in diabetes is rampant and presents a great challenge to patients as well as to their physicians. Frustration on all sides is highly evident in physician-patient interactions as well as in post-interviews with physicians and patients in our study. Strategies that physicians are using—from reciting facts and figures to instilling fear in the patient—usually are ineffective. And we've seen why. Patients tell us that they already know the facts but that this knowledge is not always enough to keep them toeing the line of compliance.

Our investigation of the language and structural patterns of accounts given by patients in our post-interviews has provided us with rich information that was unavailable to the physicians during their interactions with these patients. As patients construct verbal bridges between the expectations and knowledge they possess and the actions they clearly acknowledge are noncompliant, they provide the analyst with crucial details about themselves and their life circumstances that seem to stand in the way—at least some of the time—of healthy lifestyle choices. By teaching physicians about the vital connection between the discursive choices they make and the subsequent moves available to their patients, we can help physicians make changes that encourage patient account-giving in their offices.

As interesting and convincing as this line of argument may be to us as linguists, I have learned through my work with physicians that the decisive test is whether these language changes ultimately result in concrete, specific changes in patient outcomes. That is, will these changes in discourse actually lead patients to better compliance that will then lead to better health? The next phase of our study is designed to address these real-life concerns. Until those results are in, I remain optimistic that those of us investigating the language of health care encounters can help physicians and patients as they struggle turn-by-turn to understand not only the physical symptoms but the sometimes more elusive reasons behind the choices made by patients as they strive for the best health they can have.

NOTES

1. I am indebted to Deborah Tannen for her many insightful comments and suggestions on an earlier draft of this chapter.
2. Some scholars and practitioners avoid the use of the term "compliance" (and, therefore, "noncompliance") because they think it conjures up an image of passive patients who have nothing to say about their own treatment plans and whose sole job it is to carry out their doctors' orders. In its place, their term of choice is "adherence." Despite these very important concerns, I have decided to use the terms "compliance" and "noncompliance" throughout this essay because they are the terms used by the physicians and the patients in this study. My use of these terms is not meant to imply anything about a given patient's level of self-advocacy or the level of collaboration between patient and physician in devising the patient's treatment plan.
3. According to the cover story in the March 5, 2001, issue of the *Washington Post* Health section.
4. Of the other three accounts, one each was related to blood glucose testing, exercise, and foot care.
5. In the United States it is customary for children to dress up in costumes and go door-to-door to collect candy on Halloween (October 31).

REFERENCES

Ainsworth-Vaughn, Nancy. 1998. *Claiming power in doctor-patient talk.* Oxford: Oxford University Press.

American Diabetes Association. 1992. *Direct and indirect costs of diabetes in the United States in 1992.* Alexandria, Va.: American Diabetes Association.

Anderson, R. M. 1985. Is the problem of compliance all in our heads? *Diabetes Education* 11: 31–34.

Benkendorf, Judith L., Michele B. Prince, Mary A. Rose, Anna DeFina, and Heidi E. Hamilton. 2001. Does indirect speech promote nondirective genetic counseling? *American Journal of Medical Genetics* 106: 199–207.

Bruner, Jerome. 1990. *Acts of meaning.* Cambridge, Mass.: Harvard University Press.

Ciechanowski, Paul S., Wayne J. Katon, Joan E. Russo, and Edward A. Walker. 2001. The patient-provider relationship: Attachment theory and adherence to treatment in diabetes. *American Journal of Psychiatry* 158 (1): 29–35.

Frankel, Richard M. 1994. *Communicating with patients: Research shows it makes a difference.* Deerfield, Ill.: MMI Co.

Frankel, Richard M., and H. B. Beckman. 1995. Accuracy of the medical history: A review of current concepts and research. In *The medical interview,* edited by Mack J. Lipkin, Samuel M. Putman, and Aaron Lazare. New York: Springer Verlag, 511–24.

Hamilton, Heidi E. 1994a. *Conversations with an Alzheimer's patient.* Cambridge: Cambridge University Press.

———. 1994b. Requests for clarification as evidence of pragmatic comprehension difficulty: The case of Alzheimer's disease. In *Discourse analysis and applications: Studies in adult clinical populations,* edited by Ronald Bloom, Loraine Obler, Susan DeSanti, and J. Ehlich. Mahwah, N.J.: Erlbaum, 185–99.

———. 1994c. Ethical issues for applying linguistics to clinical contexts: The case of speech-language pathology. *Issues in Applied Linguistics* (special issue on Ethical Issues for Applying Linguistics, edited by Jeff Connor-Linton and Carolyn T. Adger): 207–23.

———. 1996. Intratextuality, intertextuality and the construction of identity as patient in Alzheimer's disease. *Text* 16 (1): 61–90.

———. 1998. Reported speech and survivor identity in on-line bone marrow transplantation narratives. *Journal of Sociolinguistics* 2 (1): 53–67.

Larson, Elaine, Heidi E. Hamilton, Kathleen Mitchell, and John Eisenberg. 1998. Hospitalk: An exploratory study to assess what is said and what is heard between physicians and nurses. *Clinical Performance and Quality Health Care* 6 (4): 183–89.

Maynard, Douglas W. 1991. The perspective-display series and the delivery and receipt of diagnostic news. In *Talk and social structure,* edited by Deirdre Boden and Don Zimmerman. Berkeley: University of California Press, 164–92.

Mishler, Elliot G. 1984. *The discourse of medicine.* Norwood, N.J.: Ablex.

Scott, Marvin, and Stanford Lyman. 1968. Accounts. *American Sociological Review,* 46–62.

Tannen, Deborah. 1979. What's in a frame? Surface evidence for underlying expectations. In *New directions in discourse processing,* edited by Roy O. Freedle. Norwood, N.J.: Ablex, 137–81.

Tannen, Deborah, and Cynthia Wallat. 1982. A sociolinguistic analysis of multiple demands on the pediatrician in doctor/mother/child interaction. In *Linguistics and the professions,* edited by Robert J. Di Pietro. Norwood, N.J.: Ablex, 39–50.

ten Have, Paul. 1991. Talk and institution: A reconsideration of the "asymmetry" of doctor-patient interaction. In *Talk and social structure,* edited by Deirdre Boden and Don Zimmerman. Berkeley: University of California Press, 138–63.

Discourse of denial

Shirley Brice Heath
Stanford University

Those of us who study learning and socialization practices that surround oral and written language constantly hear policymakers and practitioners in education call for "more research." Implied within such pleas is the view that "best practices" for improving achievement, developing innovative effective learning environments, and making knowledge from a host of fields available for decision making will or even "should" come from research. Closely attached to calls for more research, particularly in the field of literacy learning, is promotion of the idea that collecting information from the targeted population for reading and writing instruction will lead to improved teaching methods and materials.

This essay illustrates through two cases the linguistic means that policymakers and educators often use to deflect, ignore, or twist research results and target-population data sources. The first case revolves around the recent and unexpected thrust into the policy world of my research on out-of-school learning environments, especially those centered in the arts. That research, carried out for more than a decade in regions across the United States, has centered on three questions: What parts of organized learning environments do participants regard as positive and desirable? How does language socialization take place here? What strategies of interaction, collaboration, and planful behavior are evidenced within these environments?

The second case draws from work I did in the summer of 2000 in the highlands of Papua New Guinea. I worked there with linguists and literacy workers who were attempting to determine ways to bring literacy more meaningfully into the lives of villagers living in remote areas of the country. In many of these regions, multinational corporations are closing in rapidly to extract natural resources—particularly diamonds, gold, oil, and timber. The harm being done to the environment can no longer be tracked or measured because the pace is so rapid and the devastation so intense and unrelenting. My role during my time there was to listen to villagers, linguists, and literacy workers and to help them think through possible answers to the following questions (among others): What languages, genres, and styles of information presentation are villagers most likely to use in making communal decisions about their environmental resources? What are the local practices of interaction that surround the inclusion of written information into decision-making routines that otherwise are primarily oral and visual (e.g., through the use of symbols other than those of print—maps, landmarks, etc.)?

Learning in the Arts

The development of my search for effective learning environments beyond the family and school came about through continuation of my study of families of Trackton and Roadville (Heath 1983). I have followed 300 of these families for more than thirty years, and it has become increasingly clear that changes in family structures and pressures on classroom life have created, for most young people of the United States, a trajectory of language socialization that differs radically from that assumed by child language scholars and developmental psychologists. Young people beyond the age of eight spend very little time engaged in project-based or planful learning opportunities with their parents, and classrooms that are pushed to teach to standardized test performance leave little time for sustained project-based learning. School districts increasingly cut budgets for arts and shop classes during the school day, as well as for extracurricular after-school activities such as theatre or dance. Hence the grandchildren and children of the families of Roadville and Trackton grow up in environments dominated by peer experiences and popular culture. With entertainers such as Britney Spears, Little Bow Wow, and the Spice Girls and chain compact disc, video, and fashion stores racing to enlist eight- to twelve-year-olds (now called "the betwixt" or "tweens") as consumers, shopping malls or other public spaces for display have become key language socialization contexts. Neither adult mentors nor long-term plans and productive engagement mark these learning environments.

Vying with these spaces are the relatively few youth-centered organizations that can match the appeal of "hanging out," "doing nothing," or "just being with my friends." Through a process of exemplary sampling over a decade, I sought out many of these organizations in the United States and England and, with a team of young anthropologists, recorded and observed how they operated as learning environments. Although these community organizations included athletic-academic teams, as well as community service groups, the grouping I focus on here includes only arts-based organizations. All of these organizations, however, reflected several common features. They operate as places of high risk that engage young people in tasks that challenge and responsibilities that are real. All of the organizations create learning environments that depend on young people across an age range (generally from eight to eighteen) who take on roles and responsibilities that are essential to the life of the group. Youth members work on budget planning as well as building security concerns; they design sets for theatre and plan team travel. Young people in these groups find themselves immersed in situations that force them to ask "what if?" or "how about?" or "just in case...?"

Organizations of this type that offer the highest risk—because they depend on pursuit of the imagination, the conditional, the possible—invariably are those devoted to the arts: dance, theatre, visual or graphic arts, creative writing, or music. These organizations move young people through planning, preparing, and practicing toward a performance, exhibition, or production, followed by evaluation. Through all of these stages, critique figures heavily, as young artists question one another on the meaning, process, and intention of their work. In addition, these organizations ensure continual contact by the young members with professional artists, who lead the young artists through critique and hold them to high expectations.

I have written elsewhere about the ways in which these organizations scaffold young members as they take on highly responsible roles that emphasize thinking, planning, being accountable, looking ahead, and reflecting well on the group. Mental state verbs, modals, conditionals, and complex hypothetical proposals of all sorts pepper the talk of youths who take part in such organizations. These structures become part of the habitual talk of young people, who spend approximately ten hours per week over thirty to forty-two weeks in at least one year of sustained involvement within their organizations (Heath, Soep, and Roach 1998; Heath and Smyth 2000; Heath and Roach 1999). Syntactic structures and inclusion of references to sources outside the individual experience characterize language development of these young people. Developing an ease of production with these structures enables young people to take part in group planning, self-monitoring to think about the future, and expecting to evaluate a process and its outcomes. Young people actively engage with the full organizational environment, take part in a temporal arc of effort, and bring intrinsic motivation to their activities within their youth organization (Larson 2000). Not surprisingly, the confidence, habits of thinking, and ways of speaking they develop there become part of their self-representation within other contexts, such as school, peer groups, and family settings.

Along with this context of language socialization, arts organizations depend heavily on the growth and development of skills associated with numeracy and financial record management and reporting, such as estimating, calculating, balancing alternative decisions, and justifying expenditures. Writing across a variety of genres—from grants to public relations to theatre program notes to history and biography—also advances confidence and fluency in language use. Repeated practice of these skills results from the fact that young people take on major and minor tasks that keep the organization going and account for its successes and failures. Often these groups devote some of their effort to entrepreneurial activities that bring in some funding to sustain the organization (Heath and Smyth 2000).

It is no surprise that such learning in the arts, even for young people at highest risk from a host of social and economic factors, helps engender and reinforce strong value orientations toward community commitment, social equity, academic achievement, and seeking knowledge from a variety of sources, written, experiential, and personal (Heath and Roach 1999). It also is no surprise that in terms of strategic planning and weighing of consequences the young people intensively involved in the arts organizations of the type described here expect a great deal of themselves and feel accountable for their actions.

Denial of Possibilities

What is surprising, however, is that educators and policymakers—as well as funders—actively deny the possibilities and promise of creating learning environments of this sort. Even though educators frequently call for research to show when and how high-risk young people learn, they deny the idea that what happens within community youth organizations can complement and supplement school learning or merit consideration in teacher education or classroom reform. Neither statistical evidence comparing the young people of these organizations with those of the National Education Longitudinal Survey nor long-term qualitative contextual and linguistic research leads educators, policymakers, or funders to a sense of probability. The following comments characterize their responses.

> Come on, there are teachers who do just this kind of thing in their classrooms. Just the other day, I visited a school where three teachers were combining their classes across history, English, and civics for the students to create a dramatic reading. I see the sort of thing your youth organizations do every day in the schools I visit. This kind of stuff does not have to take place after school; it's already happening within schools.

> What you're talking about will take away from schools; that's where all of America's kids are, and that's where we have to put our efforts and our resources. The kind of thing you want seems to me to be the responsibility of the parents. Why, when I was a kid, everybody got carted somewhere after school every day to do something, and parents today know how important these after-school activities are. Look at how karate clubs are thriving, and little girls still do ballet and gymnastics, don't they? You don't think for one minute, do you, that any kid is going to get into any decent college today without the extracurricular, do you?

> But the kids you found had to be special. You can't tell me these are your run-of-the mill kids from inner cities. In their cases, some kind of magic happened—they were just in the right place at the right time with the right person in charge of some after-school group. These kinds of kids would have made it even without these organizations.

These responses illustrate four strategies for denying research findings. First is "narrative avoidance," in which the respondent simply provides an engaging narrative that is intended to dispute or disprove the claim of the research. In this tactic, one apparent "counter case" is sufficient to set aside research findings that are based on dozens of organizations in various regions of the country. Counterexamples follow the belief system—and, even more important, the categorizing framework—held by those who deny research evidence. Narratives that are most effective at avoiding engagement with the findings are marked by at least four stylistic maneuvers:

- Use of diminutive descriptors to refer to components of research findings: *sort of, kind of stuff, this kind of thing*
- Assertion of speaker authority as agent of knowing and seeing contrary evidence: *when I was a kid, I see, I visited*
- Attribution to researcher of overdrawn or unreasonable claims: *what you're talking about will take away...; you can't tell me these are your run-of-the mill kids....*
- Transfer of research from the groups involved in the study to other, unrelated groups: *you don't think for one minute...decent colleges today*

In addition to the use of avoidance narratives, many rebuttals or denials reflect a second characteristic of denial discourse: assertion of dichotomies that do not exist.

American educators hold strongly to dichotomies for reasons that lie deep within what may be called "companion comparatives." Terms such as "God and country," "family and school," "either in or out, for or against," and "either right or wrong" typify public discourse, as well as explanations that authorities give to young people about rules or moral beliefs to guide their behavior. The duo of "family and school" as primary socializing forces for children and young people has no place for beliefs or category labels for community youth organizations that give young people real responsibilities for management and development. There is no companion comparative for communities as learning agents or contexts.

Moreover, people who refuse to accept research findings on positive learning consequences from the participation of young people in activities outside the control of family or school are aided by the fact that there is no fixed label or identifiable agent for the time when young people are not in school, except terms such as _nonschool_ or _out-of-school_. My research has tried to plant the term *community-based* within the field of developmental psychology as well as anthropology, but this idea has not taken root. Hence, because what I describe is seen as *nonschool* or *out-of-school*, the findings from the research inevitably become set *against* schools. This third strategy sets up the research findings on learning as somehow critical of or oppositional to schools. If assertions are made that learning is taking place *outside* of schools through creation of certain kinds of contexts and activities, the implication must be that these positive forces do not or cannot operate *inside* schools.

A final feature of denial discourse on the topic of learning within community contexts springs from the fact that those legitimated by credentials or degrees from formal education regard other types of learning as inherently noncategorizable and hence irrational and chaotic. Thus, American educators rarely take seriously agents, contexts, or conditions of learning that are not guided or directed by formal instruction. Whereas the research community, as well as educators, in other postindustrial nations (most notably Canada and England) engage systematically with lifelong learning, expert learning through retraining, professional training, and development within job settings, U.S. scholars of learning and policymakers do not regard such learning as linked to K–12 or even postsecondary schooling. Other than early childhood studies, second-language acquisition research, or examination of rehabilitation (e.g., of delinquents, convicted criminals, drug- or alcohol-addicted individuals), developmental research has given almost no attention to how learning takes place beyond highly specific formal educational contexts. Terms that apply to such situations invariably fall into patterns of category-assignment that carry negative connotations—for example, "adult education," "rehabilitation," or "retraining." In all of these cases, the labels suggest a failure to have "gotten it right" in earlier education during the K-16 years and therefore the need for a "second go" at being educated appropriately.

Reflecting on the kinds of learning habits and orientation to new knowledge and skills that young people gain when they are learning, playing, or working on their own would mean taking seriously not only "<u>in</u>formal" or "<u>non</u>formal" learning (note again the dichotomous labeling) but also the massive training and development industry that the United States and other postindustrial nations use to ensure a ready workforce. The annual budget for such work can exceed that of public schooling, but educators and developmentalists pay little or no attention to this industry, which is largely responsible for ongoing or lifelong learning. On the other hand, business interests—from managers to advertisers—focus intently on learning that goes on outside formal instruction and generally through goals linked to learning for improved work, leisure, health, or human relations. Spaces such as shopping malls or modes of transport, as well as locations of medical services, are devoted largely to promoting learning that is not school-based but complements, influences, and supplements formal educational achievements in numerous ways. Yet educators remain so tied to a semantic web in which "education" links almost exclusively to school, classroom, teacher, curriculum, formal education, and K–16 that they find it difficult to construct learning beyond this web.

Making Literacy Meaningful for Communities

In Papua New Guinea (PNG) in the summer of 2000, village representatives from several communities along the Sepik River met in the highlands with linguists and literacy "experts" to talk about the role of written language(s) in their communities. A group of Angor men from a Sepik village near the Irian Jaya border came to report on their struggle to convince villagers not to allow a multinational corporation to cut the timber in their area in return for a one-time payment that the men realized was far below the actual value of the resource. Moreover, based on the experience of other villages, these men knew that erosion and other detrimental effects on the life of the remote community would follow after communal division of the one-time cash payment. These men, all of whom had some literacy skills, instead wanted to have a portable sawmill in their own village, following the example of a distant village that had successfully established a thriving sawmill run by local men.

In the course of several meetings among literacy workers, linguists, educators, and village representatives, I asked the men to describe just how written materials could figure in their efforts to save their village timber from multinationals and to start a local sawmill on their own. My hope was that such questions from a "white skin" outsider would enable the men to explain to expatriates and nationals involved in literacy instruction their village practices around external sources of information. I particularly wanted them to make clear to everyone present which languages, for which uses, they depended on in their efforts to persuade other villagers not to take the ready-cash offer of multinational corporations. These men identified fully with their village, but they also knew that edicts came from Port Moresby, the nation's capital, and the bureaucracies there. I elaborated my question by asking them also about the uses of oral languages that had gone into their deliberations.

I asked them to describe "all the pieces of paper, all the pieces of writing that have come through your plans so far...[what are] the many kinds of reading and writing you have had to do." Robert Litteral, a linguist (whom the villagers referred to as Bob) who had worked in the area for decades, translated my questions into either the local language or Tok Pisin, the *lingua franca* known to all of these village members, and one of the men responded in Tok Pisin:

> Ismoe: It is like I said before. Bob went to Moresby and he got the pamphlet from the Environment Conservation [Commission?] and brought it back. This council teaches how about things [connected to the environment] and how to look after the money of sawmill businesses. I read all these things and I had an idea. I already was thinking that I would like to do a similar business in my village, so later I went back to the village and talked with the other three neighboring villages.

Litteral then repeated my question about their talk: "When you went and talked with all the people in the other villages, how did you go about that? What did you do? Did you stand up and talk, sit down and talk, for a short time, once or several times? Did you go yourselves or did others go? OK, when you went, how did you create interest in the idea or talk with people about this idea?"

> Ismoe: Yes, well, to do this I did not stand up and just talk, we did it in our ways. We sat down with some of the big men of the village, and some of the younger men came too. And we tried to find out the thinking. We pooled our thinking together and we talked with them all. And some of the big men were there listening, and they were in agreement with our thinking. We didn't stand and talk; no, we sat down at the regular meeting place near one of the houses in the shade and we talked with everyone.

Litteral expanded:

> When the Local Government Council was going on, the people went to the council meeting, and they came back. Then they met with everyone at the village. They were in the village and spoke about things they had heard at the council meeting, and people responded to the talk about it. So they talked about it in the village, sitting down. They didn't stand up like learned or knowledgeable men and teach others.

Subsequent discussion revealed that the men had read brochures written in Tok Pisin and talked over the meaning of the brochures in Tok Pisin with officials in Port Moresby. When they returned to their own village, however, they spoke in their local language at the Council and in related informal meetings. The men agreed that because some of their villagers could read the native language, having brochures in their language would have helped. They went on to acknowledge, however, that they knew that their own recordkeeping, reports, and documentation supporting their local sawmill and rejecting the offer of the multinational corporation would need to be in English. For this material, the village would be dependent on one of their members who had become a teacher and received a diploma from a teacher's college.

Some nationals from other locations, such as Western Highlands Province, added to the account by the Angor men of how information moved across languages and means (oral, written, mapped, and "walked"—as in walking the property lines by use of landmarks designating boundaries). Rambai Keruwa, from the Kaugel community, noted that he could attribute his reading development not only to influential and supportive teachers in his local village school but also to having seen an adult man bring reading materials to the village and talk by reference to them. The man read and talked in English; Keruwa decided that he would do the same, realizing that through English he would have access to new information. Within his village, people who are literate read on their own and then orally pass on the information they have gained. To read aloud or display one's reading abilities in public—except for designated institutional individuals, such as teachers and pastors—is to bring shame to others who may not be able to read. Similarly, reading while engaged in a conversational setting within the village would not be tolerated or even useful because reading aloud becomes a performance in which readers and listeners cannot gain meaning at the same time. Keruwa emphasized, "People are more comfortable if the presenter reads the information in his or her own time, digests it, and then explains, in their own ways, the information that they want the people to know about." In short, there is more credibility in discussing, explaining, and interpreting something than in just reading from a page. Thus, knowing "how to read" within a village means knowing how to interpret reading within talk that conforms to local norms of interaction, respect, and validation.

The linguists, educators, and literacy "experts" present—many of whom were expatriates—found that these first-hand accounts challenged two primary ends of both school instruction and adult literacy teaching: the value of reading aloud and otherwise displaying one's reading skills in public arenas. They asked questions such as, "But is what these men refer to as they describe uses of reading and writing really 'literacy,' or is it something else like development?" "How does this kind of work by a learner relate to our tasks as literacy instructors of individual learners?" Preparation as a literacy worker or educator emphasizes the importance of having individuals show their ability to read orally—a means by which the teacher gains control over knowledge about the quality and level of decoding skills of the reader.

The villagers (all of whom were literate in two or three languages—Tok Pisin, the local language, and/or English) made clear that a wide range of texts in several languages could be made accessible to villagers, as long as oral patterns of information transmission were honored. Helped by representatives from other villages across Papua New Guinea, the men developed a list of types of texts (from forestry brochures to instructions for ordering parts for the sawmill) and the preferred language(s) for each, as well as arenas for oral transmittal of information (e.g., within the Local Council or informal meetings).

Strongly evident was the fact that uses of written language can (and probably will) remain broad. Moreover, information from written sources will become available to many villagers if a few knowledge brokers from each village can successfully meet local oral transmission norms. Reading *per se* is likely to remain a largely covert, rather than overt, literacy practice in PNG villages until more opportunities to learn to read in local languages are available. Of special import to educators, linguists, and literacy workers (particularly those accustomed to promoting reading aloud within church services or council meetings) was the revelation that the range of texts being accessed by villagers who can read is broad. Moreover, readers find ways to share written information with their extended family, the village, and sometimes other villages as well. The range of these types of texts shared in these ways surpassed in number and variety those of non-PNG members of the group, who found it difficult to admit that most of their reading was individual and not shared or distributed to others by word of mouth. For PNG villages, the texts shared in almost all situations would not be present during talk about the texts, whereas on some occasions the actual presence of the written material would amount to validation, but no one would read aloud.

None of this information about ways that different societies make use of literacy is new. For several decades, scholars have illustrated a host of ways that communities transfer, transform, and complement information that comes in written forms. Much of this research draws from first-hand accounts by readers of the ways in which oral language and other means of communication surround uses of written information. Yet belief systems instilled in training to be a literacy worker or teacher make denial of such accounts easy. Within Papua New Guinea and many other parts of the world, people who are most responsible for enabling villagers to learn to read find ways to dichotomize and to renarrativize local knowledge. They raise questions such as the following: If the ability of an individual reader to decode cannot be evidenced by overt public performance, is what is taking place actually *literacy*? Such overt oral transmission of knowledge from written material, particularly with regard to matters of importance to entire communities, seems to be something else—such as community development, public health, or environmental education—not *literacy*.

A second question that emerges is this: If someone is trained to teach and test for the acquisition of reading and writing skills, should the uses, retention, or expansion of these skills be of concern to the literacy instructor? Training to be a literacy worker or teacher instills the idea that these responsibilities should reside with the learner as an individual achiever. In other words, the transfer of individual literacy skills to the public arena seems to lie outside the purview or responsibility of literacy teachers. Yet, as was evident in the accounts given by the villagers, their individual acquisition of reading and writing skills through literacy instruction had taken root in their individual habits and had spread knowledge ultimately primarily through their oral skills. Complex strategies of summarizing, explaining, casting into future scenarios, and transforming into action were demanded of the literate because they could not simply read from a page or text to enable others to use written information.

International groups such as the World Health Organization, UNESCO, and the United Nations increasingly argue that raising the literacy level of the poorest nations of the world will enhance opportunities for regional development, improved health, and sustained educational interests among the residents of those nations. The Papua New Guinea illustration indicates that the portability of literacy skills to any of these ends will spring inevitably from ensuring that individual readers also acquire highly complex strategies for using written information for communal transmission. Yet literacy workers and their trainers find it easy to deny that their responsibilities extend beyond ensuring decoding skills and individual performance of interpretation of reading abilities.

Final Comments

In both of the cases I discuss in this essay, the discourse of denial carries similar bases of rejection: Agents without legitimation by formal instruction or education institutions have assumed authority over learning. In the first case, parents, politicians, and public-school advocates overclaim benefits of the formal instruction of schools in the face of research findings that show the positive effects of other organized learning environments. In the second case, villagers took authority over their own learning to guide them to use their literacy skills in ways that were compatible with oral language habits and social norms of their region. When faced with this authoritative experience, "trained" literacy workers were led to question fundamental meanings of reading and writing as distinct from development work. The two cases illustrate the boundaries that education installs to keep out what Clifford Geertz calls "local knowledge" or "experience-near" understandings. Geertz warns:

> To grasp concepts that, for another people, are *experience-near,* and to do so well enough to place them in illuminating connection with *experience-distant* concepts theorists have fashioned to capture the general features of social life, is clearly a task as delicate, if a bit less magical, as putting oneself into someone else's skin (Geertz 1983: 58; emphasis added).

The "experience-distant" concepts that theorists "fashion" entail categories and expectations of learning processes that are not easily dislodged in spite of direct-experience accounts or research findings. It probably is fair to say that throughout human history, the learning that sticks by and for individuals has to come through as "experience-near." Yet it remains extremely difficult for most people whose learning has been heavily filtered through institutional experience to acknowledge and appreciate the disassembled aspect of noncategorized learning contexts and agents. Institutional processes seem to work to implant discourses of denial that renarrativize and reaffirm the "experience-distant." Such discourse rarely emerges into frontal assault on "experience-near" learning; instead, the discourse of denial works effectively to set aside, shelve, or ignore whatever challenges conceptual or categorical unity or methodological agreement. Meanwhile, the truth and actualities of the seemingly off-hand, temporary movements toward learning illustrated in the two cases given here manage to maintain themselves and to fill institutional gaps. They remain to reflect environments and agents that no doubt will continue to sustain what may be the deepest and most central connection among people who are neither bound by nor bonded to institutions: the joint moral obligation to adaptation.

REFERENCES

Geertz, Clifford. 1983. *Local knowledge.* New York: Basic Books.

Heath, Shirley Brice. 1983. *Ways with words.* New York: Cambridge University Press.

Heath, Shirley Brice, and Adelma Roach. 1999. Imaginative actuality. In *Champions of change: The impact of the arts on learning,* edited by Edward. B. Fiske. Washington, D.C.: President's Committee on the Arts and Humanities.

Heath, Shirley Brice, and Laura Smyth. 2000. *ArtShow.* Washington, D.C.: Partners for Livable Communities.[Resource guide accompanying hour-long documentary film titled *ArtShow;* available from Partners for Livable Communities.]

Heath, Shirley Brice, Elisabeth Soep, and Adelma Roach. 1998. Living the arts through language-learning: A report on community-based youth organizations. *Americans for the Arts* 2 (7): 1–20.

Larson, Reed. 2000. Toward a psychology of positive youth development. *American Psychologist* 55 (1): 170–83.

Implementing a district-wide foreign language program: A case study of acquistion planning and curricular innovation

G. Richard Tucker
Carnegie Mellon University
Richard Donato
University of Pittsburgh

Federal legislation enacted in the United States—the Goals 2000: Educate America Act—calls for American students to leave grades four, eight, and twelve having "demonstrated competence over challenging subject matter including English, mathematics, science, [and] foreign languages, ..." Although every European country has a national policy for introducing at least one foreign language into the elementary school curriculum of every child (see, for example, Pufahl, Rhodes, and Christian 2000; Dickson and Cumming 1996), it is estimated that foreign languages are offered in only approximately 31 percent of the elementary schools in the United States (Rhodes and Branaman 1999). If American students are to complete grades four, eight, and twelve with demonstrable proficiency in a foreign language, the number of programs at all levels will have to be significantly expanded and improved, particularly at the elementary level.

The importance of including foreign language study in the elementary school also is supported by research on the amount of instructional time required for developing functional proficiency in a foreign language (Carroll 1967) and by the widely held professional view that language competence can only be achieved by children who follow well-articulated, sustained sequences of foreign language instruction (Donato and Terry 1995). Expanded foreign language instruction in the elementary school will provide students with an extended opportunity to achieve the goals that have been articulated and disseminated as the National Standards for Foreign Language Education (Phillips 1998) as well as an opportunity to develop truly functional ability in a language other than their first language.

A major objection to incorporating foreign language instruction into the elementary school curriculum seems to be that there is not enough time in the instructional day (Baranick and Markham 1986). Our present national concerns with systemic educational reform and competitiveness make this a critical time to explore more fully the factors related to implementation of elementary school foreign language programs. Tucker, Donato, and Murday (2001) review several of the major issues that often are raised with regard to foreign language education in the elementary school (FLES) for English language speakers in the United States: which model of instruction should be implemented (ban immersion or standard FLES model); at what grade level foreign language instruction should begin; in what language(s) instruction should be offered; what are realistic proficiency expectations for elementary school students studying a particular language within a given model; and how we can best assess the language proficiency of young children. Very little empirical research has been conducted on these critical issues in FLES, and responses to these questions often rely on opinions or impressions about the early language learning experiences of American youngsters (see, for example, Donato, Antonek, and Tucker 1994; Donato, Tucker, and Antonek 1996; Donato et al. 2000; Gilzow and Branaman 1999; Met 1998; Tucker, Donato, and Antonek 1996).

The major purpose of this essay is to describe systematic planning and subsequent implementation and formative evaluation of a system-wide Spanish program in a school district in suburban Pittsburgh, Pennsylvania. The school system is relatively small, with approximately 2,800 students from mostly European-American, working-class families. For this description we draw on two major sources of data: our own experiences and observations as consultants to this program over a six-year period (as of spring 2001) and analysis of a series of extensive interviews carried out with various stakeholders who constituted the planning committee for the program. In the sections that follow we discuss the origins of the program, with particular emphasis on active participation by all senior administrators—including the superintendent—in a year-long planning effort that culminated in choice of language, teacher selection, curriculum development, and in-service training for all primary school faculty members; the ways in which the language program, which ultimately is intended for all children in the district, has been incorporated into the core curriculum for the district; the status of the program currently in its fifth year of implementation, including some findings from continuing formative evaluation of the students' Spanish language development; several prominent themes that emerged from the interview data; and our reflections on a successful and satisfying collaboration.

Origins of the Spanish Program

In May 1995, we (along with then-graduate student Janis Antonek from the University of Pittsburgh) were invited to attend an informal meeting with the superintendent of Chartiers Valley School District and several members of his administrative staff. The invitation resulted in part from our previous research examining diverse aspects of implementation of a Japanese program at the elementary school level (see, for example, Donato, Tucker, and Antonek 1996; Tucker, Donato, and Antonek 1996) and partly from the fact that one of us (Donato) directs the major foreign language teacher preparation program in the region. This meeting marked the beginning of a mutually beneficial and thoroughly enjoyable school district-university partnership, which continues to the present day.

The superintendent began the initial meeting by articulating a vision for his students and for his district—a vision that included doing something different, something daring. He proposed that a new program be developed so that *all* of the district's pupils would study a common foreign language throughout their entire scholastic career. He described how American secondary school graduates in the twenty-first century will be competing for positions in which numeracy, literacy, problem-solving, and communication skills will be increasingly valued and how students with bilingual language proficiency will possess a comparative advantage in comparison with their monolingual English-speaking counterparts.

Several questions were raised at that first meeting. Was the vision plausible? If so, in which language(s) should instruction be offered? Were teachers available? Would the community support such a program? Would members of the school board support such a program—and provide the necessary budgetary authorization? Could the school district and the local universities (Carnegie Mellon and the University of Pittsburgh) work collaboratively to their mutual benefit?

The group formed a Foreign Language Program Committee to oversee planning and implementation of a new and innovative foreign language program. Committee members consist of the district's Director of Instruction, who chairs the group; the superintendent; principals from the primary, intermediate, and middle schools; selected teachers; the chair of the secondary school foreign languages department; and the university collaborators. As of March 2001 the group had met on twenty-seven occasions to plan, review accomplishments, and make decisions concerning priorities for future work. As appropriate, subgroups or individuals carry out specific activities, which they report back to the committee.

Choice of Language and Timetable for Implementation

One of the first issues with which the group dealt was the choice of language(s). Several options were considered, including French, German, Japanese, and Spanish. At the time (academic year 1995–1996) the district offered a foreign language exploratory (FLEX) program comprising French, German, and Spanish strands for middle school students, with regular programs of study in these languages available to students in grades nine through twelve on an elective basis. In addition, members of the university partnership proposed that Japanese be considered because of their work with an innovative local program. Several factors were evaluated, such as the likely availability of certified teachers and appropriate materials, potential community support, the perceived utility of proficiency in the target language for graduates, and so forth. For pragmatic reasons, the committee decided to select only one language and to make its study compulsory for all children.

The committee decided that it would be useful to conduct a community survey to ascertain the level of support for such a program and to obtain feedback concerning the choice of language. A survey instrument—the FLES Community Climate Survey—was developed by a committee member, piloted, revised, and administered to a representative sample of parents, as well as to all members of the school board. The results revealed broad general support for an innovative foreign language education program and support specifically for the teaching of Spanish. Approximately 65 percent of the respondents preferred a program that introduced children to Spanish (the other respondents were split among Japanese, German, or French or indicated that they had no preference). Respondents also indicated that this new FLES program should have the goals of developing cultural knowledge (93 percent), engaging students in the excitement of language learning (80 percent), and building basic language proficiency (19 percent).[1]

The second major question with which the committee wrestled was whether to begin the program from the bottom up—that is, at the kindergarten level; from the top down—that is, working backward a year at a time from grade nine (where foreign language instruction then began); or from both ends to meet in the middle. After much discussion of issues such as scheduling, teacher availability, and the necessity of developing long-term articulation, a decision was made to propose to the school board implementation of a Spanish FLES program in September 1996 for all kindergarten children in the district. The proposal recommended extending the program with systematic introduction of new cohorts of kindergarten youngsters in subsequent years (i.e., to grade one in September 1997, to grade two in September 1998, and so forth). The Board of School Directors formally approved this plan in April 1996 and authorized an initial five-year pilot project. In January 2001 the board reviewed the progress of the foreign language program to date and recommended budgetary authorization to extend the program for an additional five-year period, thereby ensuring that the district will have a fully articulated foreign language program from kindergarten through grade twelve for all students by academic year 2004–2005.

Development of an Action Plan

After deciding on the target language (Spanish) and the implementation model (bottom up), the committee next turned its attention to recruiting an appropriately certified teacher for the first cohort of students, planning for curriculum development activities, informing community members about the new program, and systematically informing other teachers and administrators working in the system about the program. These activities continued during the late winter and spring of 1996. A major benchmark was the hiring of the first kindergarten Spanish teacher, who was a dually certified graduate in elementary education and in Spanish from the University of Pittsburgh. The early hiring of the teacher—a procedure to be followed in subsequent years—meant that she was able to devote a substantial block of time to curriculum development activities during the summer months before the start of the program. She worked with other curriculum specialists in the district and in continuing consultation with Donato. Curriculum development activities benefited from and reflected work that had been done on the national (foreign language) standards, as well as innovative work that had been completed by other staff members in the school district on the standards for the arts.

The Spanish Program and its Incorporation into the Core Curriculum

The Spanish program began in September 1996 in all eleven kindergarten classes in the district, comprising a total enrollment of 223 students. Each class met for twenty minutes per day, five days per week—a model subsequently followed in grades one through four. The Spanish specialist goes to the students in their regular classroom and, in effect, team teaches with the regular classroom teacher.

In the first year of the program, a strong collaboration between the regular kindergarten teachers and the language specialist developed almost immediately; this collaborative style has continued across grade levels to date, and we believe that it continues to mark this program as unique (see Donato, Antonek, and Tucker 1994 and Tucker 1998 concerning the problem of marginality of FLES programs). Rather than expressing indifference toward the new program by working neither to support it nor to repudiate it, the kindergarten teachers—and subsequently the teachers in grades one through four—have all established close contact with the FLES teachers and freely shared ideas and materials during the curriculum development phase of the program as well as during the teaching. Many also have studied Spanish actively during the FLES lessons in their classrooms. The fact that the Spanish program and its first teacher were clearly positioned from inception as an integrated part of the kindergarten program led directly to the program becoming an equal participant in the total school curriculum.

The curriculum was developed by following the school-district template for planned courses of study. That is, each thematically organized unit (e.g., colors and shapes, numbers, greetings, calendar and weather, clothing and body parts, fiesta and foods) was specified according to student learning outcome; content, materials, and activities; and procedures for assessment. The main focus of each lesson is on vocabulary building and comprehension rather than production. The curriculum reflects this orientation in its assessment procedures, including activities such as coloring, baking brownies, movement activities, and game playing. Every attempt is made to integrate Spanish with ongoing activities in art, music, library activities, physical education, and the computer curriculum. The integrated nature of the Spanish class is explicit and obvious in the curriculum. Children learn numbers by accompanying jumping jack calisthenics with counting, listen to age-appropriate fairy tales in Spanish, and are introduced to days of the week in Spanish when they are learning them in their regular classes. The Spanish teacher uses Spanish whenever possible in the classroom for classroom management, as well as outside the classroom to greet her students in the hallways. She makes extensive use of manipulatives and visuals and brings in a wide variety of authentic materials. Her classes are enriched with visits by Spanish speakers and through a partnership begun in collaboration with students studying Spanish at the secondary level (e.g., the Foreign Language on Request Elementary Spanish [FLORES] program).

The teacher keeps parents informed about the goals and content of the program by means of a monthly newsletter, as well as frequent tape-recorded updates on the "homework hotline." There also have been several special presentations for parents and other interested community members at regular back-to-school nights and an informational videotape that was prepared for broadcast on a local cable channel. In addition, on several occasions parents have been asked to complete questionnaires designed to elicit their attitudes toward various aspects of the program. During the course of the 1996–1997 school year, the committee continued to meet regularly to monitor the implementation of the program, to plan for an assessment of student progress during spring 1997, and to begin planning for extension of the program into grade one together with the introduction of a new kindergarten cohort in September 1997—a model that has been followed successfully to the present (March 2001).

Expansion through the Primary Level

The committee continued to meet quarterly to discuss various aspects of the program and to plan for its expansion in the 1997–1998 school year. Another dual-certified teacher from the University of Pittsburgh program was hired, and the teachers spent time with Donato during summer 1997 revising the kindergarten curriculum in light of the first year's experience and developing the curriculum for the new grade one program.

When classes began in September 1997, all kindergarten and grade one children in the district participated in the Spanish FLES program. They followed the model established during the first year—namely, twenty minutes of instruction in Spanish, five days a week, with a specialist teacher who comes to their home classroom. The curriculum for the second year of the program built on concepts and vocabulary learned during the first year and expanded students' participation in the lesson to include more oral production. That is, the curriculum retained its integrated, thematic focus but moved toward greater oral participation in the lessons by students.

The committee addressed several major issues during the 1997–1998 school year. In general, committee members wanted to ensure that parents of current students, parents of prospective students, members of the school board, and other teachers in the district were as well informed about the program as they could be. To this end the committee drafted and piloted a "report card" for parents that was intended to convey information about the content of the curriculum and whether their children are progressing to master the material presented. The reporting procedure underwent several revisions in an attempt to create a report that capitalizes on what children can do well rather than on where they are deficient.

Parents receive a checklist of several functional language abilities (e.g., saying the date and month, identifying classroom items, telling time) with an indication of whether the child has *mastered* the material or is *progressing*. Care has been taken to design the report card so it will not discourage children by sending the unintended message to parents that their children lack an aptitude for language study or are not progressing adequately. Given that we do not know what constitutes "adequate achievement" at this level of instruction, we felt that it was important to highlight achievement over failure in a formal report procedure that would inspire confidence in parents concerning their children's ability to learn another language and bolster the image of the program in the home. This report card also is an innovative development because the school district previously had not assigned grades or provided other formative information to parents about children's progress in foreign language programs at the primary grades. The "Spanish Progress Report K–5," as it is called, is distributed to all K–4 students and their parents twice a year (at the end of the first and second semesters). Four areas are assessed: listening and reading comprehension, communicative ability in speech and writing, cultural awareness, and responsibility for work and class participation. Students are assessed for each area as either "proficient," "progressing," or "needing improvement." The progress report collaboratively devised and agreed upon by the steering committee uses a rubric that does not imply failure to provide feedback on the students' ability at the time of reporting.

In addition, several back-to-school nights with a focus on the Spanish program were held for parents; an evening orientation program for parents of prospective new pupils was held; an informational video featuring children and teachers in the program was shown on local cable television; and an in-service program was presented in the spring to inform other teachers in the middle and intermediate schools about the FLES program.

This same general model was followed for the 1998–1999 school year, with the recruitment of another dual-certified teacher, as the program expanded to include all students from kindergarten through grade two.

Expansion to Intermediate Level and Middle School
The committee continued to meet quarterly to discuss various aspects of the program and to plan for its expansion in the 1998–1999 school year. Another dual-certified teacher was hired, and curriculum development work continued. The committee addressed several major issues during the 1998–1999 and 1999–2000 school years, including planning for the program's expansion to grade three and then grade four (where it is at present) as well as beginning the process of thinking carefully about the expansion into the middle school that will not occur until 2002–2003. Indeed, this careful advance planning is a distinguishing characteristic of the program and the work to date—a characteristic that unfortu-

nately rarely is present in the implementation of innovative FLES programs (see, for example, Curtain and Dahlberg 2000).

Themes of Success: A Model for Other Districts and the Nation

Several features set the program at Chartiers Valley apart from other foreign language program initiatives. A comprehensive review of the history of the program reveals several themes that contribute to the vitality, health, and longevity of the program. In particular, five emerging themes characterize the program's past and present and anticipate its positive future.

First, a hallmark of the program is the overarching concern for *careful and collaborative planning and evaluation* each year as the program expands. This feature is worthy of repetition as a major contributing factor to the program's success.

Second, consonant with the theme of careful planning, *program expansion* is carried out consecutively each year, rather than to students in all elementary grades in a single year. Knowing what lies ahead and what must be prepared for each upcoming year provide necessary time for developing a well-articulated curriculum on the basis of annual assessments of students' expanding abilities.

Third, an overriding concern of teachers and the committee is that students make *progress in proficiency*. All stakeholders share a common goal: As students progress in the program, so too will they progress in their linguistic and cultural knowledge. Proficiency outcomes are critical to the success of foreign language programs because observations of early language learning programs often reveal that children are faced with repetitions of the same content presented in the same way from one year to the next (see Donato et al. 2000 for evidence of this assertion, as well as possible explanations). A repetitive curriculum and failure to adjust instruction to the expanding abilities of the child will result in student outcomes that will undermine the value of foreign language instruction in the eyes of school boards and parents—and ultimately will fail to motivate students to continue their study (Rosenbusch 1995).

A fourth theme that contributes to the overall quality of the program is the *quality of its foreign language faculty*. Each year a teacher is hired who is certified in both foreign language education and elementary education. This practice of ensuring high-quality, well-prepared teachers who understand how children learn and develop safeguards against the demise of the program. As FLES history has taught us, teachers who import approaches and methods of foreign language instruction from the upper grades to the elementary school usually do not provide the type of instruction that is appropriate to the learner. On the other hand, teachers who understand how children learn present age-appropriate lessons that take into account the capacity and natural curiosity for language learning that young children bring to the classroom.

The fifth theme, which is related closely to hiring qualified and appropriately prepared teachers, is the teachers' orientation to their work. Over the years we have observed that the teachers are truly *"reflective practitioners"* who make instructional decisions and modifications on the basis of classroom observation and evidence. Specifically, teachers have conducted systematic classroom-based investigations of student production beyond word-level; the frequency of instructional tasks that require unplanned, spontaneous interpersonal communication; and the effect of wait-time on student participation, among other issues. As the director of curriculum pointed out, these teachers, newly inducted into the profession, truly are in training for educational leadership positions in the near future.

Current Program Status: Formative Evaluation of Student Progress

Members of the committee have believed throughout that it is important for all stakeholders (e.g., pupils, parents, teachers, members of the school board) to conduct regular systematic assessments of student progress near the end of each school year. In addition, the university partners decided that it would be useful to document as fully as possible the process of program development and implementation in a manner analogous to that described by Markee (1997).

Assessment of Student Progress

To carry out the first of these objectives—systematic assessment of student progress—a curriculum-based interview protocol was initially developed, pretested, and revised with the assistance of the university partners. At the end of the first year of program implementation (June 1997), forty-four pupils (two boys and two girls from each of the eleven classes) were randomly selected to participate in a ten- to twelve-minute interview conducted by the high school Spanish coordinator and one of the primary school counselors. The subtasks of the interview provided a basis for assessing the students' listening comprehension (e.g., responding to a command, such as *point to the letter M on the rectangle,* with an appropriate action), their range of vocabulary (asking the child to name in Spanish a range of visuals, such as *elephant, book, school*), and their emerging sense of grammaticality (by asking them to make grammaticality judgments and by asking them to perform sentence repetition tasks with increasingly long sentences that were designed to exceed short-term memory capacity). Interviews were recorded for later transcription and analysis. In addition, the students were asked to draw a picture in their art class that later served as the "stimulus" for a picture description task. This general framework has been followed for the past four years, with gradual refinement of the assessment instruments (thanks to assistance from Sue Todhunter of the University of Pittsburgh and Rocio Dominguez of Carnegie Mellon University), to ensure that the tasks were age- and grade-appropriate and that the language forms and functions sampled were representative of the language use in their classrooms. In general, the results of the end-of-year testing show repeatedly that listening comprehension exceeds oral production, production is limited to learned material, production begins as single-word utterances and formulaic expressions, language mixing is common, and children can be expected to develop good pronunciation in Spanish.

The children in the program and their parents also have been unanimously positive about the Spanish program and in wanting it to continue. Likewise, the views of the regular classroom teachers were positive and supportive. None expressed the view that the Spanish program was somehow detracting from other elements of the school district's program. The classroom teacher noted that "we are most pleased with the level of achievement our students have attained [and] inspired by the enthusiasm they demonstrate in so doing."

Student Progress and Early Language Learner Guidelines

Most recently we attempted to benchmark the progress of the students in relationship to the American Council on the Teaching of Foreign Languages' (ACTFL) Early Language Learner Guidelines. For this purpose, in winter 2001 we designed a teacher assessment instrument to assess student proficiency on a variety of tasks. Teacher assessment has been an accurate indicator of student ability and correlates highly with independent measures of proficiency (Donato et al. 2000). Based on the descriptions in the Early Language Learner Guidelines for students, we devised a "can do/can't do" assessment that was distributed to all FLES teachers working in the program.

Our Teacher Assessment of Student Progress, drawn from the major categories of the guidelines, asked teachers to respond to items that relate to how well and how accurately the children understand and speak Spanish, their vocabulary repertoire, the communication strategies they use, and their cultural knowledge. An additional category was added that asked teachers to report on the quantity of language their students could produce (e.g., word-level, phrase-level, and so forth). We tallied teacher ratings and compared them across all grade levels. The results of the teacher assessment indicate that children in the program after five years of instruction performed as predicted by the guidelines. When we compared the teacher responses for each grade level, the results fell into two categories: what all children in all grades can do versus indicators of expanding language ability. It was necessary to analyze the teacher assessment in this way because the guidelines reflect overall outcomes for various program models (e.g., high school programs versus thirteen years of instruction) rather than specific outcomes for each year in a given sequence of instruction.

Specifically, we found that all teachers, regardless of grade level, reported that the majority of their children had developed the ability to do the following in Spanish:

- Use memorized material
- Imitate pronunciation well
- Speak with accuracy when presenting practiced material
- Understand key words and phrases in Spanish

- Comprehend and say everyday vocabulary
- Pick up Spanish vocabulary from other sources
- Know cultural facts about Spanish-speaking countries
- Say words, phrases, and full sentences.

When we examined closely the items for which differences were reported, we observed systematic growth and progress in language ability. In addition, when we examined interindividual difference by grade level, we found that these specific items shared a common feature: the ability to use language in ways that go beyond word-level, formulaic utterances and memorized material. That is, the six items that were assessed differently by the teachers were complex language tasks requiring discourse-level competence, negotiation of meaning, linguistic creativity, cultural appropriateness, and literacy skills. The analysis also indicated that these tasks did not develop randomly, nor were they equal in complexity. As Table 10.1 indicates, the kindergarten children could not perform any of these advanced tasks, whereas the students in grade four were reported to control them all. In between the kindergarten class and grade four, we observed systematic growth in advanced ability at intervals in grades one to three. Thus, this analysis of differences revealed

Table 10.1. Teacher Assessment of Advanced Language Skills

Task	Can't	Can
Less complex		
I Recombine to make short sentences	K	1–4
I		
I Understand simple stories	K	1–4
I		
I Use invented spelling	K	1–4
I		
I Clarify meaning	K–2	3–4
I		
I Use cultural expressions	K–2	3–4
I		
I Tell a story	K–3	4
More complex		

that as students moved through the program, the teachers at each higher grade level reported that their students could perform more advanced tasks.

The conclusion from this analysis is clear. Students demonstrate solid progress over the years in their language skills and cultural knowledge and develop more advanced language functions throughout their language study. The analysis indicates dramatically that these students clearly are advancing in their proficiency, that the curriculum is well articulated, and that, with each passing year, the children can say and do more with their new language.

Collaborating on Curricular Innovation: Insider's Perspective

As described elsewhere (Tucker, Donato, and Murday, 2001), we drew on Markee's (1997) definition of curricular innovation to develop an interview protocol that allowed us to construct a narrative report by uniting the opinions and perspectives of the stakeholders themselves and our own participant observations of the district's experience in collaborating on the design and implementation of the district-wide Spanish FLES program. The interview protocol, which is described in detail in Tucker, Donato, and Murday (2001), was designed to elicit participants' recollections of topics such as the early stages of program development, as well as their opinions of the relative success of implementation to date, problems likely to be encountered in the future, and comparisons with implementation of other curricular innovations in the district. The thirteen interviewees included the superintendent, a member of the school board, the director of instruction, principals, regular classroom teachers from various levels, and two of the Spanish teachers.

All participants expressed remarkable enthusiasm for the FLES program and reported that they considered it to be a success to date. During our analysis of the interview data, six overarching and consistent themes emerged across respondents:

- A vision that resonated
- Careful planning
- Empowerment
- Support of, and for, the teachers
- The physical contribution of consolidation
- Concerns for the future

We turn now to a brief consideration of five of these themes in the form of discussion and analysis of the collective thinking of the respondents that emerged during our interviews.

Articulating a Shared Vision

The superintendent wanted a foreign language program for the Chartiers Valley school system "because of a sense that American education was behind [the rest of the world] with regard to exposure to foreign languages." From the time he first proposed the idea of a foreign language program beginning at the elementary level as part of the district's plans for consolidating several community schools in one new facility, his vision resonated positively throughout the group. That the language be Spanish was not particularly important; instead, most respondents "felt strongly that a foreign language should be introduced, but it didn't matter [to them] which one."

The members of the steering committee—which had representatives from administration, teachers, community members, parents, and students—all agreed that for their students to be viable citizens for the twenty-first century, "[they] needed knowledge of another language." Students should be prepared to compete for jobs in a global market, where other students would have the benefit of school systems that emphasized the learning of several languages. The student representatives expressed dissatisfaction with the status quo; after several years of foreign language instruction at the secondary school level, they often could remember no more than a few key phrases. Many of the respondents also echoed this frustration with regard to their own language experience in school.

In addition, the respondents reported that a foreign language program would help elevate the reputation of the Chartiers Valley School District. As one respondent pointed out, "This definitely seemed a way of making them better, and improving their reputation as a leadership district . . . . It was also a way to show the people that this was something they could do for the children, to improve cultural awareness, and improve their self esteem as well." Not only would it show their willingness to try innovative new programs, but it would demonstrate their dedication to doing things that benefit the students.

Careful Planning
All respondents reported that the success of the program was traceable in large part to the careful planning that went into the development and implementation of the program. The most crucial part of this planning was the involvement of all of the stakeholders: the school board and administrators, of course, but also the teachers, parents, student representatives, community members, and university partners. All stakeholders were continually encouraged to "raise their concerns so that they could be addressed, instead of complaining in isolation later." As one administrator pointed out, "This one was done right. Sometimes when school districts make a decision to implement a program, they're not always careful to get all of the stakeholders to buy in."

Repeated again and again among the respondents was the sense that anticipation of concerns prevented them from becoming obstacles. As one respondent mentioned, "They anticipated concerns, and they were built into the action plan. . . . The proactive nature minimized problems." In addition, the program is under constant scrutiny and evaluation and is revised as needed. As one respondent put it, the steering committee "helps them keep on top of things, and anticipate issues." This factor gives the respondents confidence in contemplating potentially problematic issues that they feel will need to be addressed in the future.

Empowerment

The notion of "empowerment" was central to many of the interviews. Respondents were unanimous in feeling "ownership" of the foreign language program from the beginning. The early discussions surrounding implementation of the program were seen as drawing on "the philosophy of teamwork in the district." Respondents reported that they were "never hesitant to voice a very small concern because . . . you know any comments are treated with respect and addressed."

This empowerment that teachers, department heads, principals, and others felt clearly was the result of strong leadership provided by the superintendent, who regarded his position as one that would "allow him to guide 'the powers that be' toward the inclusion of the program [centrally within the core curriculum for the district]." It is noteworthy that both the superintendent and the director of instruction have personally participated in *all* meetings of the steering committee over the past five and a half years. Members of the Foreign Language Committee were carefully selected to include representatives from the key constituent groups: administration, building management, supervision, classroom teaching, and the university partners. Many respondents regarded this strategy as a new and desirable approach to curricular innovation for Char Valley.

Support of, and for, Teachers

Another central thread that was woven throughout the interviews was that of support of, and for, the teachers. This support took many forms. For example, there is a continuing search for teachers with dual certification (in elementary education and Spanish) so that classroom teachers would not be expected to learn and then teach Spanish—as has been done with many other programs in the United States, often with less than optimal results. A good deal of attention was paid to ensuring that the Spanish program was incorporated into the regular curriculum of the primary school with a minimum of disruption. Care was taken to provide assistance to the Spanish teachers through continuing linkage with the university partners and for classroom teachers through systematic provision of in-service training.

Respondents also noted that the Spanish teachers "had the support of the classroom teachers; they've really accepted it, they're learning the language and speaking it with their students, and they reinforce what they're learning all throughout the day." The principal of the primary school noted that he devotes a good deal of attention to ensuring that the regular classroom teachers are "attempting to implement the Spanish instruction in their daily lessons as well."

Concerns for the Future

Respondents were asked to discuss their long-term prognosis for the program, which brought several concerns related to the future of foreign language learning in the district sharply into focus. The most resounding theme reflected a realization that issues of articulation will be critical if the district is to have a coherent and viable foreign language program across thirteen years of instruction. Several respondents mentioned the need to rethink the curriculum in the middle school (grades six through eight) and high school (grades nine through twelve). As the chairperson of the high school foreign language department stated, "There will need to be drastic changes in the curriculum in the later years of schooling," though she hastened to add that she regards this "as a wonderful problem." Similar comments from several other respondents made clear that the district anticipates the effect of such a program on all levels of language instruction and recognizes the centrality of language instruction for the total school curriculum.

What is striking in the interview data are the possible solutions envisioned to the "wonderful problem" of restructuring a foreign language curriculum upward toward high school. Many respondents provided concrete suggestions for a well-articulated program model, course content, and teaching personnel. The second-grade teacher spoke of later courses containing challenging subject matter in Spanish that could be taught by highly qualified instructors who are trained to deal with academic content. According to the intermediate school principal, the "domino effect" of an elementary foreign language program on later years of instruction requires careful planning and active preparation for the language curriculum in the upper grades. Her suggestions included recruiting highly qualified teachers with teaching certificates in both elementary education and foreign language instruction and constant attention to the curriculum to ensure that it is developmentally appropriate for the learners and reflective of advances in the field of language learning. The intermediate school principal—a non-foreign language specialist—anticipated that students will be better able to acquire "additional foreign languages because of their early learning experiences with Spanish," thus possibly foreshadowing expansion of foreign language offerings to students in the high school.

From Local Themes to Professional Practice

We believe that the profile that emerged from the interviews provides important lessons for others who may embark on similar curricular innovations. This study has examined, in actual practice, key elements in developing an apparently successful educational innovation and in so doing has told the story of one district's lived experience with FLES. The direction and decisions of this district rested on the concerns of several important constituents and reflect Markee's (1997) observation that innovative projects are affected, positively or negatively, by complex sociocultural variables such as cultural beliefs; political climate; historical and economic conditions; administrative attitudes; institutional support; and technological, sociolinguistic, and language planning factors (see also Holliday 1994). Viewed globally, these themes—vision, planning, empowerment, support, and future concerns—refract and reflect all of the sociocultural variables listed by Markee and attest to their importance, as well as the need to acknowledge and address these factors openly in designing and implementing new programs. Others in the profession who are contemplating development of a program such as the one we have described here or monitoring and evaluating current FLES programs might be well advised to benchmark successes and failures against these themes.

Reflections on a Successful and Satisfying Collaboration

Several factors have contributed to the success of this project to date. The first factor that comes to mind is the key role played by the superintendent. Through his active participation in all of the committee meetings, he has provided immediate and visible credibility and value to the activity. He continually reminds committee members that they are embarking on an innovation by "navigating uncharted waters" that will have far-reaching consequences for the school district in terms of its visibility and reputation. We also have been struck by the extent to which committee members—themselves mostly monolingual and monocultural—have embraced the goal of multiple language proficiency and cross-cultural competence for their students and themselves "act as if" they were multilingual and multicultural. Throughout our association with the committee, we have found the representatives from the district to be continually and genuinely concerned with providing the best possible education for their students. We have never heard a disparaging remark about a pupil, a parent, or a community member; to the contrary, committee members express genuine knowledge about and concern for the students' educational, social, and personal well-being. We have found it enormously satisfying to be a part of this committee.

What are some of the issues that have intrigued us over the past five and a half years? Clearly, we have appreciated the opportunity to attempt to extend the generalizeability of some of our ideas about language program evaluation to another setting. Perhaps more important, however, we have enjoyed the challenges—in the words of the superintendent—of "navigating uncharted waters" in helping to write a curriculum for the elementary grades; in examining the relationship between what goes on in the language arts curriculum to what should be accomplished in the FLES curriculum; in thinking through and sharing with other committee members various issues related to the introduction of second-language literacy in relationship to native language literacy; in examining the complex set of issues related to reporting student progress to parents (we are intrigued, for example, by how parents evaluate the progress of their children in areas in which the parents themselves have no experience); and, more generally, with the responsibility of injecting substantive issues from time to time into what otherwise might become a procedural dialogue. We have enjoyed witnessing the genesis of this program and being a part of this collaborative achievement thus far, and we look forward to its continuation in the future.

Yet we are far from finished. The program committee has now turned its attention to curriculum revision and development, materials selection, and so forth for expansion of the program to the middle school (grades six, seven, and eight), and committee members have begun to think about the ways in which the current high school Spanish program will need to be thoroughly revised for subsequent cohorts of students who will bring to the high school language class a "beyond-the-basic" level of proficiency. The district and the current Spanish teachers will face a major challenge in developing a rich, content-based Spanish program that will allow these students to continue to develop cognitive and academic language proficiency in English and Spanish by the time of their graduation. This concern for articulation is well founded in light of the failures of FLES programs in the 1960s (Rosenbusch 1995). One commonly observed phenomenon during that period was that former FLES students often repeated basic language lessons when they entered high school. This repetition of previously learned material resulted in a severe lack of motivation in students and diminished their interest and enthusiasm for language study. The source of this instructional discontinuity in language study has been traced to the lack of clearly articulated shared goals and outcomes for language learning in a seamless sequence of instruction. It is not surprising that in foreign language education today, articulation programs and studies still dominate the professional literature, grant-funded projects, and conference presentations. The committee is fully aware of these issues and is taking steps to assure that transitions between instructional units and course outcomes will expand student proficiency rather than recycle rudimentary skills each year.

NOTE

1. It is interesting to note that these desired outcomes are quite similar to the rank-ordering of goals expressed by parents in our longitudinal study of a Japanese FLES program (Donato, Antonek, and Tucker, 1994; Donato, Tucker, and Antonek, 1996; Tucker, Donato, and Antonek, 1996).

References

Baranick, William, and David Markham. 1986. Attitudes of elementary school principals toward foreign language instruction. *Foreign Language Annals* 19: 481–89.

Carroll, John B. 1967. *The foreign language attainments of language majors in the senior year: A survey conducted in U.S. colleges and universities.* Cambridge, Mass.: Harvard University Graduate School of Education.

Curtain, Helena A., and Carol Ann Dahlberg. 2000. Planning for success: Common pitfalls in the planning of early foreign language programs. ERIC Digest; available at www.cal.org/ericcll/digest/0011planning.html.

Dickson, Peter, and Alister Cumming, eds. 1996. *Profiles of language education in 25 countries.* Slough, Great Britain: National Foundation for Educational Research.

Donato, Richard, and Robert M. Terry, eds. 1995. *Foreign language learning: The journey of a lifetime.* Lincolnwood, Ill: National Textbook Co.

Donato, Richard, Janis L. Antonek, and G. Richard Tucker. 1994. A multiple perspective analysis of a Japanese FLES program. *Foreign Language Annals* 27: 365–78.

Donato, Richard, G. Richard Tucker, and Janis L. Antonek. 1996. Monitoring and assessing a Japanese FLES program: Ambiance and achievement. *Language Learning* 46 (3): 497–528.

Donato, Richard, G. Richard Tucker, Jirada Wudthayagorn, and Kanae Igarashi. 2000. Converging evidence: Attitudes, achievements and instruction in the later years of FLES. *Foreign Language Annals* 33 (4): 377–93.

Gilzow, Douglas F., and Lucinda E. Branaman. 1999. *Lessons learned: Model early foreign language programs.* Washington, D.C., and McHenry, Ill.: Center for Applied Linguistics/Delta Systems.

Holliday, Adrian. 1994. *Appropriate methodology and social context.* New York: Cambridge University Press.

Markee, Numa. 1997. *Managing curricular innovation.* New York: Cambridge University Press.

Met, Myriam C., ed. 1998. *Critical issues in early second language learning: Building for our children's future.* Glenview, Ill.: Addison-Wesley Scott Foresman.

Phillips, June. 1998. Introduction: Standards for world languages—On a firm foundation. In *Foreign language standards: Linking research, theories, and practices,* edited by June Phillips and Robert Terry. Lincolnwood, Ill.: National Textbook Co., 1–14.

Pufahl, Ingraid, Nancy Rhodes, and Donna Christian. 2000. *Foreign language teaching: What the United States can learn from other countries.* Report prepared for U.S. Department of Education's Comparative Information on Improving Education Practice Working Group 4 Policy Priority: Foreign Language Learning. Washington, D.C.: Center for Applied Linguistics. Available at www.cal.org/ericcll/countries.html.

Rhodes, Nancy C., and Lucinda E. Branaman. 1999. *Foreign language instruction in the United States: A national survey of elementary and secondary schools.* Washington, D.C., and McHenry, Ill.: Center for Applied Linguistics/Delta Systems.

Rosenbusch, Marcia. 1995. Language learning in the elementary school: Investing in the future. In *Foreign language learning: The journey of a lifetime,* edited by Richard Donato and Robert M. Terry. Lincolnwood, Ill.: National Textbook Co., 1–36.

Tucker, G. Richard. 1998. Focus: Reflections on the Stories Teachers Tell. In *Stories teachers tell: Reflecting on professional practice,* edited by Douglas K. Hartman. Lincolnwood, Ill.: National Textbook Co., 213–19.

Tucker, G. Richard, Richard Donato, and Janis L. Antonek. 1996. Documenting growth in a Japanese FLES program. *Foreign Language Annals* 29 (4): 539–50.

Tucker, G. Richard, Richard Donato, and Kimmaree Murday. 2001. The genesis of a district-wide Spanish FLES program: A collaborative achievement. In *Perspectives and issues in educational language policy: A volume in honor of Bernard Dov Spolsky,* edited by Joel Walters and Elana Shohamy. Philadelphia: John Benjamins, 235–59.